# From Teilhard to Omega

# *From Teilhard to Omega*

## Co-creating an Unfinished Universe

### EDITED BY ILIA DELIO

ORBIS BOOKS
Maryknoll, New York 10545

ORBIS BOOKS
Maryknoll, New York 10545

Fathers and Brothers
MARYKNOLL™

Fourth Printing, December 2017

Library of Congress Cataloging-in-Publication Data

From Teilhard to Omega: Co-creating an unfinished universe / Ilia Delio, editor.
    pages    cm
   Includes bibliographical references and index.
   ISBN 978-1-62698-069-3 (pbk.)
   1. Creationism. 2. Creation. 3. Evolution (Biology) – Religious aspects – Christianity. 4. Evolution – Religious aspects – Christianity. 5. Teilhard de Chardin, Pierre. I. Delio, Ilia, editor of compilation.
BS651.I64 2013
261.5'5 – dc23
                                                  2013024678

# CONTENTS

# TEILHARD WORKS CITED

AE     *Activation of Energy*, translated by René Hague (London: Collins, 1970)

AM     *The Appearance of Man*, translated by J. M. Cohen (New York: Harper, 1965)

CE     *Christianity and Evolution*, translated by René Hague (London: Collins, and New York: Harcourt Brace Jovanovich, 1971)

DM     *The Divine Milieu: An Essay on the Interior Life*, translated by Bernard Wall (New York: Harper & Brothers, 1960)

FM     *The Future of Man*, translated by Norman Denny (New York: Harper & Row, 1964).

HE     *Human Energy*, translated by J. M. Cohen (London: Collins, 1969)

HM     *The Heart of Matter*, translated by René Hague (London: Collins, and New York: Harcourt Brace Jovanovich, 1978)

HP     *The Human Phenomenon*, translated by Sarah Appleton-Weber (London: Sussex Academic Press, 2003)

HU     *Hymn of the Universe*, translated by Simon Bartholomew (New York: Harper & Row, 1965; London: Collins Fontana Books, 1970)

LT     *Letters from a Traveler*, translated by Bernard Wall (New York: Harper & Row, 1962)

MM     T*he Making of a Mind*, translated by René Hague (New York: Harper and Row, 1965)

MPN     *Man's Place in Nature: The Human Zoological Group*, translated by René Hague (New York: Harper & Row, 1966)

OS     *L'Œuvre Scientifique*, ten volumes, edited by Nicole and Karl Schmitz-Moormann (Olten und Freiburg im Breisgau: Walter-Verlag, 1971)

PM     *The Phenomenon of Man*, translated by Bernard Wall (New York: Harper & Row, 1959)

# INTRODUCTION

In his book *Christ of the 21st Century,* Ewert Cousins described a new age of consciousness that has dawned with the rise of mass communication, modern science, and technology. He called this new age the "second axial period" because it is a new breakthrough in human consciousness around the globe. Whereas the first axial period gave rise to a consciousness of the individual as free and autonomous, the second axial period is marked by a consciousness of community and ecological relatedness. This new consciousness is largely the result of human creativity and inventiveness, especially computer technology, air travel, and media communications. For the first time since the appearance of human life on our planet, all of the tribes, all of the nations, all of the religions are beginning to share a common history. People are becoming more aware of belonging to humanity as a whole and not to a specific group. This second axial period is communal, global, ecological, and cosmic. It is not merely a shift from first-axial-period consciousness; it is an advance in the whole evolutionary process, challenging world religions to bring about a new integration of sacred and secular energies into a total global human energy.[1]

Cousins indicated that the bridge from the first to the second axial period is still under construction, and he called the bridge builders of this new age "mutational" persons. In genetics, a mutation is an alteration in the nucleotide sequence of an organism's genome which may result in discernible changes in the organism's behavior. Similarly, a mutational person is one who thinks outside the ordinary sequence of events and whose insights can inspire others to think in new ways. One of the outstanding mutational persons of the second axial period was the Jesuit scientist Pierre Teilhard de Chardin (1881–1955). Teilhard was a trained paleontologist, steeped in the science of evolution and human origins, and yet deeply committed to Christ. He devoted his life to bringing Christianity and evolution together into a unified vision. Christianity, he said, is a religion of evolution, and until we realize that religion is the core of evolution the earth will continue to shrink in resources and compress humanity into a nameless mass. He was keenly aware of the events of his day including war, overpopulation, and industrialization. He said, "the earth is becoming a place, like boarding a train at rush hour, where we cannot breathe" (AE, 342). The conditions will only worsen, he indicated, unless we evolve.

From a scientific perspective, evolution is the way nature works. Physical reality is not composed of fixed, stable structures but a flow of information

and energy in organized forms that interact with other forms and their surrounding environments. Evolution is a process that includes lawful regulated
patterns in nature, spontaneous events, and long periods of time in which
new entities complexify and emerge in the direction of increasing consciousness. Nature is more like a dance or a community at play than a clockwork
mechanism. Today we know that evolution pertains to all aspects of human
life including culture, religion, and economics. Evolution is not merely an
explanation of physical life but a whole new *weltanschauung* that affects
every aspect of created life. It is only through a deep feeling for the human's
past and the history of the cosmos that one can begin to envision the new
humanity for the future. The human person is integrally part of evolution in
that we rise from the process but in reflecting on the process, we stand apart
from it. Using a phrase of Julian Huxley, Teilhard wrote that the human person "is nothing else than evolution become conscious of itself" (PM, 220). If
we see the struggles of our age in view of evolution, we see not the demise of
humanity but a signal to move forward.

Teilhard spent many years in the deserts of China searching for artifacts of
human origins. Like the desert Fathers of old, he was removed from the noise
of urban life and pondered deeply the meaning of Christianity in an age of
evolution. His unique blend of science, Jesuit spirituality, and profound spiri-
tual-mystical insight produced a body of writings that set forth new directions
for theology, philosophy, culture, and science itself. He worked tirelessly to
make known that religion and science are not antagonistic but two sides of
the same conjugate. Religion, he said, does not belong to the individual but
to the whole of humankind. The earth discloses its need for a god (CE, 119)
because the cosmos itself is on a journey into God.

To what end are we to evolve as a human community or as an earth community? Here the genius of Teilhard shines forth in the way he envisioned the
cosmos related to Christ. The cosmos is seen principally as a process with an
end or goal. Evolution shows direction toward greater complexity and finds
meaning in conscious, intelligent life. Conscious, personal life finds its depth
not in isolated monads but in the emergence of a human community of love.
Christ is the universal Omega and the evolver, the one who brings to the world
the phylum of love which provides the true direction for the convergence of
the human community around its center.

Yet here is Teilhard's point of mutation. As a trained scientist, he realized
that we live in a culture deeply conditioned by the insights and theories of
modern science but in the context of the church, its theology and liturgy, we
live in a premodern world. Christian theology no longer has an effective cosmology that enables believers to relate to the world in its physical character
in a way that is consistent with their religious symbols. In the stable medieval

cosmos, Christian hope had a fixed aim, life with God in heaven above. But we have yet to reframe our hopes in light of an expanding universe where openness to the future and increasing complexity have supplanted the crystalline heavens. To evolve into a more fruitful and unitive life up ahead, we need to reshape our religious understanding of the world by engaging our faith with the best insights of science concerning the nature of the physical world. Teilhard provides a vision of "science charged with faith," not a naïve optimism but a call to wake up from our medieval slumber and to see the core of religion—love, truth, goodness, and beauty—written into the very fabric of the cosmos.

Our research began with appreciation for Teilhard's original insights. Yet we realized that his ideas were developed within a certain period of history, prior to the Second Vatican Council and at the dawn of the computer age. What he began in his own time was rich and vital to the forward movement of life; but he was limited in what he could achieve, not only because of the period of history in which he lived, but because he was prohibited by the church from publishing his spiritual writings. Teilhard established new directions for thinking about God, Christianity, and science itself but left development of these directions to future generations. We set as our goal, therefore, to build on his ideas. In this volume, thirteen scholars seek to take off where Teilhard left off, opening up new windows to the divine mystery, to the evolving human person, and to the new energies of love needed for the forward movement of life. The essays in this volume are mutational essays. They are intended to lead the reader into the depths of Teilhard's vision for Christian life in evolution, and beyond Teilhard, to where he did not go. They will shed new insight on God and evolution, secularity and spirituality, and the wisdom needed to forge the future. Most of all, they will disclose a new understanding of God coming to us from the future, inspiring us to wake up from our mediocrity and enkindle the fire within us in order to build a world together.

In an evolutionary universe, nature is incomplete and subject to ongoing creativity. What will we become in a thousand years or in ten thousand years? What will the church become? What will be the future of world religions? Teilhard opens new windows onto the future and peers into the rich possibilities for life up ahead. We seek here to build on his vision, to illuminate it and forge a path for the future fullness of life, as we journey toward Omega.

## Notes

1. Ewert H. Cousins, *Christ of the 21st Century* (Rockport, MA: Element, 1992), 7–10.

*Part One*

# THEOLOGY
# AND EVOLUTION

Since the emergence in our consciousness
of the "sense of evolution" it has become
physically impossible for us to conceive or
worship anything but an organic Prime-
Mover God, *ab ante*.

Who will at last give evolution *its own* God?

—TEILHARD DE CHARDIN
*Christianity and Evolution*

*Chapter 1*

# TEILHARD DE CHARDIN

## *Theology for an Unfinished Universe*

### JOHN F. HAUGHT

In one of his loveliest poems, Gerard Manley Hopkins (1844–1889) exclaims: "Nothing is so beautiful as Spring." The great poet is enraptured by "weeds, in wheels," thrush's eggs like "little low heavens," birds' echoes that "rinse and ring the ears" and pear tree leaves and blooms that brush "the descending blue." Hopkins asks: "What is all this juice and all this joy?"

The glorious excess of spring, he answers, is "A strain of the earth's sweet being in the beginning in Eden garden." Sin has now obscured the world's original integrity, but in the flush of springtime sacramental reminders of a paradisal plenitude—of what Hopkins elsewhere calls the "dearest freshness deep down things"—break through the smudged surface of Earth. Spring-time glory recaptures imperfectly and fleetingly the creation that had been made perfect by God in the beginning. We should hold fast then, Hopkins continues, to the vernal revival of primordial innocence: "Have, get, before it cloy... and sour with sinning."

Like generations of Christians before him, Hopkins displays here a spiritual orientation nourished by remembrance more than expectation, by regret more than promise. His fellow Jesuit Teilhard de Chardin (1881–1955), on the other hand, regards the passing glories of nature in a different light. The flowering of life need not turn us nostalgically back to "earth's sweet being in the beginning." Evolution, after all, rules out the possibility that paradise ever existed in Earth's history. Teilhard has no intention of forsaking the faith of pre-Darwinian and prescientific Christianity, but he wants us to realize that the universe and Earth are still coming into bloom. The sweet being of Earth has, in some sense, not yet appeared. Teilhard would agree with Hopkins that our world has been "bleared, smeared" and "wears man's smudge." The juice has indeed soured. To the Christian evolutionist, however, the vulnerability of sweet Earth to sin's scourge is a signal that the creation needs time to ripen and that there is still room for hope. For Teilhard, autumn rather than spring was the happiest time of year. It is almost as though the shedding of leaves opened his soul to the limitless

7

space of the up-ahead and the not-yet, liberating him from the siren charms of terrestrial spring and summer.

The divergent spiritual sensitivities of Hopkins and Teilhard, both Jesuit priests, reflect a tension that runs through the heart of Christian spirituality. Both visionaries, melancholic by nature, felt the menace of despair, and they both scanned the natural world for hints of a perfection that would allow them to lift up their hearts. However, they looked in different directions for sacraments of hope. Hopkins found spiritual comfort in seasonal reminders of a primordial innocence. He felt in the depths of nature an inexhaustible freshness now largely lost but still ready to break through unrestrainedly on occasion to remind us of what once was. Teilhard, more thoroughly schooled in the natural sciences as they had taken shape after Darwin, looked toward the future of a still unfinished universe for a reason to hope.

He found the basis for spiritual renewal in the awareness that "creation has never stopped." "The creative act," he concluded, "is one huge continual gesture, drawn out over the totality of time. It is still going on; and incessantly even if imperceptibly, the world is constantly emerging a little farther above nothingness" (PU 120–21). It is toward the world's future rather than the primordial past or an eternal present that the human soul may strain to find that for which it longs.

Hopkins, though conversant with the science of his day, did not live long enough to ponder the religious meaning of the new story of nature that was emerging in the geology and biology of the nineteenth century. Born thirty-seven years after Hopkins, however, Teilhard had scientific training that led him to realize that creation could never yet have played host to Eden. Science forbids any literal belief that the world came into full flower in an opening instant of divine creativity now eclipsed by sin. Both Hopkins and Teilhard agree that the universe as it exists now is not what it is intended to be, and both would agree that it is in need of redemption. For this reason it is still possible even for an evolutionist to be deeply moved by Hopkins's sentiments. However, if we follow Teilhard, it makes a considerable difference to Christian theology and spirituality that creation was not completed on the first day and that the world is still aborning. It means there is room for something unprecedented to take shape up ahead in the cosmic future (HP 162–63).

## God and the Unfinished Universe

Although traditional theology allows for "new creation" and understands divine creativity as sustaining the world continually, theologians of the past cannot have realized fully that the imperfection of the world at present is—at least in some sense—a function of the fact that it is still coming into being. Only in the twentieth century did the notion that the universe is historical, that it is an ongoing story, begin in earnest to reshape the minds and imaginations of a few scientific observers. Teilhard, as it happens, was one of the first among them. Of course, the judgment that the historical universe is still-in-the-making and hence unfinished is not strictly speaking a scientific claim but instead a philosophical one. Yet for Teilhard it is a characterization completely compatible with the data of scientific observation.

For the most part, however, even well into the twenty-first century, human thought, including Christian theology, has failed to reflect deeply on what it means that we live in a still-becoming universe. With rare exceptions, Christian thought has not yet looked carefully at the dramatic implications of evolutionary biology and astrophysics for our understanding of God and the world. Ecclesiastical institutions and most religious education still cling at least tacitly and sometimes literally to ancient and medieval images of a fixed universe, primordial human innocence, a historical fall, and a creator who watches over the natural world from up above.

Most theologians, it is true, allow vaguely or notionally for biological evolution and Big Bang cosmology, but they have scarcely begun to focus on, and think in depth about, the potentially explosive religious implications of the new historical understanding of the universe now taking shape in scientific thought. For that matter, the wider intellectual world, including the majority of scientists and philosophers, has so far failed to contemplate carefully what the new evolutionary sciences really imply about the nature of life, humankind, and the universe, let alone God. Stunted by a stale physicalist understanding of life, the reigning academic cult of scientific naturalism—the belief that the totality of being is reducible to what analytical science is capable of finding out—has closed its eyes to the most important implications of contemporary science, namely, that the world is new each day, that the cosmos may still be only at the dawn of its creation, and that a vast and indeterminate future may still lie open before it.

As far as theology is concerned, Christian understanding of the meaning of God, Christ, redemption, morality, and human existence is still weighed down by both prescientific and early modern cosmological assumptions. Exceptions exist, of course, but most contemporary religious thinkers, church leaders, and spiritual guides make little use of science beyond references to the Hubble Deep Field, advances in genetics, and pictures of subcellular complexity. The idea of what I shall refer to here as an "unfinished universe" seems only incidental. Scientific discovery has demonstrated on multiple fronts that the cosmic process is far from being over and done with, but most earthlings, including most Christians, have yet to explore carefully what an unfinished universe really implies for our religious lives and thoughts.

Not Teilhard. That the universe is still coming into being, he insisted, "is the basic truth which must be grasped at the outset and assimilated so thoroughly that it becomes part of the very habit and nature of our thought."[1] Science's great new discovery of a still-emerging universe, however, has yet to be assimilated seriously into either theology or our devotional lives. It is far from having become habitual to Christian thought and life. If we took it seriously, I maintain, everything in Christian life and thought would not only become new, it might also make better sense than ever.

During his lifetime Teilhard often lamented the prevalent theological indifference to scientific discovery. Were he with us today he would undoubtedly deplore the ongoing Christian unresponsiveness to science. Unfortunately, when some reputable contemporary Christian writers venture to mention his ideas, more often than not they trivialize or distort them beyond recognition.[2] Much to its detriment, Christian thought still exhibits little appetite for contact with the drastic transfiguration of cosmos and consciousness that science has wrought and that Teilhard rightly considered essential to the renewal, survival, and thriving of Christian faith.

It is time now, I believe, for theology to carry forward Teilhard's pioneering work of revision. Given Christianity's increasing irrelevance to the lives and aspirations of countless thoughtful people, the task is more pressing than ever. The main problem is that science has given us a picture of the universe that seems to have outgrown the images and concepts of God that most Christians take for granted. In view of science's new portraits of the universe, what theology needs, as Teilhard wrote already in 1919, is a God "as *vast* and mysterious as the Cosmos," a deity "as *immediate* and all-embracing as Life," and an absolute that is "*linked* (in some way) *to our effort* as Mankind." Teilhard emphatically adds: "*A God who made the World less mysterious, or smaller, or less important to us, than our heart and reason show it to be, that God—less beautiful than the God we await—will never more be He to whom the Earth kneels.*" "Of this," he says "we must be quite clear: the *Christian Ideal* (as normally expressed) has ceased to be what we still complacently flatter ourselves that it is, the common Ideal of Mankind" (HM 212, italics in the original).

The intention of this volume, however, is not to provide yet another exposition of Teilhard's novel ideas but to take up where he left off and make fresh proposals about the relevance of his ideas for cultural, religious, and ethical existence today. Christianity, along with the whole religious world, is now facing its most critical challenges ever: the spread of fundamentalism, the rising secularism in Western cultures, and the dominance of scientific naturalism in the intellectual world. Within mainline Christianity, powerful movements toward restoration rather than renewal, some of them officially endorsed by ecclesiastical leaders, seek to reestablish spiritualities that assume, in one way or another, a prescientific—hence unnecessarily static and diminished—understanding of the cosmos. In the face of these and other trends, dramatic changes are needed for Christianity's well-being in the age of science. What Christianity requires now, especially in view of developments in science, is not "no God," as scientific naturalists propose, but a "new God," as Teilhard provocatively announces (HE, 43–47).

What must be our new thoughts about God in the context of an unfinished universe? The question needs to be asked not with the intention of moving outside of Christian tradition, but to facilitate the tradition's survival and thriving far into the future. Unfortunately, the relatively few theologians who have been involved in the work of rethinking Christian faith in the age of science often seem marginal to their peers. They are seldom taken seriously by the faithful at large, by seminary instructors, or by religious officials. The habitual neglect of science by most Christians is not likely to cease soon, but I firmly believe that the intellectual respectability of theology demands our bringing together in new ways current scientific understanding of the universe and Christianity's persistent hope for new creation.

This reworking of Christian theology has had a promising beginning with Teilhard, but he lacked the opportunity to develop his thoughts with the systematic rigor and thoroughness that his creative insights demand. Even though his ideas did influence the Second Vatican Council, subsequently his synthetic efforts have had little effect on Christian life and thought at large, not to mention the intellectual world and human culture.

## Where to Begin?

For Teilhard theology must never lose sight of the fact that *the universe is still coming into being*. What does it really mean for Christian faith, then, that we live in an unfinished universe? At the very least it means an end to the idea that God's creation has at any time been perfect or paradisal. Once we have fully absorbed the scientifically incontestable fact that Earth was not Eden in the beginning, serious reflection on Christian faith can have the effect of ennobling and adding new zest to faith and life. How so? It may do so by making us realize that our lives here and now are tied into a universe that still has a future, a universe that can become much "more" than it is now. The cosmos as portrayed by contemporary science is a work in progress, still undergoing a creative transformation that began (only) fourteen billion years ago and that still winds its way toward who knows where. Strictly speaking, science does not itself characterize the universe as transformative, unfinished, or dramatic since these are interpretations from which scientific *method* abstracts. However, they are generalizations that I believe (along with Teilhard) are completely consistent with the results of scientific *discovery*. The point is, each of us is part of an immense cosmic drama of transformation, a fact that may give new significance to our lives and works no matter how ineffectual these may sometimes seem.

Human beings, as our religious traditions agree, have always had restless hearts, and our happiness has always been tied to beliefs that our deepest aspirations can, at least eventually, be satisfied. Without a horizon of expectation we succumb to the "sweet decay" of hopeless lethargy.[3] The shadows of prescientific cosmology, however, still often restrain human expectation by channeling our aspirations toward a timeless spiritual heaven outside of the physical universe. No doubt, an exclusively otherworldly expectation is understandable given the hopeless political and economic conditions in which so many human beings have lived. A universe that seems to undergo no significant transformation itself can easily be left behind in the ecstasy of final release from this vale of tears. Even today, otherworldly preoccupations may render Christians unnecessarily indifferent to social, economic, and environmental ills.

An exclusively otherworldly optimism, moreover, provides no substantive resistance to contemporary scientific naturalism and its unquestioned conviction that the universe itself is pointless. Lack of interest by theologians in the new scientific cosmic story only weakens their intellectual opposition to the current academic cult of cosmic pessimism. Cosmic pessimism is the belief that nature has no purpose and that whatever meaning exists in the world is our own human creation. This belief is taken for granted by most scientific thinkers today, but with the aid of the new idea of an unfinished universe, theology may point out that cosmic pessimism, which is usually taken as the epitome of hard-nosed realism, is not as self-evidently justifiable as it seems to most contemporary intellectuals. Geology, evolutionary biology, and cosmology now situate Earth, life, and human existence within the framework of an immense cosmic drama of transformation that is still going on. Since the drama is still being played out, none of us is in a secure position to declare with absolute certitude here and now that it makes no sense ultimately.

Once we fully realize that the drama of creation is still going on, it is not inevitable that we take the route of despair. Nor is it required that Christians today have exactly the same thoughts about the creator, sin, virtue, the meaning of life, and human destiny as before. And if the world is still emerging, we need no longer think of Christ and his mission in exactly the same way as previous ages did. As far as the life of the church is concerned, its worship, sacraments, and spirituality may need to undergo a refashioning that our religious ancestors could never have envisaged on the basis of their "fixist" understanding of the natural world. Fidelity to traditional theology and spirituality will, of course, be essential to the shaping of our new identity as Christians in an unfinished universe, but we shall not feel obliged to imprison our souls and aspirations in depictions of the cosmos that now seem too small for any thoughtful and educated person.

Those who absorb the newly emergent scientific world story not only conceptually but also imaginatively and emotionally will respond to Immanuel Kant's three vital questions in a new way. They will still ponder what we can know, what we must do, and what we may hope for, but they will do so, with vastly different cosmological assumptions from those of previous generations. Certainly Hopkins's preevolutionary lamenting of the souring of innocence by sin will still move us, but in the age of evolution and Big Bang cosmology our awareness that things are not what they were intended to be may arouse a new kind of hope and spiritual adventure.

Christians who profess to love God and to have been saved by Christ, I believe, will lose nothing and gain everything by transplanting their devotion to the new incalculably larger setting offered by contemporary biology and cosmology. Our sense of the creator, the work of the Holy Spirit, and the redemptive significance of Christ can now grow by immense orders of magnitude. The Love that rules the stars will now have to be seen as embracing two hundred billion galaxies, a cosmic epic of fourteen billion years' duration, and perhaps even a multiverse. Our thoughts about Christ and redemption will have to extend over the full breadth of cosmic time and space.

## A Metaphysics of the Future

Teilhard began this work of widening Christian faith and hope cosmically, but his ideas met with the censorship of his church. He was not permitted to publish his major writings, a prohibition that forbade the kind of scholarly exchange that might have allowed him to refine his thinking in several sensitive areas of theological inquiry. In 1962 the Holy Office in Rome issued a *Monitum* (warning) to seminaries and Catholic universities not to expose students to Teilhard's "dangerous" ideas. It also happened to be the opening year of the Second Vatican Council whose *Pastoral Constitution on the Church in the Modern World* ironically came to embrace and promote Teilhard's encouragement to rethink Christian faith in harmony with our new understanding of an evolutionary universe.[4] It is past time, I believe, to allow Teilhard's suggestions about the need for reform in theology to be carried out more systematically than either he or Vatican II were able to accomplish. The present essay, of course, can do no more than point toward some themes that will need to be explored in much more depth.

I begin by affirming Teilhard's passionate insistence that theology's indifference toward science, especially evolution and cosmology, is a great obstacle to the renewal of Christian faith.

Thinking about human life, ethics, and worship without also attending to science's picture of an unfinished universe will have at least two negative consequences. First, it will only perpetuate the impression that Christian faith is now intellectually implausible. Second, it will "clip the wings of hope" (CE, 79) and sap the "zest for living" that any theological vision must sponsor if it is to prove challenging enough to merit wide acceptance (AE, 231–43).

If hope is to have wings and life to have zest, nothing less is needed than a theological vision that opens up a new future for the world. I call such a way of looking at reality a *metaphysics of the future.*[5] By this I mean simply a vision of being that gives primacy to the future over the past and present. Philosophers and theologians conditioned to thinking of the world and God in the context of medieval notions of being will no doubt raise conceptual objections to this expression. They will assume that since the future does not yet exist it cannot be ontologically foundational in our efforts to understand the world and God. However, those who take seriously the biblical understanding of reality based on the ancient Hebrew discovery of the future can hardly object. Those who dwell within a worldview rooted in the motifs of promise and hope will rightly suspect that Platonic, Aristotelian, Thomistic, and most modern philosophies have blunted the futuristic edge and thrust of early Christian life and thought.

No matter how brilliant or conceptually attractive they may have been, most of the philosophical systems that Christian theology has tried out for more than two thousand years are not ready-made to frame adequately either contemporary science or, for that matter, the kind of expectation that animated the lives of our biblical ancestors. Consequently, I freely employ the intellectually unsettling expression metaphysics of the future to designate theology's need for a worldview that can accommodate both biblical hope and contemporary science, especially biology and cosmology. I can think of no better way of capturing both the universe's openness to unpredictable, surprising new outcomes and the shocking theme of anticipation central to biblical faith. The idea of a metaphysics of the future may be conceptually unclear, but there is a reason for its opacity, a reason rooted in the nature of the universe itself. A sense of darkness, a realization that the intelligibility we seek is always partly obscured by shadows, is inevitable in any universe that is still *in via.* As long as the universe is not yet fully actualized it cannot possibly be fully intelligible to those who journey along with it (CE, 79–86; 131–32).

Intelligibility is a goal we can only anticipate, not control. Like truth, intelligibility is something for which we must wait, since—if it is to be a continuous source of nourishment—we can never possess it. Consequently, I believe that a metaphysics of the future is an appropriate philosophical setting for contemporary theology as it reflects on our unfinished universe. In any case, a startling new mode of thought is needed to counter two dominant metaphysical alternatives that have persistently clipped the wings of hope. I call these rivals respectively the metaphysics of the past and the metaphysics of the eternal present.

The first and most deadening of these prevalent alternatives, the metaphysics of the past, is the physicalist worldview that now dominates scientific thinking and much intellectual life all over the planet. It is the largely unquestioned sense of reality ensconced in many of the world's universities and research centers. A handy compendium and endorsement of this worldview is E. O. Wilson's celebrated book *Consilience*.[6] Intellectually speaking, this way of seeing is the main roadblock to a truly hopeful vision of reality. I am referring to it as a metaphysics of the past because it assumes that the foundation of all being as well as the ultimate explanation of all present actualities lies in the mindless physical components that made up the early physical universe. According to a metaphysics of the past, the only reliable way to understand the world here and now is to dig back into the earliest episodes of cosmic history and then trace the stages that have led gradually, blindly, algorithmically, and deterministically, from an original state of diffused elemental bits of matter to the staggering biological and cultural complexity of the contemporary world.

A metaphysics of the past expects to explain present realities completely by going far back temporally, and deep down analytically, to retrieve the subatomic units that led to atoms, then molecules, cells, organisms, and eventually human brains and their cultural products. It assumes that we can arrive at the goal of complete explanation by viewing present reality, including the complexity of organisms and minds, as nothing more than "simplicity masquerading as complexity."[7] According to this starkly reductionist worldview, the human mind can reach an adequate understanding of natural reality *only* by using the analytical tools of contemporary science to uncover the "really real" regime of lifeless and mindless elements that made up the earliest stages of cosmic becoming.

A metaphysics of the past professes to have planted human thought on the firmest foundation excavated so far in the history of human inquiry: pure matter. And since the insensate material ground of all being is essentially lifeless and mindless, scientific naturalists now take for granted that nonlife rather than life is the ground state of being. Nonlife is "the intelligible par excellence," as the philosopher Hans Jonas has critically commented.[8] Science thus assures us that ever since the beginning, and for all subsequent ages, there can be no real novelty. Instead, the universe is merely the working out of a completely deterministic series of blind causes and effects. Consequently, according to scientific naturalists, cosmic pessimism is the only realistic attitude for intelligent people nowadays to have toward the world. This metaphysics of the past forbids the arrival in the natural world of anything truly new. Hence it is the fundamental contemporary intellectual challenge to Christian hope.

However, as Teilhard rightly points out, the materialist enshrinement of an inanimate and mindless physical past as the goal of our long human search for complete intelligibility is nothing more than the result of an "analytical illusion" (AE, 139). That is, contemporary physicalism and its attendant cosmic pessimism are based on the uncritical belief that only through breaking things down into their subordinate parts can we finally satisfy the human craving to understand the world. Teilhard responds that the process of analysis by itself leads our minds ever more precipitously down (and temporally back) into the domain of dispersed units of matter—and thus farther in the direction of incoherence (HE, 172–73).[9]

Thus, physicalism (or materialism) fails to provide an ultimate explanation of anything. By itself it renders nothing truly coherent or intelligible. Analysis can help provide a scientifically essential map of the universe's particulars and constituents, and so we must not diminish the importance of scientifically reductive inquiry. It has helped us piece together, chapter by chapter, the long cosmic story of the universe up to the present. However, ever since antiquity any pure atomism has only led our minds downward and backward into increasing incoherence. Along with mechanistic forms of materialism, atomism still reigns in contemporary scientific thinking, especially in biology, even though there are now some signs of discomfort with such a simplistic worldview. However, here I want to emphasize that it is not analytical scientific method as such, but rather a metaphysically materialist atomism that, if taken as the sole road to understanding what is real, renders the world finally unintelligible.

The second unsatisfactory alternative to a metaphysics of the future is a metaphysics of the eternal present. This vision of reality is rooted in the Platonic, Aristotelian, and Neoplatonic worldviews that, to one degree or another, have provided the intellectual setting of most traditional Christian thought. For centuries the classical Western theological tradition has attached itself to a general form of thought that locates the fullness of being and intelligibility in a state of timelessness immune to all becoming. It assumes the overwhelming realness of an immaterial world lurking everlastingly in, beyond, or behind the transient sphere of terrestrial and cosmic becoming.

No doubt this metaphysical alternative has offered much solace to individual souls, but it holds out little if any hope for the final destiny of the physical universe that has given birth to each of us. Today its most ardent defenders—and they are many—fail to reflect deeply on the scientific evidence that each personal subject (or soul) is intricately woven into the fabric of a universe still aborning. Moreover, the classical understanding of the self, world, and God, as Teilhard rightly complained, provides insufficient incentive for sustained human action in the world (HE, 29; CE, 178–79).

Of course, there is something of timeless religious value to be rescued from a metaphysics of the eternal present. However, if a metaphysics of the past forbids anything truly new and surprising from ever arising in the universe, so also does a metaphysics of the eternal present. It too clips the wings of hope inasmuch as it conceives of creation as having been complete from the beginning (CE, 79). It makes little room, therefore, for the world's becoming more, since it holds that creation is virtually complete from the outset. Such an assumption cannot allow for the emergence of what is truly new, for it conceives of all created being as having been fashioned fully *in principio*.

It implies also that there was a souring of "the earth's sweet being in the beginning." Long ago there occurred a besmirching of primordial innocence that has turned the history of human life and the practice of virtue into a project of restoration rather than one of joining ourselves to a universe that is still becoming more. Its mythic imagining of the world's sweet beginning has erected tacit barriers to the hope that human moral existence here and now may have something to do with bringing what is truly new and unprecedented into being.

The metaphysics of the eternal present conceives of nature as a static hierarchy of levels of being, each graded ontologically according to the degree of its participation in the eternal perfection of God. At the lowest level of the hierarchy lies the realm of matter. Then, in ascending order of being and value, come the higher levels of plants, animals, human beings, angels, and finally God. This Great Chain of Being has been the backbone of traditional Christian reflection on God as well as the lattice around which the vine of Christian spirituality has wound itself for centuries. In spite of Vatican II's acknowledgment that our understanding of the world has now moved from a static to an evolutionary one, a metaphysics of the eternal present still rules over contemporary Christian theology, ethics, and spirituality. No matter how cleanly the classical metaphysics of being rescues its devotees from the messiness of involvement in the world, it leads Christian educators and ministers to ignore both the dramatic, emergent character of the universe and the promissory thrust of biblical faith. In the final analysis its picture of nature is not wide or deep enough to carry the full substance of Christian hope.

## Implications for Hope and Love

It is in contrast to both the metaphysics of the past and that of the eternal present that I am proposing a biblically based metaphysics of the future as the framework for contemporary theology. Teilhard himself professed to be weary of metaphysics, but this reserve is simply due to the fact that the term "metaphysics" has usually been used in reference to the two alternative worldviews that I have just sketched. Nevertheless, Teilhard turned out to be thoroughly metaphysical in the sense that he too sought an ultimate and unassailable foundation upon which to situate the emerging universe that the evolutionary sciences have uncovered. His lifelong intellectual and spiritual journey, like that of most profound thinkers, was one of looking for a bedrock solidity and consistency upon which to rest his vision of reality. He looked for this foundation first in the apparent durability of matter but eventually realized that matter dissolves into atomistic dust when subjected to ever more refined scientific analysis. The further science digs into the world's physical past, in other words, the more the world falls apart into scattered individual bits. A purely physicalist philosophy, to repeat, leads our minds downward in space and backward in time toward an ultimate incoherence (HM, 15–79).

Incoherence is another word for unintelligibility. Hence it is only in the mode of coming together or "converging" toward unity or coherence that things begin to become intelligible. Teilhard's search for a grounding of solidity and consistency, therefore, led him eventually to claim that the universe leans on the future as its true foundation (AE, 139, 239). What gives coherence, unity, and intelligibility to a still emerging, unfinished universe is not the atomized and diffused cosmic past—incoherence, in other words—but the world's being drawn toward the unity of a constantly receding and refreshing future. Overall, matter has moved over time toward an increasing complexity endowed with what Teilhard often called "spirit." At the extreme term of the convergent movement of the universe from past multiplicity toward unity up ahead, Teilhard locates "God-Omega." Only by being synthesized into the unifying creativity and love of God does the world become fully intelligible.

For Teilhard, it is the world's anticipation of deeper union or communion up ahead in the future, rather than any imagined vertical participation in a timeless and finished Perfection, that gives the world its consistency and opens it toward more being. In his dissatisfaction with the fixist or immobilist theology of the scholastics, and his frustration at the failure of both scientific naturalism and traditional theology to account for evolution's becoming *more*, Teilhard calls out for a new understanding of God. God, he suggests, must now be seen as the ultimate Center of convergence for an unfinished universe rather than as a mere overseer of a creation that had once been perfect but is now spoiled by sin and the ravages of time.

What then does it mean for Christian spirituality and theology that the universe is still unfinished? It means, at the very least, that God, understood as the ultimate Center of cosmic convergence, creates the world by drawing it from up ahead (*ab ante*) rather than by pushing it into being from out of the past (*a tergo*) or by allowing it to dangle in suspension from up above. It means that even though God is both Alpha and Omega, God is more Omega than Alpha (CE 240). It means that, in our unfinished universe, the metaphysical search for what is really real leads in the direction of the not-yet rather than the already. It means that the question of suffering, while still intractable, opens up a new horizon of hope when viewed in terms of an unfinished and hence still unperfected universe. And it means also that theology may think in new ways about the doctrines of God, creation, incarnation, sin, evil and redemption, grace and freedom, eschatology, and the virtues of faith, hope, and love (CE, 76–95).

Here I cannot treat all of these themes but will limit my remaining comments to the question of how the scientific idea of an unfinished universe can give new shape to theological and ethical reflection on the virtues of hope and love. To come immediately to the point, I want to suggest that the fullest release of human love is realistically possible only if the created world still has possibilities that have never before been realized. The idea of an essentially fixed and frozen universe, on the other hand, subtly stifles enthusiasm for the practice of love and other virtues.

Only if the beloved still has a future can there be an unreserved commitment to the practice of charity, justice, and compassion. Why so? Hope for a new future, as the theologian Jürgen Moltmann puts it, "has the chance of a meaningful existence only when reality itself is in a state of historic flux and when historic reality has room for open possibilities ahead."[10] It is a great gift to Christian faith, therefore, that science has now provided irrefutable evidence that our universe is historical, that it is still in flux and therefore open to realizing new possibilities in the future. The assumption of an essentially finished and perfected universe, on the other hand, would not allow for such openness, no matter how one looks at it.

As long as humans are given the impression that everything important has already been accomplished by God in a prelapsarian creation, can anything really worthwhile still remain for human life to accomplish—as more than one modern philosopher has asked? Might not the assumption of an initially completed universe unconsciously suppress the creative vitality needed to sustain vigorous moral aspiration?

Whether and in what sense the idea of God as Finished Perfection may also impede the full release of hope is a vital theological question that I hope to address in future writings. For now I wish only to affirm with Teilhard that the traditional theological idea of an initially completed creation based on a literal interpretation of Genesis, and fortified by ancient and medieval metaphysics, not only clips the wings of hope but in doing so circumscribes

arbitrarily the field of love's effectiveness. The assumption of an initially completed creation tends to limit the significance of ethical life to the acquiring
of virtuous habits that enhance our moral character and worthiness to inherit
eternal life, but it has little to do with building the world, a motivation that
Vatican II understood to be essential to Christian ethical life.

Consequently, if the created world had ever actually been in a state of
"sweet being in the beginning," what would be the point of moral impera-
tives here and now? If we assume, along with most classical Christian theology, an initial fall from a primordial integrity, then pursuit of the ethical
life would perhaps be motivated by a sense of shame at our rebellion against
God, by the need to restore by expiation the perfection that had been defiled
or, more nobly, by a commitment to do good simply for the sake of the good.
For many Christians this might be enough. In all cases, however, the practice
of virtue would have little to do with contributing to the creation of something truly new.

The narrative of a primordial cosmic integrity and human innocence,
original sin, expiation, restoration of innocence, and final reconciliation with
God still defines the spiritual itinerary of countless Christians. Admittedly,
this narrative allows for exemplary lives, lives moreover of spiritual adventure fraught with perils and momentary triumphs. This classic map can give
a sense of meaning and achievement to human existence as it struggles from
exile toward paradise. Nevertheless, it is hard to deny that this whole understanding of innocence, sin, and redemption is tied logically and consistently
to the prescientific assumption of an initially complete creation (CE, 79–95).

I find it doubtful, therefore, that the sense of an initially integral creation
underlying Hopkins's spiritual aspirations and that of many other Christians
can any longer be taken with intellectual sincerity, at least by scientifically
informed people. The idea of an initially fixed and finished universe, one
that fits a metaphysics of the eternal present, seems more appropriate to the
nurturing of melancholy or nostalgia than for the full liberation of our native
need for hope. Certainly Hopkins's "Spring" is a moving expression of the
universal religious sense that the world at present is not what it is intended to
be. But evolutionary biology teaches us that a strain of souring was present in
the universe long before the sinning.

The science-based idea that the universe is still coming into being offers a
more promising—and I believe realistic—framework for Christian hope and
the practice of love. I believe Teilhard's embrace of science's historical view of
the universe is one of the main reasons why his writings often lift the hearts
of his scientifically educated readers and make room for a kind of hope—an
*extensio animi ad magna*—that they had never experienced before when
reading and meditating on other theological and spiritual works.

Teilhard realized that the universe is still in historical flux and hence open to what is new. Such a metaphysical setting is congenial to meaningful hope and effective love. Teilhard's implicit metaphysics of the future offers an uplifting alternative to the academically sponsored fatalism based on the illusory analytical journey back in time toward the world's elemental past where everything eventually falls apart into sheer multiplicity. At the same time, his alternative metaphysics is justifiably critical of spiritualities that idealize an eternal present that beckons us prematurely to untie ourselves from the physical universe in which something momentous may still be working itself out.

Both science and biblical faith open up our understanding of the universe to new possibilities and hence to a worldview in which love and hope have a positively creative significance that the other two metaphysical alternatives tend to suppress. From a Christian point of view, if determinism reigned and the cosmic future were virtually closed, or if the fullness of being were already actualized in an eternal now, it would blunt Jesus's enthusiastic proclamation of the good news and his constant encouragement to trust, love, and practice justice as virtues that really matter. The Gospel writers realized that Jesus's own ethical instructions would have had little power or meaning apart from his profound impression that something radically new (the Reign of God) is still coming and not yet fully actualized. Likewise, St. Paul's ethical enthusiasm would have been empty apart from his premonition, and that of his contemporaries, that the world is still turning. Scientific cosmology now confirms the Pauline intuition that the lifting up of our hearts at the news of God's coming is remarkably continuous with the anticipatory drama we call the universe.

## Points to Ponder

+ Creation was not completed on the first day, and the world is still aborning. There is room for something unprecedented to take shape up ahead in the cosmic future.

+ The belief that the totality of being is reducible to what analytical science is capable of finding out has closed its eyes to the most important implications of contemporary science, namely, that the world is new each day, that the cosmos may still be only at the dawn of its creation, and that a vast and indeterminate future may still lie open before it.

+ Most earthlings, including most Christians, have yet to explore carefully what an unfinished universe really implies for our religious lives and thoughts.

◆ The metaphysics of the eternal present conceives of nature as a static hierarchy of levels of being, each graded ontologically according to the degree of its participation in the eternal perfection of God. At the lowest level of the hierarchy lies the realm of matter. Then, in ascending order of being and value, come the higher levels of plants, animals, human beings, angels, and finally God.

◆ In spite of Vatican II's acknowledgment that our understanding of the world has now moved from a static to an evolutionary one, a metaphysics of the eternal present still rules over contemporary Christian theology, ethics, and spirituality. No matter how cleanly the classical metaphysics of being rescues its devotees from the messiness of involvement in the world, it leads Christian educators and ministers to ignore both the dramatic, emergent character of the universe and the promissory thrust of biblical faith.

◆ Teilhard's search for a grounding solidity and consistency led him eventually to claim that the universe leans on the future as its true foundation.

◆ Only by being synthesized into the unifying creativity and love of God does the world become fully intelligible.

◆ God must now be seen as the ultimate Center of convergence for an unfinished universe rather than as a mere overseer of a creation that had once been perfect but is now spoiled by sin and the ravages of time.

◆ Both science and biblical faith open up our understanding of the universe to new possibilities and hence to a worldview in which love and hope have a positively creative significance.

## Questions for Discussion

1. How does a metaphysics of the future affect our choices for God, neighbor, and creation?

2. Describe the difference between a metaphysics of the present and a metaphysics of the future. What is the significance of the difference for you personally?

3. How does evolution change the direction of Christian faith?

# Notes

1. Neville Braybrooke, ed., *Teilhard de Chardin: Pilgrim of the Future* (London: Libra, 1964), 23.

2. See, for example, N. T. Wright, *Surprised by Hope: Rethinking Heaven, the Resurrection, and the Mission of the Church* (New York: Harper One, 2008), 84–86.

3. Jürgen Moltmann, *Theology of Hope: On the Ground and the Implications of a Christian Eschatology*, trans. James W. Leitch (New York: Harper & Row, 1967), 16.

4. Walter M. Abbott, ed., *The Documents of Vatican II* (New York: Guild Press, 1966), 203–4, 218, 233.

5. I am not certain about the precise origin of this expression. I believe it was used first by the German philosopher Ernst Bloch or perhaps some of his students, but I cannot find a specific source. In any case, I have adopted "metaphysics of the future" as an apt label for the worldview that Teilhard eventually came to embrace.

6. E. O. Wilson, *Consilience: the Unity of Knowledge* (New York: Knopf, 1998).

7. Peter W. Atkins, *The 2nd Law: Energy, Chaos, and Form* (New York: Scientific American, 1994), 200.

8. Hans Jonas, *The Phenomenon of Life* (New York: Harper & Row, 1966), 9–10.

9. For a book-length critique of the materialist assumptions underlying the analytical illusion, see John F. Haught, *Is Nature Enough? Meaning and Truth in the Age of Science* (Cambridge: Cambridge University Press, 2006).

10. Moltmann, *Theology of Hope: On the Ground and the Implications of a Christian Eschatology*, 92.

*Chapter 2*

# SOPHIA

*Catalyst for Creative Union and Divine Love*

### Kathleen Duffy, SSJ

One of the most challenging questions regarding the theory of evolution for believers today is how to describe, or at least to imagine, the role that God plays in ongoing creation when so much of the evolutionary process can now be explained from a materialist viewpoint. As science continues to discover the details of a story that astounds us with its splendor and drama, we often lose sight of that story's inner dimensions. Mechanisms for chemical reactions and nuclear fusion, for the formation of stars and galaxies, for the life processes of plants and animals are spelled out by science in great detail with little or no attention to matter's spiritual component. Does God, then, have a function, much less a significant role, in the cosmic creative process? And, if so, how can believers experience God at work in an evolutionary world?

Of course, it is impossible to answer these questions using the methods of science since we are here considering a layer of reality that is not accessible by its methods. Only through the eyes of faith are we able to perceive God's action, and then only darkly. It is the mystics who, throughout the ages, have been able to sense God acting in their lives. It is they who have sometimes been gifted with ways of seeing through to the heart of matter, to the place where God is all in all. Some have even attempted to share their mystical experiences, as much as that is possible. However, since it is only through the lens of biblical, prophetic, and sacramental imagination[1] that the deep mysteries of the Divine are able to come into focus for us, the writings of these mystics tend to appeal to our imaginations. In vivid imagery, they spark in us new realizations about the nature and action of the Divine that are absent from purely rational theological descriptions. Thomas Merton expresses the need for this mystical imperative:

> The Christian's vision of the world ought, by its very nature, to have in it something of poetic inspiration. Our faith ought to be capable of filling our hearts with a wonder and a wisdom which see beyond the surface of things and events, and grasp something of the inner and

"sacred" meaning of the cosmos which, in all its movements and all its aspects, sings the praises of its Creator and Redeemer.[2]

The Jesuit geologist and paleontologist Pierre Teilhard de Chardin was a mystic vitally aware of the need to spark religious imagination. As a practicing paleontologist, he was gifted with a keen eye for noticing primitive tools and fossils. His close encounter with the geological history of Earth's surface rock made him aware of the richness of an evolutionary view of the cosmos. As a mystic drawn to Earth's beauty, he developed an extraordinary ability for contemplative seeing, a keen sensitivity to the divine presence alive and at work in the evolutionary process as well as in his own life. As a priest, he was truly in love with Christ and aware of Christ's love and care for the world. And as a human being, he was able to incorporate these many facets of his life experience into a single whole. The result of this integration was his coming to know a God who is situated within every speck of matter, who is one with each of us in a relationship of intimate love, and who is beyond the world as the unseen source of all that we experience with our senses.[3]

Teilhard was a prolific scientist who wholeheartedly practiced the scientific method and often referred to scientific findings in his religious writings. Yet he was also critical of the philosophy of the science practiced in his day. While honoring the value of its method, he called for a more holistic approach that would take into account the inner realities that science, by definition, ignores. In his many religious essays, he attempts to articulate his mystical insights, to describe his perception of God's action, and to integrate his scientific understanding of the cosmos with his religious beliefs through the use of images that allude to aspects of human experience that are, in fact, unutterable.

In an effort to articulate his understanding of God's presence and action in the evolutionary world, Teilhard composed a poem entitled "The Eternal Feminine" (WTW, 191–202).[4] This poem, which is based on passages from the wisdom literature of the Bible,[5] seeks to portray God's action as dynamic and to explore the cosmic nature of divine love. In this paper, I intend to explore this image to ascertain whether it can enliven an appreciation for the richness of the divine presence in matter, offer a more dynamic image of God's action in an evolutionary world, and focus our attention more fully on the sacred depths of nature.

## The Poem

Mostly likely, the concurrence of two personal experiences impelled Teilhard to write this poem. The first occurred while he was pursuing his doctorate in geology and paleontology at the Institut Catholique, the Collège de France, and the Musée d'Histoire Naturelle in Paris. After not having seen each other since they were children, Teilhard and his cousin Marguerite Teillard-Chambon met and, finding that they had similar interests, immediately fell in love.[6] From that moment, they developed a deep and lasting friendship and continued throughout their lives to relate to each other what was deepest in their souls. Teilhard confided in her; in particular, he shared with her his early mystical insights.[7] She, on the other hand, knew his mind and provided him with the support and understanding that he needed. Yet, at the time, Teilhard, a priest and in his thirtieth year of age, was surprised by the strength of the passion aroused in him by the light shining in Marguerite's face (WTW, 117). In fact, he was profoundly affected by the experience. His love for Marguerite drew him out of himself, sensitized him, and stimulated his capacity for deeper and more intimate relationships (HM, 59).

Shortly after their meeting, Teilhard volunteered to serve as a stretcher bearer on the battlefront during World War I. During this time, he also began consciously preparing for his final profession as a Jesuit. Obviously, he was reflecting seriously on the meaning of human love as it relates to the vow of chastity that he was about to pronounce; presumably, he was also very much aware of the power of his relationship with Marguerite. In order to articulate the fruit of his reflection on this experience, he planned to write a poetic essay. Shortly before his religious profession, he completed the poem, entitled it "The Eternal Feminine,"[8] and dedicated it indirectly to Marguerite who was its initial inspiration.[9] On one level, Teilhard's poetic rendition of the Wisdom readings was an exercise in exploring the meaning and value of Christian virginity; however, it was actually more than an endeavor to solve a personal intellectual problem. On another level, it was his attempt to share insights into the cosmic nature of love that were sparked by this fortuitous coincidence of events.

Teilhard's eternal feminine embodies the spiritual power of matter as the feminine aspect of God's nature embedded in all of creation and captures Teilhard's profound understanding of what is occurring in the cosmos.[10] The eternal feminine has many prototypes—Beatrice of Dante's *Divine Comedy*, Goethe's eternal feminine, Sophia of the wisdom literature, and the Virgin Mary, to name but a few.[11] Like each of these prototypes, Teilhard's eternal feminine personifies the cosmic unifying and spiritualizing force at work in creation; like Wisdom, she is at play in creation and delights in its every facet; like Dante's Beatrice, she is a guide for the journey into God.

Inspired by the power of Teilhard's poem "The Eternal Feminine" to put us in touch with this deepest of mysteries and its ability to portray the immanent nature of the divine creativity, I take the liberty to rewrite Teilhard's poem, updating it with insights gained from modern science and from modern sophiology. I weave some of Teilhard's phrases together with scripture passages from the wisdom literature and with images gleaned from the work of the many others who have contemplated the divine creativity at work at the heart of matter. In order to attend to feminist concerns regarding the expression the eternal feminine, and to be faithful to biblical references, I prefer to call her Sophia, the Greek word for wisdom. In language that is both affective and effective, I allow Sophia to tell her story, to lead us through the billions of years during which she has been laboring, hoping to stimulate our ability to imagine divine action at work in an evolutionary world and to demonstrate more vividly the sacred nature of matter.

## Sophia Speaks

Like the passage from the wisdom literature that he emulates (Prov 8:22–31), Teilhard's poem opens at the beginning of time, at the moment when Sophia is embedded into the primordial energy that is already expanding into the space-time of the early universe. Only half formed and still elusive, she emerges as from the mist, destined to grow in beauty and grace (WTW, 192). As soon as the first traces of her presence become apparent, she assumes her mandate to nurture creation, to challenge it, to unify it, to beautify it, and ultimately to lead the universe back to God. With this mission as her guide, she attends to her work of transforming the world, a world alive with potential. Let us listen as she speaks:

> *From the beginning, I am being poured forth. Even before the universe comes into being, I am being formed. In the stirring of the cosmic substance, the first traces of my countenance can be read (WTW, 192), playing over the surface of the divine fire. I am the catalyst for the ongoing creative process, endowed with the power to synthesize and to sublimate the multiple. I stimulate the physical and spiritual cosmic energy that is needed to reach the fullness of life and summon the cosmos to follow my lead.*

> *From within the heart of matter, I hold together the foundations of the universe. Since everything in the universe is made by union, I labor to condense and to concentrate the elementary particles that continue to emerge from the energy ejected from the primordial fire (WTW 193, 192). In order to release the energy stored within these particles and to assist me in my task of producing greater complexity, I have developed the process of creative union and coded it into the very fabric of the cosmos. Fortified with this guiding principle, I attempt to persuade the fragments, whether similar or diverse, to come together. I begin by stirring up within the quanta of primeval energy a deep desire to hold fast*

*to something outside themselves, to attempt to unite with one another (WTW, 192–93), to become something more.*

*I am the principle of union, the soul of the world. At play throughout the expanding space-time (CE, 108), I am the magnetic and unitive force that brings disparate matter together and nurtures each newly created form, urging each one to multiply, to beautify, and to bear fruit.*[12] *With a promise of worlds beyond number, I advise the primordial force field to separate into its fundamental components: the gravitational, electromagnetic, and nuclear forces that, throughout the ages, have continued to be effective facilitators of creative power. Embedded within the elementary particles that materialize out of the energy of the Big Bang, I counter their tendency to escape from one another. I marvel as protons, which naturally repel one another, swarm about in the fiery plasma and eventually come close enough to fuse. As the early universe continues to expand and cool, it becomes possible for me to engage in further efforts that will eventually unite the matter scattered throughout the confines of space-time. Nuclei now attract electrons and form ions and neutral atoms. Soon, atoms of all sorts interact with each other and form molecules.*

*I delight as the gravitational force slowly but surely gathers the cosmic gas and dust into the clumps of matter that will form the first stars and galaxies. In the cores of the newly formed stars, nuclei respond to the strong nuclear force and fuse first into helium and then into more complex nuclei. These are the building blocks that the stars will share with the rest of the universe. As I explore the expanding universe looking for a variety of ways to implement the process of creative union, I thrill at the energy that is continually released from elementary interactions. These initial results hold the promise of much more diversity and beauty.*

*The process of creative union is a gradual process, and it is often beset with failure. Therefore, from within the fragments of matter, I encourage all possible combinations since I know that not every combination, will be productive. Whenever fragments of matter are able successfully to unite, I make sure that they do not lose their identity. However, as they come together and begin to operate as a unit, I evoke in them new possibilities for creativity, for more fruitful interactions, and for further union. Under my influence, these new creations always become more than what they would have been had they failed to unite. Each step toward union drives the cosmos toward greater spontaneity and freedom (WTW, 197),*[13] *toward greater novelty, greater integrity, and ultimately toward greater consciousness.*

*Because transitions to novel forms are often accomplished by way of intense interactions, processes that unite the elements into integrated wholes can seem undisciplined and violent at times. In fact, I often stir up a certain amount of instability in order to achieve the kind of atmosphere that makes union possible. In the early universe, for instance, new elements are formed only under conditions of great volatility and high energy, often at extremes of both temperature and pressure. This is the price of the creative process.*

## Sophia and Earth

Although the cosmos is immense, with billions of galaxies, each containing billions of stars, and many of them with intricate planetary systems, Sophia speaks with particular fondness about the emergence of planet Earth almost five billion years ago:

*I accompany planet Earth as she emerges from the recycled waste material of an exploded supergiant star. I thrill from within the fire of her molten lava as we swirl over Earth's surface, cool, and form her rocky crust. I am present in the gases oozing from her surface and forming her protective atmosphere. I encourage the waters of her great oceans to separate and allow dry land to form. I am the beauty running through this newly born planet, encouraging it to be creative, to produce novel forms. I am fire. I am determined to make something new. And suddenly there is life! All at once, the oceans swarm with one-celled organisms.* (HP, 38)

As life continues to emerge on planet Earth, Sophia becomes more differentiated and her tasks become more specialized. She tells us:

*The yearning that I embedded into the fragments of the early universe continues to be effective—living creatures spread rapidly over the face of planet Earth. Within the early life forms, I instill the sexual force in order to enhance Earth's diversity and provide new paths to union. I thrill to see the flowers that appear on the land, making Earth's face more colorful, more vibrant, and more beautiful. I urge the many species of animals to find ways to cooperate. Some are particularly clever at this: insects divide their food-finding tasks among members of their colony; birds swarm, moving as a body in order to avoid their predators. I am at work in the song of the birds, in the wild hum of insects, in the tireless blooming of flowers, in the unremitting work of cells, and in the endless labors of seeds germinating in the soil. I am the radiance by which all of this beauty is aroused and within which it is vibrant.* (WTW 194)

## Sophia and the Human

With the coming of the human, Sophia's task becomes personal. She is pleased at last to be recognized. As she begins to unveil her face (WTW, 194), she says:

> *Always ready to promote a richer, deeper, and more spiritualized union, I set about my task of alluring the highly conscious feature of the world into the elusive web of my charms. I am the fragrance drawing human persons, who are able to interact in new and interesting ways and to follow me freely and passionately along the road to unity (WTW, 192). I am the source of their affective power,*[14] *the radiance that arouses human effervescence, the magnetic force of the universal presence and the ceaseless ripple of its smile (WTW, 195). Although the gift of human freedom makes my role more difficult at times, humans often assist me in fulfilling my mandate of Creative Union by conceiving new possibilities. Their creativity brings me great delight.*

> *Especially within the human family, I stir up passionate desire for the more—for dedication to scientific discovery, for the creation of beauty, for compassion toward those in need. My love is like a tremendous vital current running through the cosmic landscape. It is the source of the passionate cosmic forces of union woven into the very fabric of the universe. It is the world's attractive power imprinted on human features. In solidarity with the most vulnerable of creation, with those who yearn for the barest necessities of life, I sit at the city gates, at the crossroads of a world in crisis, begging for mercy. I attempt to open the eyes of each person to the presence of pain and suffering in the world. Whenever and wherever possible, I encourage tender compassion, forgiveness, and sacrificial love, attitudes that characterize the sensitive soul. I am hope breaking into history, appearing in the most unexpected places.*[15] *I am love, a wild and daring cosmic love—as strong as the sexual force between lovers, as tender as the nurturing love of a parent,*[16] *as fruitful as a vineyard in late summer.*

> *Embedded within the collective human heart and brain that is weaving a web of threadless fibers (CE, 104) over planet Earth, I am the golden thread that holds the fabric of human love and knowledge together. I gather all who care to join me in my mission. What thrills me most is the rich potential that I find among so many members of the human family. Because of their ability to care for one another, to communicate with one another, and to collaborate in highly complex ways, because of their capacity to see into the future, to imagine outcomes, and to accept a goal greater than themselves, my expectations for creative union are raised to new heights.*

> *I know that the only force available to the human community capable of providing the energy needed for union is love. Only love will herald the coming of a more fully conscious form of humanity. Embedded within the fibers of this complex web of conscious interaction that surrounds planet Earth, I continue to draw the human family toward the light, to the heights, and into freedom. I now focus my activity on my next major task in the evolutionary process—teaching humanity how to bear the burden of a greater consciousness, how to harness psychic energy, and how to transform this energy so that all may be one.* (TF, 72)

## Sophia's Identity

Who then is Sophia?[17] Scripture calls her a "breath of the power of God, and a pure emanation of the glory of the Almighty. . . a reflection of eternal light, a spotless mirror of the working of God, and an image of [God's] goodness" (Wis 7:25–26). She is the presence of God poured out in self-giving love, closer to us than we are to ourselves, ever arousing the soul to passion for the Divine. From within the depths of matter, she reveals herself to us as the *ousia*—the very nature of God, residing within the core of the cosmic landscape. She resides in a world in process, a world filled with excitement and activity. From this privileged spot, she gazes lovingly at all those in her field of view, infusing them with vitality, with an appetite for growth and a desire for union. As its hidden creative power, she orchestrates the divine energy field[18] and transforms the chaos of the early universe into a cosmos of amazing potential, influencing a world that behaves according to strict natural laws, yet one that is open to novelty and surprises.

Like the cosmos itself, Sophia is alive, pulsating with energy, endlessly productive,[19] and attentive to our every need. Unknown and unseen, she draws us "away from the alienation and polarization of [self-centered preoccupation into that] unified field of divine abundance that can be perceived only through the heart."[20] Once we recognize her in our everyday lives, we want to be with her, to be loved by her, to see as she sees, to work with her on her projects. Whenever she irrupts into our consciousness, we yearn for the courage to return her gaze, since to gain sight of her is to experience the living presence of God. The more deeply we descend into ourselves, the more we are able to perceive Sophia at work in the very marrow of our being (WTW, 61). We are able to feel her, to touch her, and to live in the deep biological current that runs through the soul. She stirs our imaginations, guides us on the inward journey, assembling the disparate parts of our lives, so that we can make sense of the whole. With each flash of insight, each loving encounter, she challenges us to a life of integrity.

Attempting always to capture our attention, Sophia peers out at us from behind the stars, overwhelms us with the radiance of a glorious sunset, and caresses us with a gentle breeze. When we do take time to contemplate her presence in the beauty and dynamics of the world around us, we begin to know her more intimately. On the other side of the veil that keeps her from bursting forth, she draws us steadily out of our ego-driven selves. Once she breaks through to our true selves, we recognize her as our sister. We realize that she knows us, loves us, and inspires us; she speaks to our hearts, raises us up, and impels us on. So long as we are open to her promptings, she remains with us. However, as soon as we try to hold on to her, she eludes our grasp (WTW, 195), always encouraging us to greater depths of exploration.

Sophia is ubiquitous, dynamic, and responsive. She is the bond that links us to one another. She abides with us and is present in every encounter that brings a caress, in every impetus that moves us on, in every experience that comes as a shock, in every event that bruises or breaks us (WTW, 60). She encourages us to develop fruitful relationships with nature and with other human beings so that ultimately we will be capable of the deepest of relationships with her.[21] Shining through the eyes of the ones we love, she sets our world ablaze.

Sophia is the mercy of God in us.[22] Tender compassion radiates from her presence. She speaks to us from the faces of the poor ones of our world, seeking, in their name, kindness, empathy, and love. She sits at the crossroads of our lives, ever imploring us to work for peace, to engage in fruitful dialogue, and to find new ways of connecting with the other. She longs to open our eyes to the presence of pain and suffering in the world, to transform our hearts, and to move us to action.

## Sophia: The Sacred Depths of Nature

Awareness of Sophia's presence at the heart of matter provides a striking image of how interconnected we are to our God but also to all aspects of nature. Recently, scientists have also been noticing and pointing out how fundamental interconnection is to the understanding of our place in the cosmos: we are made from the energy that emerged from the Big Bang; the stars have fashioned the elements that our bodies need for life; the Sun's energy provides Earth with the light that plants need to produce food and the heat we need to keep warm; our lives depend critically on whether we breathe clean air and drink clean water, on the availability of nourishing food for our bodies and beauty for our souls. With the entire Earth community, we share a common journey and a common destiny. Our fellow species supply us not only with the food that we eat, but also with needed companionship. We are beginning to realize that if we destroy Earth's delicate balance, we will most surely destroy the possibility of life not only for the human species but also for other living things as well. With the help of science, we are finally coming to know our place in the Earth community and the importance of our relationships with all of its members. From this perspective alone, Earth is precious.

By helping us to imagine a world permeated by Sophia's presence, modern sophiology offers us even deeper insight into the communion that we share with all of nature. Sophia's care and concern extend to the smallest elementary particle as well as to the largest cluster of galaxies, to the most ancient form of bacteria as well as to each and every person who lives today. All are precious; all have value. Viewed from Sophia's perspective, nature can no longer be viewed merely as ours to be exploited; rather, since all of nature is filled with the divine presence, all is valuable in Sophia's loving embrace.

When we fail to appreciate Sophia's presence at work in nature, we are also more likely to fail to appreciate the sacred depths of nature. Instead, whenever we remember Sophia at play in creation, whenever we admire Earth's beauty, whenever we discover ways to advance her project of creative union, we gradually develop attitudes of gratitude and appreciation for the gifts that are ours as well as a deep respect for all of creation; we begin to understand how great is the work that has been going on throughout the world's space-time history. When we recognize Sophia's presence in nature, we respond more easily to her invitation to develop a sense of companionship with the other, to give ourselves over to Earth's beauty, and to partner with her in the work of ongoing creation. To do this enhances our dignity as human persons.

## Conclusion

Teilhard came to know the vibrant presence of Sophia at an early age. Even before he was able to understand or articulate his experience, he perceived her first in the rocks that he collected, and later in the beauty of the natural world that surrounded him. His initial contact with the light shining through Marguerite's eyes opened him to new ways of perceiving Sophia's all pervasive presence and stimulated his capacity for love (HM, 59). This encounter led him beyond his senses and toward union with the other—with nature, with other persons, and with the Divine.[23] His senses came alive to beauty and love, and his heart to ever more palpable ways of relating to Sophia's presence. He began gradually to recognize her everywhere—in the rocks that he chiseled, in the seascapes and landscapes that he contemplated, and in the faces of the dying soldiers to whom he ministered during the war.

After years of searching for what is most durable, Teilhard came to know Sophia as the cosmic Love that is holding all things together, a love that manifests itself as "the unified field of all reality."[24] He was convinced that the path to mystical seeing is mediated through the physical world and that "Sophia . . . can be known only in embodied human actions."[25] Sophia was the source of Teilhard's life. She created him, enveloped him, and penetrated him. Her constant care for creation during so many billions of years gave him confidence that she would continue to be faithful (HM, 72). Totally grasped by the divine eros, Teilhard vowed to steep himself in the sea of matter, to bathe in its fiery water, to plunge into Earth where it is deepest and most violent, to struggle in its currents, and to drink of its waters (HM, 72). Filled with impassioned love for Sophia, he dedicated himself body and soul to the ongoing work needed to transform the cosmos to a new level of conscious-ness and to transformative love (FM, 24–25).

## Points to Ponder

◆ It is only through the lens of biblical, prophetic, and sacramental imagi-nation[26] that the deep mysteries of the Divine are able to come into focus for us.

◆ Teilhard was a prolific scientist who wholeheartedly practiced the scien-tific method and often referred to scientific findings in his religious writ-ings. Yet, he was also critical of the philosophy of the science practiced in his day. While honoring the value of its method, he called for a more holistic approach that would take into account the inner realities that sci-ence, by definition, ignores.

◆ Teilhard's eternal feminine embodies the spiritual power of matter as the feminine aspect of God's nature embedded in all of creation and captures his profound understanding of what is occurring in the cosmos.

◆ Reflect on these words: *From within the heart of matter, I hold together the foundations of the universe. Since everything in the universe is made by union, I labor to condense and to concentrate the elementary particles that continue to emerge from the energy ejected from the primordial fire* (WTW, 193, 192). *I am the principle of union, the soul of the world. Especially within the human family, I stir up passionate desire for the more—for ded-ication to scientific discovery, for the creation of beauty, for compassion toward those in need. My love is like a tremendous vital current running through the cosmic landscape. I am love, a wild and daring cosmic love— as strong as the sexual force between lovers, as tender as the nurturing love of a parent.*

◆ When we recognize Sophia's presence in nature, we respond more easily to her invitation to develop a sense of companionship with the other, to give ourselves over to Earth's beauty, and to partner with her in the work of ongoing creation. To do this enhances our dignity as human persons.

## Questions for Discussion

1. Who is Teilhard's "Eternal Feminine"? How is she vital to the forward movement of life?

2. What parts of his poem speak to you directly? Does his insight of wisdom at play in the universe influence your understanding of the value of science?

3. Are Teilhard's insights on wisdom purely poetic or deeply religious? How does wisdom change our understanding of God's presence in evolution?

4. Most of Teilhard's writings on wisdom were composed during World War I. What connections do you find between wisdom and suffering?

## Notes

1. Denis Edwards, *Jesus the Wisdom of God: An Ecological Theology* (Eugene, OR: Wipf & Stock, 2008), 19.

2. Patrick Hart, ed., *The Literary Essays of Thomas Merton* (New York: New Directions, 1981), 345.

3. Adapted from the phrase "a beyond, a with and a within to the world and its history," found in Elizabeth A. Johnson, *She Who Is: The Mystery of God in Feminist Theological Discourse* (New York: Crossroad, 1997), 210–11.

4. For alternate interpretations of this poem, see, for example, Henri de Lubac, SJ, *The Eternal Feminine: A Study on the Text of Teilhard de Chardin*, trans. René Hague (New York: Harper & Row, 1971); Sister Catherine R. O'Connor, CSJ, *Woman and Cosmos: The Feminine in the Thought of Pierre Teilhard de Chardin* (Englewood Cliffs, N.J.: Prentice-Hall, 1971); and Celia Deane-Drummond, "Sophia, Mary and the Eternal Feminine," in *Pierre Teilhard de Chardin on People & Planet*, ed. Celia Deane-Drummond (London: Equinox, 2006), 209–25.

5. See, for instance, Sir. 1:1–8; 24:3–12; Prov. 8:22–31; Wis. 1:6–7; 6:12–25; 7:7–12, 24–30; 9:9–12.

6. Ursula King, *Spirit of Fire: The Life and Vision of Teilhard de Chardin* (Maryknoll, NY: Orbis Books, 1988), 43–44.

7. Many of the letters written by Teilhard to Marguerite during the war can be found in MM.

8. See de Lubac, *Eternal Feminine*, 10–24.

9. King, *Spirit of Fire*, 73. The actual dedication is to Beatrix, a reference to Dante's Beatrice.

10. Teilhard returns to this theme again in an essay entitled "The Evolution of Chastity," in TF, and more directly in the conclusion to his last major essay, "The Heart of

Matter," in HM, 58–61. He also refers to Earth's creative action in "The Spiritual Power of Matter," describing in yet other words his experience of the eternal feminine.

11. Aware of the strong feminist critiques of the eternal feminine tradition, I hope to avoid some of the major problems by considering Sophia as the manifestation of God's nature in the natural world rather than a human ideal. See O'Connor, *Woman and Cosmos*, especially 93–96, for more detail about this concern.

12. Deane-Drummond, "Sophia," 210.

13. De Lubac, *Eternal Feminine*, 15.

14. De Lubac, *Eternal Feminine*, 10.

15. Christopher Pramuk, *Sophia: The Hidden Christ of Thomas Merton* (Collegeville, MN: Liturgical Press, 2009), 263, 261, 278, 217, 218, 262.

16. De Lubac, *Eternal Feminine*, 10.

17. In *She Who Is*, Johnson enumerates and briefly analyzes the many Hebrew scripture texts in which Sophia appears (86–93). However, she notes that "debate on the interpretation of personified Wisdom remains unresolved" (90). She also indicates the many ways in which Sophia has influenced Christian pneumatology, Christology, and Mariology (94–103). My approach has been to portray Sophia as the immanent presence of God at work in the ongoing creation.

18. A phrase attributed to Joseph Bracken in Brandon Gallaher, "The Problem of Pantheism in the Sophiology of Sergii Bulgakov: A Panentheistic Solution in the Process Trinitarianism of Joseph A. Bracken," in *Seeking Common Ground: Evaluation & Critique of Joseph Bracken's Comprehensive Worldview*, ed. Marc A. Pugliese and Gloria L. Schaab, SSJ (Milwaukee: Marquette University Press, 2012), 154.

19. Pramuk, *Sophia*, 231.

20. Cynthia Bourgeault, *The Wisdom Jesus: Transforming Heart and Mind—A New Perspective on Christ and His Message* (Boston: Shambhala, 2008), 62.

21. Edwards, *Jesus the Wisdom of God*, 136.

22. Pramuk, *Sophia*, 268.

23. De Lubac, *Eternal Feminine*, 12.

24. Bourgeault, *Wisdom Jesus*, 72.

25. Christopher Bamford, foreword to *Sophia: The Wisdom of God: An Outline of Sophiology* by Sergei Bulgakov (Hudson, NY: Lindisfarne, 1993), xviii.

26. Edwards, *Jesus the Wisdom of God*, 19.

*Chapter 3*

# EVOLUTION AND THE RISE OF THE SECULAR GOD

## Ilia Delio, OSF

The new atheism has attracted considerable attention today, but apart from the public hype, it offers no substantial change or direction to modernity's problems. Religion may be the opium of the masses but atheism offers no new yeast as leaven for the masses. Surprisingly, not all atheists are happy with a godless world and perceive that a religious spirit is missing from the public center of human interaction. Paul Griffiths identifies this new sentiment as a "church without Christ."[1] Apologists for this new church adopt a very different tone from those who want to destroy any trace of religion; instead they realize that "something important is being lost, something without which a rich and meaningful life cannot be lived."[2] Two of these apologists, Jürgen Habermas and Simon Critchley, express concern that a spirit of defeatism lurks within the patterns of public reason which mark the modern secular-liberal state. Habermas states that public practical reason "no longer has sufficient strength to awaken, and to keep awake, in the minds of secular subjects, an awareness of the violations of solidarity throughout the world, an awareness of what is missing, of what cries out to heaven."[3] That is, "the secular self-understanding of the liberal state can no longer motivate its citizens to act self-sacrificially in the service of justice. Its failure to find a way to mark death is mirrored by its failure to make passionate collective action a real possibility. Such action, to be possible, requires a shared sense that what we do next . . . is a matter of infinite importance, something performed before the face of God."[4] Critchley too sees that an atheological polity cannot be for its citizens what a polity must be. It cannot form loves of a properly political kind. "Without faith—understood as the infinite demand—political action proves impossible."[5] Despite a new religious longing among these intellectual atheists, there is a rising departure from institutional religion. Recent studies show that the number of people of no religious institutional affiliation has risen to almost twenty percent in the past year. While people are leaving institutional religion, many still believe in God, acknowledging the existence of a divine presence without trying to prove or defend this presence.

In an interesting article entitled "Some Reflexions on the Conversion of the World," written in October 1936, Pierre Teilhard de Chardin saw that Christianity was facing a new world brought about by discoveries of modern science, especially evolution and quantum physics (SC, 118–27). The modern world, he wrote, is emerging and developing outside Christianity; there is a new modern spirit on the rise. Teilhard composed his article on the brink of the Second World War, having served as a stretcher bearer in the First World War. He lamented not only the failure of atheism to attain something better for the world, but he called attention to the failure of Christianity as well, which is still fixed in a three-tiered universe focused on sin, salvation, and otherworldliness. Christianity has lost its power to transform worldly life, and atheism is blind to its own shallowness, unable to offer any emotional balm, direction, or depth to cosmic life. Atheists, he claimed, do not reject Christianity because it is too difficult but because it does not address Earth's needs and the modern spirit of a scientific age. Hence we have an insuperable gap between a "religion of the earth" (atheism) and a "religion of heaven" (Christianity) enervating life from within. Teilhard felt that Christianity has something vital to offer the world if it can relinquish its medieval framework and wake up to the growing world of modern science. Our situation today calls us to reflect on this new world brought about by modern science and to see how it can grow into a believing world.

## A New Religious Spirit

The relationship between science and religion bears modernity's impasse between faith and reason, and few signs of rapprochement between these two fundamental pillars of life are visible. Teilhard overcame this impasse by forming a new religious vision in the context of modern science. He identified the antagonism between Christianity and modernity as one between premodern and modern scientific worldviews. The discoveries of twentieth-century science, especially Big Bang cosmology ("universalism" or cosmic wholeness) and evolution (nature's openness to the future), ushered in two new dimensions of life, wholeness and futurism. Contrary to the ancient Ptolemaic cosmos of order, stasis, and hierarchy, the Big Bang cosmos was now seen in its evolving capacity for greater wholeness and openness to consummation in the future. As astronomy overturned the geocentric universe with its fixed realms of heaven and hell, so geology and biology pushed the horizons of time backward into the remote past and forward into the far distant future. Life evolves across the millennia in a gradual succession of living forms. With this new sense of moving forward, from simple to complex life forms, from bacteria to humans, science shows that evolution is more than a method of collecting and classifying the facts of life; rather it is the *means* by which humanity can move forward into the future. Teilhard wrote that "science recognized itself as a means of extending and completing in man a world still incompletely formed. It assumed the shape and grandeur of a sacred duty. It [has] become charged with futurity" (HE, 171).

Teilhard did not see modern science as dispensing with religion; on the contrary, the discoveries of Darwin and Einstein brought with them a new sense of mystery in the universe, an opening up of religion from the individual to the whole. The modern world is not irreligious, he said, but the religious spirit is taking on a new form (CE, 174). To engage this new religious spirit is to recognize that a fundamental shift in human religious consciousness must take place. Modern science gives us a new understanding of space and time that demands a new understanding of ourselves in relation to God. In this new concept of space there is no containment; that is, there is no spatial location in which the infinite and finite can meet. Rather, the expanding universe is unfolding space-time, which means that our new consciousness of space no longer admits traditional religious imagery by which we conceive our encounter with God. At the same time we must also recognize that this traditional imagery was never essential to Christianity. We must therefore lay aside the old form of Christianity and engage the world as the place to find God if we are to rekindle the Gospel for our age. Teilhard states his argument most succinctly in the closing chapter of *The Human Phenomenon*:

> To outward appearance, the modern world was born of an antireligious movement: man becoming self-sufficient and reason supplanting belief. Our generation and the two that preceded it have heard little but talk of the conflict between science and faith; indeed it seemed at one moment a foregone conclusion that the former was destined to take the place of the latter. . . . After close on two centuries of passionate struggles, neither science nor faith has succeeded in discrediting its adversary. On the contrary, it becomes obvious that neither can develop normally without the other. And the reason is simple: the same life animates both. Neither in its impetus nor its achievements can science go to its limits without becoming tinged with mysticism and charged with faith. (HP, 203)

Teilhard's idea of a "science charged with faith" marks the new religious spirit of the scientific age which is nurtured by turning to the earth in a new understanding of God. The Fathers of the Church spoke of nature as a book of revelation and read this book carefully to probe the divine mystery. Throughout the centuries we see that the relation between faith and the natural world has been integral to the task of theology and the development of theological world images. Zachary Hayes asks: "If Augustine was able to speak theologically in a world conditioned by neo-Platonism, and if an Aquinas was able to construct a theology using Aristotelian categories to speak to a world wrestling with the Aristotelian world view, is it possible for contemporary theology to do a similar thing, taking a world view from the sciences?"[6] Without engaging the book of nature in the task of theology, theology can become a mere abstraction of a nonexisting God.

## Evolution and the New Religious Paradigm

The key to Teilhard's new religious vision is evolution. Although he was a trained paleontologist who studied the evolution of human origins, he had remarkably little to say about Darwinian mechanisms of change. He was, however, influenced by the developmental perspectives they presuppose. Evolution means that nature does not operate according to fixed laws but by the dynamic interplay of law, chance, and deep time; that is, one cannot understand natural processes apart from developmental categories. The interaction of forces creates a dynamic process of unfolding life, pointing to the fact that nature is incomplete; there are no fixed essences. Instead, nature is consistently oriented toward new and complex life. Teilhard described evolution as a movement toward complexified forms which, at critical points in the evolutionary process, emerge as qualitative differences: "There is only one real evolution, the evolution of convergence, because it alone is positive and creative" (CE, 87). The foundation of things is not so much a ground of being that sustains its existence from beneath, as it is a power of attraction toward *what lies up ahead*. Evolution is a general condition before which all theories, systems, and hypotheses must bow and which they must satisfy if they are to be thinkable and true. It is not background to the human story; it *is* the human story. It is neither theory nor fact but a "dimension" to which all thinking in whatever area must conform.[7] Teilhard wrote:

> For many, evolution still means only transformism, and transformism itself is an old Darwinian hypothesis as localized and obsolete as the Laplacean concept of the solar system or the Wegnerean theory of continental drift. They truly are blind who do not see the scope of a movement whose orbit, infinitely transcending that of the natural sciences, has successively overtaken and invaded the surrounding fields of chemistry, physics, sociology, and even mathematics and history of religions. Drawn along together by a single fundamental current, one after the other all the domains of human knowledge have set off toward the study of some kind of *development.... Evolution is a general condition, which all theories, all hypotheses, all systems must submit to and satisfy from now on in order to be conceivable and true* [italics added]. (HP, 152)

Teilhard saw evolution of the human person as part of the whole natural process of creativity and generativity. The human person is not the great exception to evolution but its recapitulation. We are integrally part of evolution in that we rise from the process but in reflecting on the process we stand apart from it. He defines reflection as "the power acquired by a consciousness of turning in on itself and taking possession of itself as an object endowed with its own particular consistency and value; no longer only to know something—but to know *itself*; no longer only to know, but to know that it knows" (HP, 110). He quotes a phrase of Julian Huxley, "we are *nothing else than evolution become conscious of itself*" (HP, 154). To this idea he adds, "until it is established in this perspective, the modern mind (because and insofar as it is modern) will always be restless. . . . Reflecting in the consciousness of each one of us, evolution is becoming aware of itself" (HP, 154). Thus the human person emerges from the evolutionary process and is integral to evolution. She or he is "the point of emergence in nature, at which this deep cosmic evolution culminates and declares itself" (HE, 23).[8] Hence, the human person is the arrow of evolution.

## Toward a Metaphysics of Evolution

The process of evolution is marked by convergence and complexity. Entities unite and form new levels of relatedness; as degrees of relatedness complexify, consciousness increases. Teilhard was fascinated by nature's intrinsic capacity to unite. Science can tell us about the forces of nature but it cannot explain *why* things unite at all. Teilhard was influenced by the discovery of quantum physics and knew the French physicist Louis De Broglie, who developed the double-slit experiment and helped to advance quantum physics. From his conversations with De Broglie and others, Teilhard reflected on the primordial reality of energy and the physical world of mass-energy where there is an inherent force of attraction within all dimensions of cosmic life. He was impressed by the levels of attraction in nature whereby elements unite center to center, leading to more being and consciousness. Teilhard called this fundamental force of attraction "love energy" because it is the primordial energy of union by which new complex entities emerge. Love-energy undergirds the process of attraction between particular entities in the openness toward greater union and is present from the Big Bang onward, though indistinguishable from molecular forces. As Thomas King notes: "Even among the molecules, love was the building power that worked against entropy, and under its attraction the elements groped their way towards union."[9] Teilhard realized that if there was no internal propensity to unite, even at a rudimentary level—indeed in the molecule itself—it would be physically impossible for love to appear higher up, in a hominized form. Ursula King states: "Teilhard criticized the traditional concept of love as too static, too 'spiritualized,' too divorced from its cosmic roots, from natural passion, in which all love, including the love of God, has its starting point."[10] Hence the energy of attraction that creates greater wholes in nature is one of union and relatedness (complexification), whereby more complex life emerges in the cosmos; this energy of attraction is love. "The physical structure of the universe," Teilhard said, "is love" and "the manifestation of this fundamental power" reveals itself to our consciousness in three successive stages: in woman (for man), in society, in the All—by the sense of sex, of humanity and of the cosmos" (HE, 72).

Teilhard was attentive to the new physics, especially the subatomic realm of quantum reality, and spoke of spirit and matter as two forms of energy, radial and tangential energy, that comprise a whole. There is neither spirit nor matter in the world, he said; rather, "all that exists is matter becoming spirit" (HE, 57; CE, 105). Matter is not a thing in itself but a concentrated form of energy which has mass or weight. Tangential energy attaches matter to matter, and radial energy draws matter forward. Love is radial energy (spirit) that draws tangential energy (matter) to something more than itself; that is, radial energy is a vector of tangential energy. Based on the primacy of energy, Teilhard considered the term "being" as neither an abstract concept nor a substantive entity. Rather, being is energy and hence relational. The primacy of energy means that what exists does not act toward a self-sufficient end in which relationship is extrinsic to that end; rather, union is the end toward which being directs itself. Being is existence toward more being—reflected in the process of evolution. He writes: "What comes first in the world for our thought is not "being" but "the union which produces this being" (CE, 227). Being is the outflow of union; to be is to be united. This led Teilhard to posit a new understanding of reality. Instead of a metaphysics of being which connotes stability and sameness, he suggested that a metaphysics of unity had emerged: "Let us therefore try to replace a metaphysics of *Esse* by a metaphysics of *Unire*" (CE, 227). The foundation of existence is not mere being itself (what is) but relationality (what is becoming): union is always toward more being. Teilhard coined the word "hyperphysics" to describe a principle of more being; that is, the fundamental drive of everything is toward *more being*.

Metaphysics is the study of principles underlying reality: the nature and purpose of being. Christianity inherited a metaphysics based on Greek philosophy, formed against a stable, fixed cosmos. Scholastic theologians constructed teachings on creation, salvation, and redemption based on the principles of Greek metaphysics. Teilhard's "hyperphysics" is a foundational first step toward renewing Christianity in an evolutionary universe, moving beyond a static metaphysics of being. The prefix "hyper" undergirds the primacy of love-energy, placing an emphasis not on what is timeless and fixed but on the future and what is becoming. Teilhard emphasized that what exists in evolution is incomplete and therefore open to creativity, that is, to becoming something more. Nature is not defined by fixed essences but by relationality. The openness of nature to new things means that cosmic evolution includes unpredictable, irreducible, and novel appearances.[11] Since being is not self-contained but being toward the other, existence is for the sake of giving so that something more unitive may arise. Being is first a "we" before it can become an "I." Love is the affinity of being with being and such unity is always toward more being. In his *Human Phenomenon* Teilhard wrote:

> Love alone is capable of completing our beings in themselves as it unites them, for the good reason that love alone takes them and joins them by their very depths—this is a fact of daily experience. Is not the moment when two lovers say they are lost in each other the moment when they come into the most complete possession of themselves? All around us at every moment does love not accomplish that magic act, reputed to be so contradictory, of "personalizing" as it totalizes? And if it does this on a daily basis on a reduced scale, why could it not someday repeat it in the dimensions of the Earth? (HP, 189)

The universe, therefore, is in the framework of love and is intrinsically relational. Teilhard claimed: "Love is the most universal, the most tremendous and the most mysterious of the cosmic forces" (HE, 32). The whole of reality from the lowest to the highest is covenanted or united in a bond of love.

## The Rise of God in Evolution

Teilhard recognized the import of love-energy for our understanding of reality, including God, and said that we are "making our way to a completely new concept of being" which affects our understanding of God. The "contradictory attributes of the *ens ab alio* and the *ens a se* of the world and God can now be formulated in a general synthetic function: 'God completely other in nature than the world and yet unable to dispense with it' "(SC, 182). Teilhard felt that the traditional view of God and creation, the "metaphysics of the eternally present," was inadequate for the reality of evolution. Evolution, he claimed, requires a divine source located not in the past or "up above" in a timeless present but "up ahead" in the future. Thus he suggests a metaphysics of *Esse* be replaced by a metaphysics of *Unire,* since unity marks evolution and the evolution of multiplicity is unitive.

A new integral relationship between God and nature was not unique to Teilhard but reflective of many twentieth century theologians who sought to renew a doctrine of creation compatible with our scientific age. In his Gifford Lectures, *The Rhythm of Being*, Raimon Panikkar said, "the very name of God is a kosmological notion. . . . A theology without kosmology is a mere abstraction of a non-existent God, and a kosmology without theology is just a mirage."[12] Paul Tillich identified the problem of God in a scientific age when he wrote:

> A God whose existence or nonexistence you can argue is a thing beside others within the universe of existing things. . . . It is regrettable that scientists believe that they have refuted religion when they rightly have shown that there is no evidence whatsoever for the assumption that such a being exists. Actually, they not only have refuted religion, but they have done it a considerable service. They have forced it to reconsider and to restate the meaning of the tremendous word *God*. Unfortunately, many theologians make the same mistake. They begin their message with the assertion that there is a highest being called God, whose authoritative revelations they have received. They are more dangerous for religion than the so-called atheistic scientists. They take the first step on the road which inescapably leads to what is called atheism. Theologians who make of God a highest being who has given some people information about Himself, provoke inescapably the resistance of those who are told they must subject themselves to the authority of this information.[13]

Teilhard too saw that the God of Scholasticism, forged out of Greek philosophy, no longer speaks to the world of modern science. In his *Christianity and Evolution* he summed up the dilemma of our age by saying:

> In the case of a world which is by nature evolutive . . . God is not conceivable (either structurally or dynamically) except in so far as he coincides with (as a sort of "formal" cause) but without being lost in, the centre of convergence of cosmogenesis. . . . Ever since Aristotle there have been almost continual attempts to construct models of God on the lines of an outside Prime Mover, acting *a retro*. Since the emergence in our consciousness of the "sense of evolution" it has become physically impossible for us to conceive or worship anything but an organic Prime-Mover God, *ab ante*. . . . Who will at last give evolution *its own* God? (CE, 239–40)

Teilhard seized the moment to return to a primordial mysticism at the heart of the physical world where there exists the affirmation and the expression of a strictly bilateral and complementary relationship between God and world: "In truth it is not the sense of contingence of the created but the sense of the mutual completion of the world and God which gives life to Christianity" (CE, 227). While in the case of a static world, the creator is structurally independent of his work, in the case of an evolutive world, the contrary is true. God is not conceivable except in so far as he "coincides with evolution but without being lost in, (as a sort of 'formal' cause) the center of convergence of cosmogenesis" (CE, 23). God is a "hyper-center," in other words, of greater *depth* (italics added) than we are (TF, 76). The world is not God and God is not the world, yet God is the unlimited depth of love, the center, of all that is: a love that overflows onto new life. God is not a supernatural being hovering above Earth but the supra-personal whole, the Omega, who exists in all and through all. "Only a God who is functionally and totally 'Omega,'" the absolute, ultimate whole, "can satisfy us" (CE, 75).

God and creation are so integrally united that Teilhard does not speak of a creator but of creative union. The term "creation" is not an act or event but a fundamental relatedness, a kenosis of divine love. God becomes "element" by emptying God's self into the other, the Word of divine self-expressiveness, drawing all things through love into the fullness of being. This is the basis of God's secularity, since all things are made through the Word (Jn 1:1). God is the center of every center, the creative power of everything that exists. As Teilhard wrote: "He [God] is at the tip of pen, my spade, my brush, my needle; of my heart and of my thought" (DM, 64). In every action we must adhere to the creative power of God, to coincide with it and become its living extension. He believed that without creation, something would be absolutely lacking to God, considered in the fullness not of God's being but of God's act of union. According to Christopher Mooney:

> The assertion that the world's movement towards unity "completes" God in some way is unusual and needs to be clarified. . . .Teilhard is doing nothing more nor less than asserting in an evolutionary context the paradox which is already contained in St. Paul: *the Pleroma of Christ cannot constitute an intrinsic completion of God himself,* but it will nonetheless in some sense be a real completion. . . . Teilhard wants to do away once and for all with the idea that God's continuous act of creation is one of *absolute* gratuity.[14]

Teilhard opposed the idea of an absolutely gratuitous creation which makes creation independent of God or merely contingent on God.[15] For Thomas Aquinas, creation is the outflow of divine will. God freely chooses to create. Teilhard felt, however, that this type of radical dependency between God and creation diminishes the significance of the world in relation to God. Creation is not merely gift of God or dependent on God; it expresses God's being-in-love and thus is the most apt expression of what God is—outpouring love. It is more than divine will or desire; creation is the Beloved of God and the becoming of God in love since all that God is, is poured out in creation. Thomas King wrote: "Matter is the principle of otherness. In matter God and man can become other than what they are. Through matter God and man can meet. God is not found through opposition to matter (anti-matter) or independent of matter (extra-matter) but through matter (trans-matter)."[16] We take hold of God in the finite; God is sensed as "rising" or "emerging" from the depths, born not in the heart of matter but *as* the heart of matter.[17] God and creation are so united that creation "can have only one object: a *universe*"; that creation can be effected "only by an *evolutive process* (of personalizing synthesis); and that it can come into action *only once:* when 'absolute' multiple is reduced, nothing is left to be united either in God or 'outside' God" (CE, 179). Thus, union with God is realized by passing through and emerging from matter. Teilhard wrote: "I can be saved only by becoming one with the universe" (CE, 128).

## Christogenesis

Teilhard's God-world relationship, unified in love, is the core doctrine of incarnation. He insisted that it is time to return to a form of Christology which is more organic and takes account of physics. We need a Christ "who is no longer master of the world solely because he has been *proclaimed* to be such," he wrote, "but because he animates the whole range of things from top to bottom" (CE, 89). He wrote: "Our Christology is still expressed in exactly the same terms as those which three centuries ago, could satisfy men whose outlook on the cosmos it is now physically impossible for us to accept. . . . What we now have to do without delay is to modify the position occupied by the central core of Christianity—and this precisely in order that it may not lose its illuminative value" (CE, 77). Teilhard saw his approach to the question of Christ in line with the Church Fathers. Whereas the early church sought to understand Christ's relation to the Trinity, he said, "in our own time the vitally important question has become for us to define the links between Christ and the universe: how they stand in relation to one another and how they influence one another" (CE, 176–77). He rejected original sin, the origin of a defect from a human couple, as incompatible with evolution. Rather, he opted for the doctrine of the primacy of Christ which states that whether or not sin existed, Christ would have come. God is love and from all eternity willed to love a finite other to grace and glory. Christ is first in God's intention to love and therefore to create.[18]

The primacy of Christ is wholly compatible with evolution and the ubiquity of love-energy. Whereas classical theology took as its starting point Aristotle's notion of being and the relationship between God and world as ontologically distinct, Teilhard began with evolution as the understanding of being and hence of God. What he tried to show is that evolution is not only the universe coming to be but it is *God* who is *coming to be.* By this he meant that divine love poured into space-time rises in consciousness and eventually erupts in the life of Jesus of Nazareth. He wrote, "God is entirely self-sufficient; and yet the universe contributes *something that is vitally necessary to* him" (CE, 177). In and through mass-energy and space-time, God becomes visible, intelligible, and lovable. Evolution is a cosmic birthing process toward personal unity by which the whole is gathered together in love. In *How I Believe* he wrote:

> If we Christians wish to *retain* in Christ the very qualities on which his power and our worship are based, we have no better way—no other way, even—of doing so than fully to accept the most modern concepts of evolution. Under the combined pressure of science and philosophy, we are being forced, experientially and intellectually, to accept the world as a coordinated system of activity which is gradually rising up toward freedom and consciousness. The only satisfactory way of interpreting this process is to regard it as irreversible and convergent. Thus, ahead of us, a *universal cosmic center* is taking on definition, in which everything reaches its term, in which everything is explained, is felt and is ordered. It is, then, in this *physical pole* of universal evolution that we must, in my view, locate and recognize the plenitude of Christ. . . . By disclosing a world-peak, evolution makes Christ possible, just as Christ by giving meaning and direction to the world, makes evolution possible. (CE, 128)

Incarnation does not take place *in* evolution; Christ does not intervene in creation and then become its goal. Rather, the whole evolutionary process is incarnational. Evolution *is* God coming to be at the heart of the cosmos. As Teilhard said, "it is not just something but Someone holds together the plurality of elements in a personalizing center," and this is Christ, the One engendered by the Father's love through the life-giving Spirit.

Evolution has purpose and aim, according to Teilhard, because it is grounded in Christ. From the Big Bang 13.8 billion years ago to the present, God has been creating through the word of love and incarnating creation in a unity of love. The integral relationship between incarnation and creation is the unfolding of Christ, the Word incarnate, who invests himself organically with all of creation, immersing himself in things, in the heart of matter and thus unifying the world.[19] Teilhard spoke of Christ as evolver and Omega. As evolver, Christ is divine personal love which is coming to be in evolution through the process of creative union. As Omega, Christ is suprapersonal in nature, the divine depth of love who fills all things and who animates and gathers up all the biological and spiritual energies in the universe—that is, the goal of evolution.

Teilhard did not believe that the human reality of Jesus Christ was lost in the superhuman and vanished in the cosmic. Rather, the universal Christ could not appear at the end of time at the peak of the world if he had not previously entered it during its development, through the medium of birth, in the form of an element. The universe is physically impregnated to the very core of its matter by the influence of divine nature. God is present within everything that exists as the dynamic center of love, but God is the excess of everything that exists, the overflow of love. Hence, God "is the transcendent future horizon that draws an entire universe, and not just human history, toward an unfathomable fulfillment yet to be realized."[20] Evolution is movement toward union in love in relation to a God of ever-deepening love. "God is the newest thing there is," Meister Eckhart wrote, "and if we are united to God we become new as well."[21] God and world are in the process of becoming something *more* than what they are separately because the universe is grounded in Christ, the personal center of divine union in love. Thus the *One who is in evolution* is *cause and center* of evolution and its goal. The world is being personalized through the birthing of Christ marked by the rise of consciousness and unity in love.

## The Human Arrow

Teilhard proposed that Christianity is a religion of evolution. The life, death, and resurrection of Jesus Christ means, from a Christian perspective, evolution has purpose and aim. It is not a mere plurality of unrelated things but a true unity in divine love incarnate. God is united to each personalizing element through the divine Word; hence, Christ is the One who is coming to be at the heart of evolution. The human person emerges in evolution with a unique capacity of intelligent self-consciousness and is essential to God's becoming in history. The life of Jesus shows that the human person completes the yearning of God's own love for us and God's desire for our wholeness in love. Donald Gray writes: "Man completes God's love for the creation by bringing that love to the effective realization of its goal, which is the good of the creation."[22] To love God in and through the universe through the cocreative energies of love and participation in history is the basis of evolutionary convergence and hominization.[23]

Teilhard believed that Christianity is the form of faith most fitted to modern needs: a religion for Earth's progress. It is not a matter of the church *reconciling* itself to the modern world; rather, the church must *accept* the world as science now discloses it. "The world will never be converted to Christianity's hopes of heaven," he said, "unless first Christianity is converted to the hopes of the earth" (SC, 127). By doing so, Christianity will reveal itself less as a new religion than a new humanism, a new spirit of love now present in the human person to act on behalf of God in history. Christianity is faith in the evolving unification of the world in God—unity with the natural world, unity with other religions, unity with other planets, unity with all people. Christians are to be engaged unifiers in a world of evolution, working toward the *pleroma*, the fullness of plurality in unity. Christian love is to be dynamized, universalized, and pantheized (SC, 120). The whole earth in all its natural diversity, the whole planet and planets in their diversity, all religions or spiritual yearnings in all their diversity, all of these are being drawn together from the future in a boundless love, the fullness of Christ. "It is not the religious act that makes the Christian," Dietrich Bonhoeffer wrote, "but participation in the sufferings of God in the secular life."[24] This participation is a way of love that unifies, makes whole, and lifts up what is fragmented and incomplete.

This is the type of action I believe that "unsatisfied atheists" of today are looking for—not a religion of dependence but one of empowerment that moves the earth toward unity and justice. The Marxist view sees the human collectivity in terms of a merely human future; the Christian view sees the center of universal convergence as both ultrahuman and transcendent, that is, a deepening of humanity bound together in love. Teilhard wrote:

> Fascism, Communism, democracy, have ceased to have any real meaning. My own dream would be to see the best of humanity regrouped on a spiritual basis determined by the following three aims: Universalism, Futurism and Personalism, and cooperating in whatever political and economic movement should prove techni-cally most able to safeguard these three aims. (LT, 224–25)

As life evolves toward greater unity, we are to help shape that unity toward an inclusivity of wholeness that reflects the life of Jesus who reached out to those on the margins and brought them into community. Jesus' inti-mate experience of God and his self-identity with the Father (Jn 17:20–23; Jn 10:30) empowered him to act in the name of love. Jesus showed that love is the creativity of God manifest in all aspects of life but especially in the human person.[25] Thomas Merton wrote: "Christianity does not teach man to attain an inner ideal of divine tranquility. . . . It teaches him to give himself to his brother and to his world in a service of love."[26]

Teilhard saw that creativity and invention would forge the modern path of evolution but he also saw that science alone cannot fulfill the cosmic long-ing for completion. He wrote: "However far science pushes its discovery of the essential fire and however capable it becomes someday of remodeling and perfecting the human element, it will always find itself in the end facing the same problem—how to give to each and every element its final value by grouping them in the unity of an organized whole" (HP, 177). God rises up at the heart of cosmic evolution through the power of love which science and technology can facilitate but not surpass. This divinely empowered being-in-love is the evolution of Christ in whom all things are embraced by God.

For Teilhard, the future of the earth lies not in science but in the spiritual power of world religions and the power of love. He envisioned an eventual convergence of religions so that the emergence of Christ would ultimately not be limited to a single religion but would be the convergence of psychic, spiritual energy, the unification of the whole. He wrote: "No longer is it simply a religion of individual and of heaven, but a religion of mankind and of the earth—that is what we are looking for at this moment, as the oxygen without which we cannot breathe" (AE, 240). He described the emergence of Christ as "a general convergence of religions upon a universal personal center of unity who fundamentally satisfies them all" (CE, 130). We do not know what the future of religious convergence will look like but, for Teilhard, religious convergence is integral to the emergence of Christ who is the Omega, the fullness of all beings in love. To realize this unity in love, we must build the earth together, share the earth's resources, and care for one another creating a new world through the power of love.

## Points to Ponder

◆ Big Bang cosmology ("universalism" or cosmic wholeness) and evolution (nature's openness to the future), ushered in two new dimensions of life (wholeness and futurism). The Big Bang cosmos is seen in its evolving capacity for greater wholeness and openness to consummation in the future.

◆ Evolution means that nature does not operate according to fixed laws but to the dynamic interplay of law, chance, and deep time; one cannot understand natural processes apart from developmental categories.

◆ Evolution is a movement toward complexified forms in which, at critical points in the evolutionary process, qualitative differences emerge. The foundation of things is not so much a ground of being that sustains its existence from beneath, as it is a power of attraction toward *what lies up ahead.*

◆ The word "hyperphysics" describes a principle of more being; that is, the fundamental drive of everything is toward *more being.*

◆ Hyperphysics emphasizes not what is timeless and fixed but the future and what is becoming. The foundation of existence is not mere being itself (what is) but relationality (what is becoming): union is always toward more being.

◆ The world is not God and God is not the world; yet God is the unlimited depth of love, the center, of all that is, a love that overflows onto new life. God is not a supernatural Being hovering above Earth but the suprapersonal whole, the Omega, who exists in all and through all.

◆ Evolution is a cosmic birthing process toward personal unity by which the whole is gathered together in love.

## Questions for Discussion:

1. How does Teilhard's theology provide new direction for Christian life?

2. What new insights on God do you find in this essay?

3. In what ways does Teilhard's theology challenge you?

4. Are you open to evolution and what does that mean for you personally, communally, and spiritually?

## Notes

1. Paul J. Griffiths, "Fellow Travelers? Four Atheists Who Don't Hate Religion," *Commonweal* (October 26, 2012): 24.

2. Griffiths, "Fellow Travelers?" 24.

3. Jürgen Habermas, *An Awareness of What Is Missing: Faith and Reason in a Post-Secular Age,* trans. Ciaran Cronin (Malden, MA: Polity, 2010), 19.

4. Griffiths, "Fellow Travelers?" 25.

5. Griffiths, "Fellow Travelers?" 26; see also Simon Critchley, *The Faith of the Faithless: Experiments in Political Theology* (New York: Verso, 2010).

6. Zachary Hayes, *A Window to the Divine: Creation Theology* (Quincy, IL: Franciscan Press, 1997), 87.

7. Robert G. North, *Teilhard and the Creation of the Soul* (Milwaukee: Bruce, 1967), 49.

8. Teilhard's position on human evolution put him at odds with church teaching, primarily because he rejected the idea of original sin in light of evolution. However, in the 1950 encyclical *Humani generis* Pope Pius XII stated that evolution may explain how the physical body of the human person is formed but the soul is created immediately by God: "The Teaching Authority of the Church does not forbid that, in conformity with the present state of human sciences and sacred theology, research and discussions, on the part of men experienced in both fields, take place with regard to the doctrine of evolution, in as far as it inquires into the origin of the human body as coming from pre-existent and living matter—for the Catholic faith obliges us to hold that souls are immediately created by God." See Pope Pius XII, *Humani generis*, para. 36. http://www.vatican.va.

9. Thomas M. King, *Teilhard's Mysticism of Knowing* (New York: Seabury, 1981), 104–5.

10. Ursula King, "Theories of Love: Sorokin, Teilhard and Tillich," *Zygon* 39, no.1 (March 2004): 85.

11. Philip Clayton, *Mind and Emergence: From Quantum to Consciousness* (New York: Oxford University Press, 2006), 39. Although evolution is marked by novelty in nature, it does not mean naïve optimism, which I find frequently articulated by those unfamiliar with science. A more thorough explanation of evolution would include aspects of devolution, mutations, and punctuated equilibrium over long periods of developmental processes.

12. Panikkar, *The Rhythm of Being: The Gifford Lectures* (New York: Orbis Books, 2010), 187–88.

13. Paul Tillich, *Theology of Culture* (New York: Oxford University Press, 1959), 4–5.

14. Christopher F. Mooney, *Teilhard de Chardin and the Mystery of Christ* (New York: Harper & Row, 1964), 174–75.

15. Donald Gray, *The One and the Many: Teilhard de Chardin's Vision of Unity* (London: Burns & Oates, 1969), 127.

16. King, *Mysticism of Knowing*, 66.

17. King, *Mysticism of Knowing*, 103.

18. For a more detailed discussion on the primacy of Christ, see Ilia Delio, "Revisiting the Franciscan Doctrine of Christ," *Theological Studies* 64, no. 1 (March 2003): 3–23.

19. Timothy Jamison, "The Personalized Universe of Teilhard de Chardin," in *There Shall Be One Christ*, ed. Michael Meilach (New York: Franciscan Institute, 1968), 26.

20. John F. Haught, *Deeper Than Darwin* (Cambridge, MA: Westview, 2003), 174.

21. *Meditations with Meister Eckhart*, ed. Matthew Fox (Sante Fe: Bear, 1984), 32.

22. Gray, *The One and the Many*, 128.

23. Gray, *The One and the Many*, 185–86.

24. Dietrich Bonhoeffer, *Letters and Papers from Prison*, ed. Eberhard Bethge (London: SCM, 1971), 361. Bonhoeffer's insight does not negate the place of worship; rather it amplifies the need for worship, because, as Irenaeus wrote, "the glory of God is the human person fully alive." See also Teilhard's insights in *Christianity and Evolution*, 96, especially note 1.

25. Thomas Merton, *Love and Living*, ed. Naomi Burton Stone and Brother Patrick Hart (New York: Harcourt, 1979), 147.

26. Thomas Merton, *Love and Living*, 150.

## Chapter 4

# TEILHARD'S VISION AS AGENDA FOR RAHNER'S CHRISTOLOGY

## DENIS EDWARDS

Pierre Teilhard de Chardin (1881–1955) was not only a geologist and pale-ontologist but also a Jesuit priest who developed an integrated vision of the inner relationship between the Omega of evolution and the Christ of Christian faith. In this article, I address this question: To what extent did his younger Jesuit confrere Karl Rahner (1904–1984), who was not a scientist but a theologian, take up and develop the agenda set by Teilhard?[1] I will begin to explore this question by examining Teilhard's view of the relationship between the Omega of evolution and Jesus Christ, focusing particularly on Teilhard's two late essays "The Heart of Matter" and "The Christic." (Both essays are printed in HM.) Then I will trace Rahner's explicit comments on Teilhard's work and propose that Rahner set himself a theological agenda with regard to Teilhard's vision. After noting the different methodological approaches of Teilhard and Rahner, I will explore how fundamental aspects of Rahner's Christology develop Teilhard's vision.

## Teilhard on Evolution and Christ

At the end of his life, Teilhard looked back and traced the development of his thought in "The Heart of Matter." In a first line of thought, he describes how, beginning from his early love of matter, his personal discovery of evolution enabled him to begin to see how "Matter is the matrix of Spirit," and "Spirit is the higher state of Matter" (HM, 35). What became central for him was the conviction that the evolutionary law of complexity-consciousness does not stop with the biosphere but continues into the noosphere, the sphere of the human mind and of interpersonal consciousness and love. He became convinced that evolution now takes the form of a movement toward a global convergence and union of the human, to a point of irreversibility that he called Omega. He saw the universe, the whole world of matter, as in the process of becoming fully personalized in this Omega Point.

In a second line of thought Teilhard reflects on the emergence of the Christic in his life. Beginning from his early initiation into the symbol of the

53

heart of Christ, he began to discover how the fire of love symbolized in this heart permeated everything in the universe. This discovery coincided with a view of God not simply as the God above, but as the God ahead, the God who draws all things to their completion in Christ. The incarnation of God in Jesus Christ reveals a God who is radically involved with matter. The risen Christ, sharing in the divine immensity, is at work in the whole of creation.

Teilhard tells us that his vision of reality was formed when he was able to understand together his insight into evolution of the cosmos to the point of Omega and his conviction of the presence of Christ in all things. Then he was able to see the cosmic and the Christic not only as converging, but as one:

> The cosmic sense and the christic sense: these two axes were born in me quite independently of one another, it would seem, and it was only after a long time and a great deal of hard work that I finally came to understand how, through and beyond the Human, the two were linked together, converged upon one another, and were in fact one and the same. (HM, 40)

On the one side, based on his scientific training, Teilhard saw a vision of a universe that was becoming personalized through convergence. On the other side, based on his theological commitment, he saw a vision of a person, Christ, who was becoming universalized. The result in him was his conviction of Christ as the very heart of the evolving matter of the universe: "To Christify Matter: that sums up the whole venture of my innermost being" (HM, 47). This process of christification happens through the energy of incarnation, flowing into, illuminating, and giving warmth to the universe of matter. He insists that this action of the risen Christ occurs not in a metaphysical sense, but in a physical sense (HM, 48). For Teilhard there is a wonderful confluence between Christ, who can be seen as "evolver," and the cosmic Center that emerges from evolution. In this way, he says, the "Heart of the universalized Christ" coincides with the heart of "amorized Matter" (HM, 49).

Just two months before his death, Teilhard began to write "The Christic," which he saw as bringing together the quintessence of *Le Milieu Divin*, "The Mass on the World," and "The Heart of Matter." In this essay, he argues that there is more in the total Christ than humanity and divinity. There is also the whole creation. He speaks of creation as a third "aspect," or "function" of Christ, and as "in a true sense of the word," a third "nature" of Christ (HM, 93). Teilhard asks himself how such an "immensified" view of the Christ avoids depersonalizing him. He finds the answer to this precisely in the union between the Omega of evolution and the Christ, since this constitutes a divine milieu in which all opposition between the universal and the personal is wiped out. What is most cosmic is now most personal and what is most personal is most cosmic. For Teilhard, then, cosmogenesis reveals itself first

in biogenesis and then in noogenesis, and culminates only in a true christogenesis.

Teilhard's work was resisted by some other biologists, and not simply
because of his bold linking of evolution with Christ. The philosopher of science Ernan McMullan has pointed to a neo-Lamarckian tendency in Teilhard
that may help to explain the violence of the opposition to him on the part of
some leading neo-Darwinian biologists.[2] Teilhard divides the energies that
propel the universe forward into two types, tangential and radial (HP, xxii,
30–32, 37, 227–32). Tangential energies are those that are normally associated
with the natural sciences. But Teilhard introduces another form of energy,
the radial, as necessary to account for the evolutionary process. This radial
energy is fundamentally psychic in nature. It can be discerned by seeing
the larger patterns of evolutionary process, rather than through the normal
modes of inference at work in biology. Teilhard himself writes of this as a neo-
Lamarckian addition to Darwinism (HP, 97–98). Rahner, by contrast, will see
God as acting at a metaphysical level through secondary causes, in a way that
is not accessible to science, which does not fill gaps in the scientific account,
and which leaves science with its own integrity.

Toward the end of "The Christic," Teilhard asks himself why it is that he
seems to be the only one who has seen this vision: "How is it, then, that as I
look around me, still dazzled by what I have seen, I find that I am almost the
only person of my kind to have *seen*? And so I cannot, when asked, quote a
single writer, a single work, that gives a clearly expressed description of the
wonderful 'Diaphany' that has transfigured everything for me?" (HM, 100).
This is a poignant question, made all the more so by the difficulties Teilhard
experienced with restrictions on his theological work by church authorities
during his lifetime. Since Teilhard wrote "The Christic," of course, other theologians, including Henri de Lubac, have taken up and defended his vision
and, in our own time, scholars working in the area of science and theology,
such as John Haught, continue to build creatively on his thought.[3] I will focus
on some key aspects of Rahner's response to Teilhard's vision.[4]

## Rahner's Explicit Comments on Teilhard

Cardinal Karl Lehmann was Rahner's assistant from 1964 to 1967. In an interview, he notes that Rahner did not see himself as a disciple of Martin Heidegger, Joseph Maréchal, or any other thinker, and then he goes on to speak
of Rahner's relationship to the thought of Teilhard:

> It is also difficult to document where Rahner is dependent on some-
> one else's thought. There are only faint clues, not that he wanted to
> cover that up, but his primary concern was his own independent
> thinking. Many maintain, for example, that he borrowed much from

Pierre Teilhard de Chardin. That's not true. He did not read much Teilhard de Chardin, but he did have a seminar in Innsbruck on him. When others made their presentations during the seminar it stimulated new ideas for Rahner to think about.[5]

Rahner himself seems to have agreed that while he had not read Teilhard closely, he had been influenced by his ideas in a more general way. In response to an interviewer, Rahner recalled how a Dutch theologian had complained that while Rahner's thought had been largely inspired by Teilhard, Rahner had failed to acknowledge Teilhard. Rahner comments:

I could only answer that at least up to that time I had read practically nothing of Teilhard de Chardin. But if you concluded from this that Rahner's theology is independent of Teilhard, I would answer that I don't make any such claim. I would conjecture that in the investigation of someone's thought, that there is obviously an "atmospheric communication" of a non-literary kind.[6]

It is this atmospheric communication and its effects in Rahner's Christology that I will explore in the rest of this article. Rahner is sparing in his direct references to other thinkers, but in fact he does mention Teilhard de Chardin many times. Sometimes Rahner refers to Teilhard simply as an example, as when he lists Teilhard with Augustine, Aquinas, and Pascal, as orthodox Christian thinkers who have different understandings of the human.[7] In another instance, reflecting on the future of the Jesuits on the two hundredth anniversary of their suppression in 1773, Rahner invokes the name of Teilhard to bring to mind the way Jesuits have been seen in "leftist" or "progressive" terms.[8] In an article where he is discussing the difficulty of theologians and natural scientists finding common ground, Rahner writes: "So it happens, for example, that a Teilhard de Chardin is recognized by theologians as a natural scientist but not as a philosopher and theologian, whereas the natural scientist will think of him as a theologian who has not quite managed to keep up to date with the most recent findings of the natural sciences."[9]

In a late article on natural science and faith, Rahner speaks of the church's resistance to the heliocentric system of Copernicus and then says of Teilhard: "In reprimanding Teilhard de Chardin and repressing his endeavors it manifested too little understanding for an ontology in which created being is conceived in principle and in the very beginning as being which is in the process of becoming within an entire evolution of the cosmos, which is still in the process of becoming."[10] In one of his important articles on Christology and evolution, Rahner describes his understanding of the self-transcendence of matter to spirit and, in a footnote, points out that "a similar line of thought, though developed from a different starting-point, is to be found in Teilhard de Chardin's *Man's Place in Nature*."[11] Rahner also consciously uses Teilhard's language of Christ as Omega Point.[12] In his article on evolution in *Encyclopedia of Theology*, Rahner uses Teilhard's concepts of the "noosphere" and speaks of the relationship between growth in "complexity" and in "interiority," in a way that seems to echo Teilhard's law of complexity-consciousness.[13] Naturally, Rahner refers to Teilhard's work in the introduction he agreed to write to Robert North's book *Teilhard and the Creation of the Soul*.[14]

Rahner's most fundamental contribution to an evolutionary Christology is undoubtedly his "Christology within an Evolutionary View of the World," first published in English in 1966. It contains three references to Teilhard. In the first, Rahner makes an important methodological distinction between his own work and that of Teilhard:

> To put it another way: we will try to avoid those theorems with which you are familiar from your study of Teilhard de Chardin. If we arrive at some of the same conclusions as he does, then all to the good. Yet we do not feel ourselves either dependent on him or obliged to him. We want to confine ourselves to those things which any theologian could say if he brings his theological reflection to bear on the questions posed by the modern evolutionary view of the world.[15]

I read this as Rahner saying that he may well arrive at some of the same conclusions as Teilhard, but he will attempt to get there on the basis of a theological methodology, rather than through the unitary approach of Teilhard and his attempt at a full integration of science and theology. In a second reference to Teilhard in this same article, Rahner says that he can go no further in applying his concept of self-transcendence without "the more *a-posteriori* method proper to the natural sciences and with the aid of concepts such as are developed by Teilhard, for instance."[16] In the final reference, Rahner defends Teilhard against the accusation that he does not have a proper concept of sin: "It is also well-known that Teilhard has been reproached with rendering sin harmless in this way—a reproach which H. de Lubac has surely invalidated most lucidly in his most recent book about Teilhard."[17]

In a late discussion on the love of Jesus, Rahner points to the difficulty of connecting the Teilhardian Christ-Omega with Jesus of Nazareth, and with the Jesus whom Christians seek to love here and now.[18] Finally, about the same time, in 1982, Rahner published a short article on "Christology Today" where he said, among other things: "It would do no harm for a present-day Christology to take up the ideas of a Teilhard de Chardin and to elaborate them with more precision and clarity, even though in his work it is not very easy to find an intelligible and orthodox connection between Jesus of Nazareth and the cosmic Christ, the Omega Point of world evolution."[19] I see this comment as more than a suggestion for other theologians. I propose that it might be seen as a description of what Rahner had tried to do in his own theology. He had taken up aspects of Teilhard's agenda, and tried to develop these in ways that showed their intelligibility and their orthodoxy in the light of the Christian tradition. Before exploring three of the ways in which Rahner took up this project in his Christology, I will make a brief comment on their very different methodologies.

## Two Methodologies

Teilhard's methodology can be characterized as a unitary one. He brings together science, the interpersonal, and the religious into a unity of knowledge. Thomas King, a helpful guide to Teilhard's thought, points out that, for Teilhard, the unifying theme of all knowledge is evolution. Evolution does not remain simply a biological concept but becomes a universal one. Evolution is understood as far broader than biology, but biology still remains dominant in Teilhard's thought. As King says, "By his broad understanding of evolution Teilhard is introducing a biological model by which to understand the universe."[20] Teilhard sees the universe in bodily terms, as an organism, and then unites all fields of knowledge within his biological and evolutionary model. He sees everything as interrelated and understands these interrelations as increasing and progressively converging in evolutionary process. As opposed to reductionists of both materialist and idealist kinds, Teilhard seeks to manifest a unity of the without and the within, of the bodily and the spiritual. He sees the material and biological universe coming to consciousness in the human. In the human, the universe can itself turn to God in love.

Rahner's methodology is radically different. It is true that he shares with Teilhard a great unifying vision of God's action in creation, redemption, and in final fulfillment, which I will discuss in the next section. But Rahner's methodology can be distinguished from Teilhard's in four important ways. First, unlike Teilhard, Rahner sees God's action with regard to creation as occurring not at the physical or psychic level, but at the metaphysical level of a God who acts dynamically in and through created entities. In principle, this divine action is not open to scientific investigation. Second, Rahner writes only as a systematic theologian thinking within the Christian tradition, who seeks always to show the way that new theological approaches and insights remain faithful to what is central to the tradition. Third, while Rahner has a strong sense of the reciprocity of matter and spirit, and hence of science and theology, and while he engages with science creatively and often, he does this in a dialogical stance, conscious of the difference between science and religion, rather than through any attempt at the kind of full integration that Teilhard undertakes.[21] Finally, as opposed to Teilhard's unitary approach to knowledge, Rahner insists over and over again on the irreducible pluralism of knowledge today in all disciplines, including theology. He is deeply convinced that any one thinker can have only a partial approach to truth.[22] With their different methodologies in mind, I turn now to consider three ways in which Rahner builds on Teilhard in his Christology.

## Divine Self-Bestowal:
## The Unity of Creation and Redemption

In Christian theology there have been two traditional views about the relationship between Christ and the whole creation. In one view, the incarnation is thought to have been caused as a remedy for human sin. In the other, associated with Franciscan theology, particularly Duns Scotus (c. 1266–1308), God's plan of creation always had the incarnation of Christ as its center. Long ago, N. M. Wildiers drew attention to the importance of this Scotist position for Teilhard de Chardin.[23] Rahner, too, follows this Scotist line of thought and develops it. He holds that God freely chooses, from the beginning, to create a world in which the Word would be made flesh and the Spirit poured out.[24] It would be hard to overestimate the importance of this insight for Rahner's theology. Harvey Egan has said that the briefest possible summary of Rahner's theological enterprise can be found in "his creative appropriation of Scotus's view that God creates in order to communicate *self* and that creation exists in order to be the recipient of God's free gift of self."[25]

One of Rahner's most characteristic theological concepts is his idea of divine self-bestowal. What is revealed in the Christ event, in the life, death, and resurrection of Jesus and in Pentecost, is a God who gives God's self to us in the Word made flesh and in the Spirit poured out in grace. God is revealed as a God who bestows God's very self to creatures. Based on what is revealed in Christ, Rahner sees this divine self-bestowal as defining every aspect of God's action in creation and redemption. The story of the universe and of life on Earth, and everything that science can tell us about its evolutionary history, is part of a larger story, the story of divine self-bestowal.[26] When God wills to bestow God's self in love, creation comes to be as the addressee of this self-bestowal. This means that the story of salvation is the real ground of the history of nature, and not simply something that unfolds against the background of nature.[27] The evolution of the universe, and of life on Earth, exists *within* this larger vision of the divine purpose to give God's self to us.

Once sin exists, of course, the incarnation is the radical event of divine forgiveness and reconciliation. But at a more original level, the incarnation expresses the meaning and purpose of creation, the self-bestowal of God to a world of creatures. Creation and incarnation are not separate and independent acts of God, but are, in all their distinctiveness, united in the one act of God: they are "two moments and two phases of the *one* process of God's self-giving and self-expression, although it is an intrinsically differentiated process."[28] For Karl Rahner, self-bestowal in love characterizes God's action in creation, grace, incarnation, and the final fulfillment of all things in Christ. In this radically Trinitarian theology of self-bestowal, I believe that Rahner achieves what Teilhard sought, a way of showing an inner connection between creation and Christology that is thoroughly theological and deeply grounded in God's self-revelation.

## Evolutionary Christology—
## Creation's Self-Transcendence

Working simply as a theologian, Rahner asks how Christology might be understood in terms of the evolutionary worldview proposed by contemporary science. At the heart of his contribution on this issue is his concept of self-transcendence. Rahner comes to this concept in a transformation of scholastic theology's understanding of the God-world relationship that builds on Aquinas. In this view, God's action with regard to creatures had been understood as the dynamic creative presence by which God sustains creatures in being (*conservatio*) and enables them to act (*concursus*). Rahner takes up and develops this fundamental metaphysical position into something new with his concept that God gives to creation itself the capacity for self-transcendence. In this new vision, divine self-bestowal and creaturely self-transcendence are mutually interrelated. It is precisely the creative presence of God in self-bestowing love that enables created entities to go beyond what they are to become something new.

Rahner's idea of the God-given self-transcendence of creatures is explored particularly in his evolutionary Christology, but it functions in his anthropology, his eschatology, and many aspects of his work.[29] In all the transitions to the *new* in the history of the universe, particularly when matter becomes life, and when life becomes self-conscious spirit, Rahner proposes an evolutionary dynamism that is truly intrinsic to creation, but which occurs through the creative, saving power of the immanent God. The idea of *self*-transcendence indicates that at the empirical level, the emergence of the new is completely open to explanation in scientific terms. But at a deeper, theological and metaphysical level, it is the immanent presence of the divine being that enables creation to become more than it is in itself.

Rahner proposes the following pattern of evolutionary self-transcendence that brings out the inner connection between evolution and Christology. The material universe transcends itself in the emergence of life, and life transcends itself in the human. In human beings, the universe further transcends itself, becoming self-conscious and free and capable of personal response to God's self-bestowal in grace. The Christ event is the radical self-transcendence of the created universe into God. In his humanity, Jesus, like us, is part of the evolutionary history of life on Earth, and a product of the long history of the universe. As a creature, and unlike us, Jesus in his life and death is wholly open to God, and lives a radically free response of love to God's self-bestowal.

Considered from below, Jesus Christ can be seen as the self-transcendence of the evolving universe into God, the culmination of the process of evolutionary emergence, although one that has not yet reached its final fulfillment. Considered from above, Jesus Christ can be seen as God's irreversible bestowal of God's very self to creation. In this one person, we find the event of salvation: God's irreversible self-giving to creatures and full creaturely acceptance of this self-bestowal, united in the one person.[30]

In this theology, Rahner builds an evolutionary theology in a critical engagement with two fundamental parts of the Christian tradition. First he engages with Aquinas's metaphysical view of the God-world relationship, transforming it with his concept of self-transcendence. In doing so, he preserves Aquinas's view of a God who works consistently through secondary causes. God is not seen as an interventionist, but as one who works in and through the regularities and the laws studied by the sciences.[31] This means that God is not an alternative to what science can discover. Gaps in science are to be filled by science, not by invoking God. God is not an alternative to natural selection, but works through natural selection, through randomness and lawfulness, through all the processes of nature, which it is the role of science, not theology, to discover.

The second aspect of the tradition that Rahner takes up, and transforms, in this theology is the Christological teaching of the Council of Chalcedon. Rahner's view of Jesus as both the evolutionary self-transcendence of creation to God and God's self-bestowal to creation, united in the one person, as the event of our salvation, respects and dynamically develops the doctrine of the two natures united in the one person of Chalcedon.

## Resurrection as Deifying Transformation of Creation

A third fundamental dimension of Rahner's evolutionary thought is his eschatological theology of the resurrection of Christ. He contrasts the traditional Western juridical focus on the death of Jesus with the theology of the East, where the resurrection plays a fundamental role in the theology of salvation: "The redemption was felt to be a real ontological process which began in the incarnation and ends not so much in the forgiveness of sins as in the divinization of the world and first demonstrates its victorious might, not so much in the expiation of sin on the cross as in the resurrection of Christ."[32] Along with this Eastern theology, Rahner sees salvation as ontological rather than juridical, understands salvation as a deification that involves human beings and with them the whole creation, and sees the resurrection of Christ as the beginning of this divinizing transfiguration. He thus locates a basis for something like the Teilhardian vision in the theology of great Eastern thinkers like Irenaeus and Athanasius.

According to Rahner, what happens in the death of Jesus is that a piece of this evolutionary, fleshly world is handed over freely into God, in complete obedience and love. In the resurrection, God irrevocably adopts creaturely evolutionary reality as God's own reality. Because of the unity of the world that springs from the creator, this is an event for the whole world. What occurs in the resurrection of Jesus, as part of the physical, biological, and human world, is *ontologically* and not simply juridically "the embryonically final beginning of the glorification and divinization of the whole of reality."[33] As Rahner puts it in another place, the resurrection is "the beginning of the transformation of the world as an ontologically interconnected occurrence."[34] The final destiny of the world is not only promised, but already begun. The risen Christ is the "pledge and beginning of the perfect fulfillment of the world." He is the "representative of the new cosmos."[35]

On this basis, Rahner holds that we Christians are really "the most sublime of materialists." Matter will last forever, and be glorified forever in Christ. But, Rahner believes, it will also undergo a transformation, "the depths of which we can only sense with fear and trembling in that process which we experience as our death."[36] In this way, Rahner holds with Teilhard that the transfiguration of the world has already begun in the risen Christ and is "ripening and developing to that point where it will become manifest."[37] In dialogue with Eastern patristic theology, Rahner argues that the resurrection of the crucified one is the beginning of the transfiguration in Christ, not only of humanity, but, with humanity, in ways that are appropriate to different creatures, of the whole universe.

## Conclusion

Earlier I referred to Teilhard's lament that he could not quote a single writer that gave expression to the insight into the relationship between Christ and evolution that had transfigured everything for him. I have proposed that Rahner can be counted as one who does this. I also referred to Rahner's suggestion at the end of his life that present-day Christology should take the up the ideas of Teilhard de Chardin, elaborate them with precision and clarity, and show an intelligible and orthodox connection between Jesus of Nazareth and the cosmic. It has been proposed that this formed something of an agenda for Rahner throughout his life. Rahner stays with a more traditional metaphysical notion of divine action than Teilhard, and I think this enables his theology better to respect the integrity of science, including neo-Darwinism. And he places evolutionary theology in a profoundly trinitarian and incarnational theology of a God who bestows God's self to us in the Word and the Spirit.

At the same time, he transforms the metaphysical tradition of divine action by showing how God's self-bestowal enables creation to transcend itself in evolutionary emergence. In a way that is faithful to Chalcedon, he shows how Jesus Christ can be understood as both the evolutionary self-transcendence of the universe to God, and God's radical self-bestowal to the universe, united in one person. Finally, he builds on the Eastern patristic tradition to show that the resurrection of Jesus can be seen as the beginning of the deifying transformation of human beings and with them of the whole universe in Christ. Rahner takes up some of Teilhard's agenda in a theology of divine self-bestowal, a self-bestowal in love that enables not only creaturely self-transcendence but also the transfiguring deification of human beings and of the whole universe in Christ.

## Points to Ponder

+ The evolutionary law of complexity-consciousness does not stop with the biosphere but continues into the noosphere, the sphere of the human mind and of interpersonal consciousness and love.

+ The universe, the whole world of matter, is in the process of becoming fully personalized in this Omega Point.

+ The incarnation of God in Jesus Christ reveals a God who is radically involved with matter. The risen Christ, sharing in the divine immensity, is at work in the whole of creation.

+ Teilhard saw a vision of a universe that was becoming personalized through convergence.

+ There is more in the total Christ than humanity and divinity. There is also the whole creation.

+ It is precisely the creative presence of God in self-bestowing love that enables created entities to go beyond what they are to become something new.

+ Rahner proposes an evolutionary dynamism that is truly intrinsic to creation, but which occurs through the creative, saving power of the immanent God. The idea of *self*-transcendence indicates that at the empirical level, the emergence of the new is completely open to explanation in scientific terms. But at a deeper, theological and metaphysical level, it is the immanent presence of the divine being that enables creation to become more than it is in itself.

- ◆ The Christ event is the radical self-transcendence of the created universe into God.

- ◆ As a creature, yet unlike us, Jesus in his life and death is wholly open to God, and lives a radically free response of love to God's self-bestowal.

- ◆ The resurrection of the crucified one is the beginning of the transfiguration in Christ, not only of humanity, but, with humanity, in ways that are appropriate to different creatures, of the whole universe.

## Questions for Discussion

1. What aspects of Teilhard's Christology speaks to you personally? Similarly, what aspects of Rahner's Christology appeals to you? What is the common ground between these two systems of thought? What are the differences?

2. Does Rahner's Christology adequately address the mystery of Christ in our evolving cosmos? If so, how? If not, why not?

3. Rahner holds definitely to the two natures of Christ defined at Chalcedon (451 AD) while Teilhard posits a "third nature" of Christ, the organic or physical. What difference do these distinctions make to the salvific work of Jesus Christ in light of evolution?

4. Teilhard sought to unify knowledge while Rahner held to plurality and hence distinct scientific and theological epistemologies. What is your own position on science and religion?

## Notes

1. This chapter had its origin in a paper delivered at the International Symposium in Commemoration of the 400th Anniversary of Matteo Ricci 1552–1610: The Genesis and Development of East-West Dialogue, held at Fu Jen Catholic University, Taipei, Taiwan, April 19–22, 2010. It was first published as a journal article in *Pacifica* 23 (June 2010): 233–45.

2. Ernan McMullin, "Natural Science and Belief in a Creator: Historical Notes," in *Physics, Philosophy and Theology: A Common Quest for Understanding*, ed. Robert John Russell, William R. Stoeger, and George V. Coyne (Vatican City: Vatican Observatory, 1988), 68–70.

3. See John F. Haught, *Christianity and Science: Toward a Theology of Nature* (Maryknoll, N.Y.: Orbis Books, 2007), particularly 65–81, and *Making Sense of Evolution: Darwin, God, and the Drama of Life* (Louisville: Westminster John Knox, 2010), particularly 137–48.

4. Some of these themes have been taken up in a thesis by H. K. Kodikuthiyil, "Faith Engaged in Dialogue with Science: A Comparative Study of Pierre Teilhard de

Chardin's and Karl Rahner's Reception of the Theory of Evolution" (PhD diss., Catholic University of Leuven, 1998). See also Leo O'Donovan, "Der Dialog mit dem Darwinismus: Zur theologischen Verwendung des evolutiven Weltbilds bei Karl Rahner," in *Wagnis Theologie*, ed. Herbert Vorgrimler (Freiburg: Herder, 1979), 15–29.

5. Karl Lehmann, "He Simply Was Unique: In Conversation with Karl Cardinal Lehmann, Mainz," in *Encounters with Karl Rahner: Remembrances of Rahner by Those Who Knew Him*, ed. and trans. Andreas R. Batlogg and Melvin E. Michalski (Milwaukee: Marquette University Press, 2009), 118.

6. Karl Rahner, "The Importance of Thomas Aquinas: Interview with Jan van den Eijnden, Insbruck (May 1982)," in *Faith in a Wintry Season: Conversations and Interviews with Karl Rahner in the Last Years of His Life*, ed. Paul Imhof and Hubert Biallowons, trans. Harvey Egan (New York: Crossroad, 1990), 53.

7. Karl Rahner, "Christian Humanism," *Theological Investigations* IX (London: Darton, Longman & Todd, 1972).

8. Karl Rahner, "The Jesuits and Their Future," in *Karl Rahner: Spiritual Writings*, ed. Philip Endean (Maryknoll, NY: Orbis Books, 2004), 170.

9. Karl Rahner, "A Small Question Regarding the Contemporary Pluralism in the Intellectual Situation of Catholics and the Church," *Theological Investigations* VI (London: Darton, Longman & Todd, 1969), 25.

10. Karl Rahner, "Natural Science and Reasonable Faith: Theological Perspectives for Dialogue with the Natural Sciences," *Theological Investigations* XXI (New York: Crossroad, 1988), 25.

11. Karl Rahner, "Christology in the Setting of Modern Man's Understanding of Himself and of His World," *Theological Investigations* XI (London: Darton, Longman & Todd, 1974), 218.

12. On Christ as Omega Point, see Rahner's "Thoughts on the Possibility of Belief Today," *Theological Investigations* V (London: Darton, Longman & Todd, 1966), 13; "Evolution: II. Theological," *Encyclopedia of Theology: The Concise Sacramentum Mundi* (London: Burns and Oates, 1975), 481.

13. Rahner, "Evolution: II. Theological," 481.

14. Robert North, *Teilhard and the Creation of the Soul* (Milwaukee: Bruce Pub. Co. 1967), ix.

15. Karl Rahner, "Christology within an Evolutionary View of the World," *Theological Investigations* V (London: Darton, Longman & Todd, 1966), 159–60.

16. Rahner, "Christology within an Evolutionary View," 167.

17. Rahner, "Christology within an Evolutionary View," 185.

18. Karl Rahner, *The Love of Jesus and the Love of Neighbor*, trans. Robert Barr (New York: Crossroad, 1983), 20.

19. Karl Rahner, "Christology Today," *Theological Investigations* XXI (New York: Crossroad, 1988), 227.

20. Thomas M. King, "Teilhard's Unity of Knowledge," in *Teilhard in the 21st Century: The Emerging Spirit of Earth*, ed. Arthur Fabel and Donald St. John (Maryknoll, NY: Orbis Books, 2003), 34.

21. See Karl Rahner, "Natural Science and Reasonable Faith," *Theological Investigations* XXI (New York: Crossroad, 1988), 16–55.

22. See, for example, Karl Rahner, "Pluralism in Theology and the Unity of the Creed in the Church," *Theological Investigations* XI, 3–23.

23. N. M. Wildiers, *An Introduction to Teilhard de Chardin* (London: Collins, 1968), 130–41.

24. Karl Rahner, "Christology within an Evolutionary View of the World," 184–87.

25. Harvey D. Egan, "Theology and Spirituality," in *The Cambridge Companion to Karl Rahner,* ed. Declan Marmion and Mary E. Hines (Cambridge: Cambridge University Press, 2005), 16.

26. Karl Rahner, "Christology in the Setting of Modern Man's Understanding," 219.

27. Karl Rahner, "Resurrection: D. Theology," in *Encyclopedia of Theology,* 1442.

28. Karl Rahner, *Foundations of Christian Faith: An Introduction to the Idea of Christianity,* trans. William V. Dych (New York: Crossroad, 1982), 197.

29. Karl Rahner, *Hominisation: The Evolutionary Origin of Man as a Theological Problem* (London: Burns and Oates, 1965), 98–101; "Christology within an Evolutionary View of the World," 157–92; *Foundations,* 178–203.

30. Rahner, *Foundations,* 193.

31. Karl Rahner and Karl-Heinz Weger, *Our Christian Faith* (London: Burns and Oats, 1980), 78–79.

32. Karl Rahner, "Dogmatic Questions on Easter," *Theological Investigations* IV (London: Darton, Longman & Todd, 1966), 126.

33. Rahner, "Dogmatic Questions on Easter," 129.

34. Rahner, "Resurrection: D. Theology," 1442.

35. Rahner, "Resurrection: D. Theology," 1442.

36. Karl Rahner, "The Festival of the Future of the World," *Theological Investigations* VII (London: Darton, Longman & Todd, 1971), 183.

37. Rahner, "The Festival of the Future of the World," 184.

*Chapter 5*

# HUMANITY REVEALS
# THE WORLD

### François Euvé, SJ

One of the most difficult and fascinating questions we are facing today is the question of the specificity of humanity among the other living beings that compose the natural world. Is humanity unique in the cosmos? Is it a species among millions of species, no more important or significant than others? Is the emergence of the human phenomenon only an accident in the cosmic history or is it the result of a determined or "guided" process? Our scientific knowledge of the progressive emergence of humanity from other living forms, associated with an increasing ecological sensitivity, challenges the traditional vision of the peculiarity of the human being, if not its superiority.

The Christian tradition, according to the Bible (Gen 1:26), holds that the human being is created the image and likeness of God. The Second Vatican Council adds that "according to the almost unanimous opinion of believers and unbelievers alike, all things on earth should be related to man as their center and crown" (*Gaudium et spes*, 12). Does it mean that "especially in its Western form, Christianity is the most anthropocentric religion the world has seen"?[1] Does it mean that the technological revolution of the modern times, the idea of a human dominion over nature and a capacity of transforming it, with all its problematic outcomes, should be seen as a direct consequence of the biblical exhortation to "subjugate the earth"?[2] If this is the case, it would be difficult to harmonize the Christian view of the human person with the ecological sensitivity which we think is so necessary today.

My contention is that Pierre Teilhard de Chardin brings an original contribution to these questions. His reflection can help us think about the "human phenomenon" in a way which is coherent with the scientific worldview (and, at least partly, with ecological sensitivity) and the Christian tradition. As a scientist he was fully aware of humanity's belonging to the natural world but he was also aware of something different, of being able to give meaning to the process of evolution. He tried to avoid two extremes: the modern defense of an anthropocentrism that gives way to a radical transformation of nature, including human nature ("transhumanism" can be seen as a good expression of this tendency[3]); or, on the other side, the reduction of the human phenomenon to a purely natural one, maybe accidental.[4] His position can be summarized in a dialectical formula, proposed by Thomas M. King: "The universe is needed to illumine man and man is needed to illumine the universe."[5] Both are needed to understand the entire process, and no reduction is possible of one to the other. Modern science has taught us that, as a biological species, humanity comes from other living forms through a very long evolutionary process combining chance and necessity. To understand the human phenomenon, we need first to know the historical process of the evolution of life as contemporary biology tries to unfold it. Indeed, humanity is integrally part of evolution but, with the emergence of thought or consciousness, the process has led to a turning point. The capacity of reflecting upon the natural process puts humanity in a unique position in nature. As Thomas King puts it, humanity is "both continuous and discontinuous with evolution."[6]

This does not mean that humanity occupies a preponderant or dominating position over other natural beings. It is insufficient to say that humanity has freed itself from cosmocentrism in the benefit of anthropocentrism.[7] That is true in the sense that human behavior does not depend any more entirely on natural influences. But the acquired capacity of freedom gives humanity a responsibility to share this gift with the other creatures. The capacity of "centration" (consciousness, freedom) yields a capacity of "decentration" (self-givenness) in favor of others, not only human persons but, at least potentially, all natural beings.

This dialectical path is partly founded on a scientific, evolutionary worldview. Science alone cannot define what humanity is. It cannot say that the conscious human person is able to or should give or sacrifice self for the benefit of others. Something else is needed. This something else can be identified within the Christian perspective through the figure of Jesus of Nazareth. As one human person among others, Jesus is not extrinsic to the evolutionary process (he is "son of Adam"). As all other human beings, he stems from a biological lineage, though a long natural and cultural process. But this natural heritage is not enough to say what Christ truly is. Jesus Christ is the model of the human person, insofar as we can contemplate in his life accomplished freedom and the capacity of complete self-bestowal.

My thesis here is that humanity reveals the world in the sense that liberty (or consciousness), which characterizes the human person, reveals the historical structure of the world. Liberty here is not to be construed as self-affirmation (centration) which entails a dominion over other beings, but rather in a relational perspective, a capacity of self-givenness which Teilhard calls decentration, following the example of the one who "emptied himself" (Phil 2:7) "so that God may be all in all" (1 Cor 15:28). It is revelation in the sense that it does not come only from a scientific examination of the natural processes; rather, something else is needed. But this something else is not incoherent with the scientific picture of the world.

To understand the relevance of Teilhard's thought we will begin by his scientific examination of the human phenomenon. This will lead us to understand the importance he gives to consciousness and freedom, a freedom that finds its fulfillment in relationship with the other in a process of decentration. In short, the history of humankind reveals the history of the cosmos.

## Scientifically Studying the Human Being

Understanding the human being is traditionally a philosophical issue, expressed in the famous three Kantian questions: What must I know? What ought I to do? What should I hope? The development of modern science has changed the panorama. The scientific method, so successful in its treatment of physical phenomena, can be stretched to include human ones. The question is not theoretical but truly existential, as Teilhard writes: "It becomes more and more necessary for us, in order to live, to understand man" (AM, 132). The scientific study of the human being seeks to exhibit its continuity with the natural world and rejects the traditional idea of a distinction of the human person, usually expressed by the notion of "soul," that completely isolates the human in the universe. In the ancient, prescientific vision, "man was the center of creation . . . the geometrical center and the central value of a universe formed of spheres concentrically planned around the earth" (VP, 216). But since the emergence of modern science, humanity seems to have become an insignificant object, neither the bigger nor the smaller in the universe, occupying a not very interesting place, lost between the two infinites. Facing such evaporation of the human specificity in modern thinking, a sensitive thinker could be tempted to reject the scientific path in the profit of a more "humanistic" way of looking at it. Are not literature, art, or at least "human" sciences better ways to understand what the human is rather than "natural" science?

Teilhard does not easily reject the scientific method. It would have been much easier to disqualify the scientific discourse as essentially unable to reach the very essence of the human person since free will, which lies at the core of the human person, cannot be defined, because of the risk of falling into a contradiction. But it is possible to further scientific investigation. If, for example, we look more precisely at the human organism, it appears to be the most complex system in the universe, complexity being defined as "an organized, and consequently centered heterogeneity" (VP, 222). Teilhard's anthropology is first of all an effort to make of the human being an object of scientific study. His enterprise was recognized by some anthropologists, such as Georges Gusdorf, who considered Teilhard as "the greatest name in French anthropology since Broca."[8] He was surprised by the lack of interest in the scientific world for this particular yet familiar object: "Almost nobody has yet decided to put the main question: 'But what exactly is the phenomenon of man?'" (VP, 162). He does not ignore the existence of "human science" (*Geisteswissenschaften,* distinct from *Naturwissenschaften* in the German-speaking area or *Sciences morales* apart from *Sciences naturelles* in French), but he considered it as a kind of "protection" from the methodology of the natural sciences in order to avoid "desecrating the 'soul'" (VP, 162). This situation reflects the modern dualism of mind and body or liberty and nature. The fear that humanity could be reduced to a material system led to a strict separation of two uncorrelated disciplines. But in light of evolution, such a separation can no longer hold.

The scientific study of the human being is indeed ambivalent. In fact, we often observe a reduction of the human phenomenon to a purely physical object by the hard sciences. Neuroscience is a significant case study, which can encourage more philosophically oriented thinkers to erect once again a protective barrier against such an undesirable invasion. But this strategy would be a poor and insufficient answer to the challenge. It is probably better to accept the scientific path but to pursue it to its latest consequences. A significant text is the essay Teilhard wrote in 1925 on "Hominization." His aim was "to express as objective and simple a vision as possible of humanity considered (as a whole and in its connections with the Universe) as a phenomenon" (VP, 51). In this perspective we must first look at the human phenomenon as pure natural scientists, not from inside (introspection) but from outside, objectively. This implies not differentiating *a priori* between the human and the nonhuman (animals, plants, stones) beings: "Though the human and non-human are intimately linked in nature, we persistently look on them from two different points of view; in practice if not in theory, researchers and thinkers almost always act as if even viewed by science (although it is only concerned with appearances and antecedents) man were a certain universe, and what is not man, another" (VP, 51).

This way of proceeding is deliberately naturalistic. But even this method would be able to make us aware of some traits that partly escape a purely naturalistic worldview. The human being, for example, shares many traits with our nearest cousin, the ape. On the zoological level a dominant characteristic is continuity between the manifold expressions of life. Humanity is not outside the vast ensemble of life. If we are to understand natural beings on the basis of our understanding of humans, we need to maintain the continuity between them. Yet, even if the human being is physically not very differentiated from other animals, the human manifests some specific elements, of which I would like to highlight two. The first is the capacity to transform its environment and thus to become able to act upon the very evolutionary process. Humanity "alters the face of the earth to an extent which should warn us that its appearance marks the beginnings of a new phase for our planet" (VP, 58). A *reversal* occurs in the evolutionary process: the evolution of humanity is no longer dependent only on biological processes. The second element is the ability to establish mutual relationships so to weave a network all over the planet. This is not only the fact of spreading all over physical space, but also the qualitative phenomenon of the links that the different parts of humanity are able to create. One can object that these relations are not always friendly. Divisions, hostility, wars exist. But despite all these hostile forces, Teilhard sees a unification process as irreversible. This marks the "elaboration of a common consciousness" (VP, 59). While this process is specifically human, at the same time it is nothing else than the extension of the evolutionary process which finds its fulfillment in humanity. Teilhard wrote: "Our aspirations and powers of invention reveal themselves as this same organogenic power of life hominized. And, reciprocally, the whole evolutionary process of the organic world becomes comprehensible when placed in analogy with the developments of our human world" (VP, 71).

## From Matter to Consciousness and Freedom

In a great number of texts Teilhard highlights the novelty of humanity: "Man, connected though he is to the general development of life, represents an absolutely new phase at the termination of that development" (VP, 62). He "is not simply a new species of animal (as we are still too often told). He represents, he initiates, *a new species of life*" (AE, 325). "Man, viewed zoologically, constitutes a new stage [*un palier nouveau*] (perhaps a supreme stage) in the series of fundamental stages through which life—and therefore terrestrial matter—is compelled to pass" (VP, 66). To describe this phenomenon one can employ the concepts of "single points," "changes of state," or "critical state" (VP, 65). But at the same time scientific discourse is reluctant to accept a true novelty. In this lies the limitation of the scientific worldview which tends to eliminate the dimension of time, as Bergson already noted. The usual tendency in science is to reduce the unknown to the already known: "Man is an embarrassment to science only because it hesitates to accept him at his full significance, that is to say as the appearance, at the goal of a continuous transformation, of an absolutely new state of life" (VP, 167). The existence of novelty signifies that a threshold has been passed. We must take into account the dimension of time which means adopting resolutely a historical perspective. In the paragraph dedicated to the theme "Man, the Key to Evolution," Teilhard begins by criticizing the universal tendency, especially in science, to find in matter a principle by which to understand things. This is not a good path for understanding the world as development or evolution. The historical "spring" of the universe does not lie in its material components or in its beginning but in the process itself. We cannot know the final achievement of the historical development, but we can find in humanity some kind of anticipation of this achievement, since humanity represents the most complex system we know. Teilhard wrote, "Let us try therefore to understand the biosphere by the Noosphere" (VP, 67). In an evolutionary (historical) process the meaning is revealed in the fulfillment of the process, not in its beginnings: "Nowhere are things less comprehensible than at their beginnings" (AM, 57).

The next step consists in correlating complexity and consciousness. This is much more difficult since consciousness is not a scientific, objective notion. In fact a reversal must happen, since we must give up the external, objective vantage point for a more internal one. The objective (naturalistic) path has led us to become aware of the novelty of the human phenomenon in the evolutionary process. It cannot say more. To get further, we must adopt another perspective. How can we define consciousness? In the *Human Phenomenon*, the term indicates "every kind of psyche, from the most rudimentary forms of interior perception conceivable to the human phenomenon of reflective consciousness" (HP, 25). This means that "inside, consciousness and spontaneity are three expressions of one and the same thing" (HP, 25). Consciousness is first grasped from our own experience as human beings, the "I" looking *inside* itself. Since we experience consciousness in our own existence, we can generalize this experience to other human beings, even if we have no direct access to their inside. And since human beings are the most complex structures in the universe, we deduce that there is an intimate connection between complexity and consciousness. We observe that the human organism is "both supremely *complex* in this physical-chemical organization (measured by the brain) and, at the same time, viewed in one's psychism, supremely *free and conscious*" (AE, 101). So we can draw this conclusion: "Spiritual perfection (or conscious 'centreity') and material synthesis (or complexity) are but the two aspects or connected parts of one and the same phenomenon" (AE, 60–61). The ultimate step is the affirmation of free will. Consciousness means freedom. The human person appears to be "the most mobile thing in the world" because he or she belongs to a new state in the universe "in which everything is still free and everything still has to be created" (AE, 327).

Thanks to this freedom, the human person can transform the world. Nature is no more a mere reference for human action, because "when nature attained the level of man it was obliged, precisely in order to remain true to itself, to change its ways" (AE, 17). The novelty of humanity resides precisely in a turning point: the blind evolutionary forces produce an organism that is able to act upon these forces, to modify them and maybe to give a direction to the evolutionary movement. Even in the elementary life forms, autonomy is already present: "the corpuscle . . . at certain higher levels of internal complexity, manifests strictly autonomous phenomena" (MPN, 20). The notion of consciousness can be generalized to other beings than human. We can do that, not after an objective observation of the nonhuman beings (we have no direct access to the inner side of beings), but after our own experience extrapolated to other instances thanks to the continuity we have recognized between all world beings.

We can stop here a while, wondering whether we are still in a scientific perspective. Complexity is a scientific concept. Is consciousness? We doubt it. Speaking of a within indicates that we have no direct access to what is in question. In his 1921 conference "Science and Christ," Teilhard is aware of the limitation of the scientific method, which is analytical and can result in an "infinitely dissociated world" (SC, 26). Science, as such, dissociates the world because it looks at it in the direction of the past. We must "reverse our direction," he said, if we are to understand true reality: "The *only consistence* beings have comes to them from their *synthetic element*, in other words from what, at a more perfect or less perfect degree, is *their soul, their spirit*" (MPN, 29). The synthesis is the very process by which the world is evolving toward new, more synthetic and unitive stages. Teilhard's insights seem to justify anthropocentrism. While he rejected the old anthropocentrism, he seems to promote a new one (VP, 216–33). But the term "centrism" needs to be understood within evolution, since the notion of center implies a static picture of reality.

## Centration, Decentration, Super-Centration

The freedom of the individual being, conceived as autonomy regarding its environment, is not its fulfillment but the first stage, which can be defined as centration (the more centered the being, the more autonomous it is from its environment). Inside a historical worldview no static state can be thought of as accomplished, full being. Movement is not a transitory stage between two fixed positions, the second of which could be considered more accomplished than the first. Movement and change are the rules of a universe which is still in genesis, in which everything still has to be created. In a lecture given in 1943 entitled "Reflections on Happiness," Teilhard presents the evolutionary process as a dialectical one in three steps. This is more visible in the case of the process of human personalization. But, insofar as the human person is "psychically the highest of all livings beings and the one best known to us" (TF, 117), what occurs in the human person unveils a more general process at a universal level.

The first is centration, in which an organism gets its own identity, its inner unification, the feeling of its ownness. This implies a work on oneself by which one introduces "more order and more unity" into his or her ideas, feelings, or behavior (TF, 117). This step corresponds to the process that leads toward more autonomy, more freedom, less dependency on the surrounding reality. Teilhard identifies this process as what the spiritual tradition calls chastity.[9] This implies also a difference from the other organisms. A child discovers that he or she is different from his or her mother's body. But to become a fully accomplished person that child must get into another kind of relationship with others and the world. Friendship and love are types of union with other persons which can have a deep influence on the development of one's personality.

Thus we discover a second step, which can be called decentration. One has to overcome the temptation to believe that real identity is reached by withdrawing oneself from the rest of the world. One could think that the more one is isolated, the more one is oneself. But this idea ignores the fact of our interdependence, not only with other people but also with other world beings and the entire universe. This second step is not only the awareness of the cosmic dimension of our life, but the discernment of something "infinitely more important than any private undertakings, the development of a vast world that calls for all his good will and fills him with enthusiasm" (WTW, 42). If the risk associated with centration is isolation or self-sufficiency, the converse risk here is a pantheistic dilution in an impersonal universe. If the decentration can be called "love" (TF, 118), it is because it affects not beings in the neutral sense of the word, but *persons*. In fact the example proposed by Teilhard of a molecule, which, "in common with all the other similar molecules," forms a "definite corpuscular system from which [it] cannot escape" (TF, 118), can be misleading, since it seems to reduce the thinking being to the stage of a passive being that finds its place in a "mechanical ensemble." Interpersonal relationship is not of this type because personal links affect the person much more than physical ones. One can even say that, at least ideally, an interpersonal relationship gives more personality, and not less, to each of the two beings it involves: "union differentiates," as Teilhard states (HP, 186).

For Teilhard there is a third stage he calls super-centration. The decentration toward another self is not enough to achieve the fulfillment of life. In fact one can wonder whether the other involved in an interpersonal relation is really other. Is it not the otherness that gives a relation its fundamental character, avoiding any kind of reduction or assimilation? One can see the need of a more radical other that will fulfill the relation. In fact our experience shows us that the otherness of our partner does not hinder but enhances the quality of the relation. If God is the wholly other, God can be the proper partner for such an accomplished relation. The communion which stands at the horizon of the whole process demands that the ultimate center is a person toward whom all beings must converge. If Christ is the Omega Point, it is because he is in conjunction with the two previous steps. The Gospel shows that Jesus was at the same time a fully existing human person, with full liberty, of which perhaps the most significant expression is his words "I am" (*Egô eimi*), and that he was totally committed or decentered to others. As the good shepherd, he "lays down his life for his sheep" (John 10:11). The death on the cross is the radical expression of this, prefigured in the image of the wheat grain that must fall into the earth and die if it is to yield a rich harvest (John 12:24).

The threshold of death shows that the evolutionary process by which an organism reaches the fulfillment of its life is not a linear, progressive one, but one that goes through a rupture, a negation of itself. This manifests, inter alia, the difference between transhumanism and Teilhardian "ultrahumanism." If the former seeks to eliminate death by the reward of a kind of eternal life (in practice a mechanical one) and, at the same time, suppress the individual by its annihilation into an anonymous system, the latter sees death as a necessary step to be crossed toward a truly accomplished life, which is, at the same time, both personal and communal. As we have seen, for Teilhard communion does not suppress the person but gives one full personality.

## The Risk of History

There is, on the one hand, a link between the presence of liberty in human action and, more generally, spontaneity in nature, and, on the other, the evolutionary or, better, historical characteristic of nature. This was the contribution of Bergson, whose famous book *Creative Evolution* was so inspiring for Teilhard. In 1926, Teilhard wrote: "History is gradually invading all the disciplines from metaphysics to physical chemistry" (VP, 168). Contemporary culture is in the process of discovering time in a new way.[10] History should be understood in the radical sense of the word. Evolution is often conceived as a process of unfolding, which is almost as determinate as the process that leads from an acorn to an oak tree. Indeed, even such a process is not entirely determined from the very beginning. Accidents can happen. But the result is not surprising: looking at the acorn, taking into account the experience we have, we can predict with a great probability the kind of tree it will produce. But history, for the most part, is unpredictable. The irreversibility of the process leads "towards ever more improbable and more fully organic constructions" (SC, 95). On the biological level this unpredictability depends on the chance component of the processes. But it could also be linked with the free decisions of the human actors. Once again the distinction between the two levels is not easy to establish. The existence of unpredictability does not necessarily mean that liberty is at work. But conversely one can interpret the "spontaneity" of the natural processes as a first spark or manifestation of an element that with the appearance of the human being will be called freedom.

The unpredictability of history entails the existence of risks. The final result of the evolutionary process is not guaranteed in advance. "Hominization has unleashed an immense force on the world: this is the material fact that we have studied so far. But at the same time it has introduced, correlatively, into the conduct of life formidable risks, in which human knowledge discovers the problem of evil at its origins" (VP, 74). The possibility of new realizations, the appearance of novelty that enriches the world, includes, at the same time, the danger of failure. What can help us evolve in spite of all these threatening elements? Teilhard answers: "A crisis of cosmic nature and magnitude, the social ferment which is today pervading human populations can only be dominated and guided by a clearer and more conscious faith in the supreme value of evolution" (VP, 76). This faith is not certitude, since no absolute guarantee can be given, nor is it arbitrary, a game of heads and tails. Rather, faith should be supported by the coherence of the evolutionary phenomenon, "the coherence of the deep movement which, starting from matter, culminates in spirit" (VP, 79). To be successful, human action should be supported by lawfulness that allows a certain level of predictability. Hope is not only wishful thinking but should be able to rely on historical phenomena. Teilhard thought he found this coherence in "orthogenesis," and he dedicated some texts to the defense of this idea. It is defined as "the fundamental drift as a result of which the stuff of the universe is seen to behave as though moving toward corpuscular states continually more complex in their material arrangement and, psychologically, continually more interiorized" (MPN, 90). He was always willing to cling to the phenomenon, the tangible, even if he was aware that this tangibility could be deceptive. This question was (and is still) very disputed. Among biologists, there is a strong tendency to give chance a leading role in the evolutionary process, with the result that the "purpose" of a process is deprived of any scientific basis. Other positions exist as well. For example, Simon Conway Morris champions the idea of a certain "trend" in evolutionary lines.[11] This is not the right place to debate these positions. One can simply note that the question of purpose or meaning of world history cannot be entirely disconnected from any scientific reference, even if science itself cannot prove firmly one purpose or another (or the absence of it). Due to its analytical method, science is not equipped to answer meaning questions. But the ultimate destiny of the cosmos should have visible marks on the phenomenal level. The debates dealing with the direction of evolution show that it is difficult to find support for the meaning of evolution in the scientific—objective—discourse. It is difficult to attribute a law to the process, the unfolding of which is at the same time determined by free decisions. This seems to be an ambiguity in Teilhardian thought. As Michael Polanyi reminds us, meaning cannot be found in pure objectivity. Teilhard seems aware of this when he says in a very short formula in the foreword to the *Human Phenomenon*: "In the act of knowledge, object and subject are wedded together and mutually transform each other" (HP, 4). More precisely, in his article "Science and Christ or Analysis and Synthesis" he differentiates between analysis as the traditional scientific method, and synthesis, which is necessary to grasp the meaning of the process (SC, 21–36). If we adopt a historical perspective, the difficulty is that the synthesis can be reached only at the end of the process. Any knowledge can only be an anticipation of the final result. But this result already exhibits some marks in the concrete, physical, phenomenological reality. Teilhard is right in saying that, even if our action influences the unfolding of history, its meaning is not only a projection of our own desires on the physical world, but the result of an interaction between autonomous yet related instances.

## Conclusion

As we have seen, Christianity is often accused, especially among ecologically sensitive people, of being too anthropocentric and thus of having inspired the rise of modern technology and the problematic consequences thereof. For some religious thinkers it seems as if the ideal should be to put aside the most specific aspects of the biblical tradition for the sake of a more general spiritual message that would give a greater importance to the cosmos. We should adopt cosmocentrism or at least biocentrism instead of anthropocentrism. A revival of stoicism is characteristic of our time: the functioning of nature should be the pattern human action must follow. True liberty is to conform human behavior to physical nature. There is a certain grandeur in this attitude, of which the philosophy of Spinoza is probably the best illustration. The biblical message does not stand in opposition to it, as if it would promote a human action entirely disconnected from any natural link. The Bible inserts the human being in the cosmos, but the way it does it must be translated into a more contemporary lexicon. The Teilhardian dialectic seems a good way of proceeding, which avoids the traps of two opposing positions. The defense of human free will, that is, the capacity of acting, or transforming the world, is associated with a call to decentration for the benefit of the other instances. This other is not only the fellow human. It could be, as well, other living or nonliving beings. Love is given a scope much broader than the understanding we have of it. To a certain extent, this is coherent with the scientific revolutions of Copernicus and Darwin, whose discoveries overturned any notion of a center. In the Christian tradition even God is hardly a center. Jesus' life exhibits an essential and radical capacity to be decentered for the benefit of others. Is this not an expression of the creating love of God?

## Points to Ponder

♦ Humanity is integrally part of evolution but, with the emergence of thought or consciousness, the process has led to a turning point. The capacity of reflecting upon the natural process puts humanity in a unique position in nature.

♦ The fear that humanity could be reduced to a material system led to a strict separation of two uncorrelated disciplines.

♦ "Though the human and non-human are intimately linked in nature, we persistently look on them from two different points of view; in practice if not in theory, researchers and thinkers almost always act as if even viewed by science (although it is only concerned with appearances and antecedents) man were a certain universe, and what is not man, another."

♦ Even if the human being is physically not very differentiated from other animals, the human manifests some specific elements, of which I would like to highlight two. The first is the capacity to transform its environment and thus to become able to act upon the very evolutionary process. Humanity "alters the face of the earth to an extent which should warn us that its appearance marks the beginnings of a new phase for our planet. . . ." The second element is the ability to establish mutual relationships so to weave a network all over the planet. This is not only the fact of spreading all over physical space, but also the qualitative phenomenon of the links that the different parts of humanity are able to create.

♦ Man, connected though he is to the general development of life, represents an absolutely new phase at the termination of that development. He is not simply a new species of animal (as we are still too often told). He represents, he initiates, *a new species of life.*

♦ The existence of novelty signifies that a threshold has been passed.

♦ Nowhere are things less comprehensible than at their beginnings.

♦ Consciousness means freedom. The human person appears to be "the most mobile thing in the world" because he or she belongs to a new state in the universe "in which everything is still free and everything still has to be created."

♦ The unpredictability of history entails the existence of risks. The final result of the evolutionary process is not guaranteed in advance.

♦ The functioning of nature should be the pattern human action must follow.

## Questions for Discussion

1. Is humanity unique in the cosmos? Or is it a species among millions of species, no more important or significant than others? Is the emergence of the human phenomenon only an accident in the cosmic history or the result of a determined or guided process?

2. Does Teilhard's notion of evolution give rise to a new anthropocentrism (centrality of the human person) or does he evoke a new biocentrism (centrality of life)?

3. How do you understand the relationship between the human person and the natural world? What are some problems with this relationship today? What is Teilhard's understanding of this relationship for the future fullness of life?

4. What is the import of this statement for the church and world today: "The functioning of nature should be the pattern human action must follow."

## Notes

1. Lynn Whyte, "The Historical Roots of Our Ecologic Crisis," *Science* 155 (1967): 1205.

2. Pierre Hadot, *The Veil of Isis: An Essay on the History of the Idea of Nature* (Cambridge, MA: Harvard University Press, 2006), 130.

3. Eric Steinhart, "Teilhard de Chardin and Transhumanism," *Journal of Evolution and Technology* 20, no. 1 (2008): 1–22; Ilia Delio, "Transhumanism or Ultrahumanism? Teilhard de Chardin on Technology, Religion and Evolution," *Theology and Science* 10, no. 2 (2012): 153–66.

4. Jacques Monod, *Chance and Necessity*, trans. Austryn Wainhouse (New York: Knopf, 1971).

5. Thomas M. King, *Teilhard's Mysticism of Knowing* (New York: Seabury, 1981), 49.

6. King, *Teilhard's Mysticism of Knowing*, 33.

7. See Karl Rahner, *Theological Investigations*, VI (New York: Herder, 1971), 8–9.

8. See Claude Cuénot, *Pierre Teilhard de Chardin: Les Grandes Étapes de son Évolution* (Paris: Plon, 1958), 426.

9. See "The Evolution of Chastity" (TF, 60–87). In "Science and Christ" (SC, 34) the three stages are expressed as "purity" (or "concentration," "unification of man in himself"), "charity" (or "fusion of multiple individuals in a single body") and "self-denial" (or "deconcentration of every man in favor of a more perfect and more loved Being").

10. This rediscovery of time is exemplified in the scientific work of Ilya Prigogine.

11. Simon Conway Morris, "Evolution and the Inevitability of Intelligent Life," in *The Cambridge Companion to Science and Religion*, ed. Peter Harrison (Cambridge: Cambridge University Press, 2010), 148–72.

*Part Two*

# A NEW PHILOSOPHICAL VISION

Should we not take a lesson from physics, which had no hesitation in changing its geometry when the pressure of facts demanded it?

Should we not, then, simply decide at last to create a higher metaphysics which includes a further dimension?

—TEILHARD DE CHARDIN,
*Christianity and Evolution*

*Chapter 6*

# THE INTEGRAL VISIONS OF TEILHARD AND LONERGAN

*Science, the Universe, Humanity, and God*

### Patrick H. Byrne

The animating concern of this collection of essays is the current fragmentation of the many intellectual achievements of the sciences and humanities. Ilia Delio's invitation to contribute to this volume observed the lamentable state of affairs that our "educational system has become silos of specializations, with the humanities and sciences kept worlds apart." I would hasten to add that the sciences themselves are now so specialized that even members of the same science department have great difficulty communicating with one another. The purpose of this volume, therefore, is to highlight the integrative vision of Pierre Teilhard de Chardin, SJ, as a response of lasting worth to this state of affairs. In my contribution to this project, I hope to show how the approaches of Teilhard and his fellow Jesuit Bernard Lonergan, SJ, complement each other in articulating this integral vision.

In this essay I explore further striking parallels, as well as some significant differences, between Teilhard and Lonergan in their approaches to the question of the unity of the fields of human knowledge, of the universe, of evolution, and of humanity with God. But beyond these comparisons and contrasts, I think there is an important complementarity between their approaches and their works. In the sections that follow I first summarize Teilhard's account of the evolution of the universe and humanity, as well as his understanding of how God in Christ Jesus is the final and crucial unifier of all evolution. I will then propose that the enthusiastic reception that Teilhard's work received is due in important ways to the symbolism he developed to communicate his vision of unity. Then I will briefly explore some of the criticisms his work received, and propose that to some extent this was because his symbolic modes of communication were not appreciated for the kind of meanings they expressed. Then I will present a parallel account of Lonergan's thought on evolution. And finally, borrowing from Lonergan's own way of thinking about theological method, I will propose that his "functional specialties" of systematics and communications provide an illuminating way of

thinking about the relationships between the work of these two thinkers—
that they complement one another, and that both need each other.

## Parallels between Teilhard and Lonergan on Unity

Teilhard and Lonergan were two of the twentieth century's most remarkable
Jesuit thinkers. The two shared a love of God incarnate in Christ Jesus, as well
as a love of modern science and the world it has revealed. Born into a time in
history where both their own religious community and the community of scientists regarded each other with great skepticism and antagonism, Teilhard
and Lonergan devoted themselves to the task of seeking the underlying unity
of their great loves for Christ, science, and the universe it envisions.

Both found the most profound inspiration for their visions of unity of
the evolving universe with God in the writings of St. Paul. Teilhard frequently
cited as a source of his thought Colossians 1:17 ("He himself is before all
things, and in him all things hold together.").[1] Lonergan, on the other hand,
was inspired at an early age by Ephesians 1:10 ("[God] has made known to
us the mystery of his will . . . to gather up all things [*panton anakephalaiosis*]
in [Christ], things in heaven and things on earth.").[2] Each understood Paul's
phrase "all things" to apply to the entirety of the natural and human universe,
and set about to elaborate Paul's vision of unity in the context of modern science and history. Both also strongly affirmed that evolution has a direction,
in spite of prevailing extrascientific opinions to the contrary. Both conceived
of the evolution of the universe and life as an ascent through time involving
successive emergences of entities that are dramatically distinct from and irreducible to one another. They contend that evolution brings about an objective
hierarchy (i.e., higher orders) of entities from the earliest physical state to the
advances of human culture and the entry of God into human history. Both
claim that the evolutionary dynamism of the universe becomes conscious in
humanity. For Teilhard, humanity discovers that it *"is nothing other than evolution become conscious of itself"* (PM, 221). For Lonergan, "the tension that
is inherent in the finality of all proportionate being becomes in [humanity] a
conscious tension."[3] (There are, however, significant differences in the ways
they understand consciousness and its relationships to evolution, which will
be explained later in this article.)

Again, both Teilhard and Lonergan remark on the challenges facing
humanity once our advances in knowledge brought us face-to-face with the
enormousness and complexity of the evolving world—and with the fact that
we ourselves participate in that unfolding. This challenge can be a source of
great anxiety. According to Teilhard, our anxiety could be set at ease if we
could believe that we are "contributing infinitesimally . . . to the building of
something definite" (DM, 56). For Lonergan our intellectual advance "reveals

to [humanity] a universe of being in which . . . [we] are but infinitesimal components in the history of [humankind]."[4] For Lonergan this anxiety is overcome
by discovering the unity and the destiny of the dynamic evolution of the universe, and approving it, and cooperating with it.[5]

There are of course differences, some quite significant. Some of the differences have to do with more detailed aspects of the positions they shared;
some differences have to do with the fundamental assumptions that ground
their shared assertions.

## The Unity of Evolution and Its Stages according to Teilhard

It will be helpful to begin this comparison with an overview of evolution and
its stages as Teilhard portrays them. In *The Human Phenomenon*[6] Teilhard
covers the now very familiar stages in the evolution of the universe, but he
does so by using language that underscores his overarching vision of the
unity of all natural and human evolution in Christ. "Fuller being is closer
union. Such is the kernel and conclusion of this book" (PM, 31, 35). The
human phenomenon appeared to Teilhard as a continuous unity—"a whole
which unfolds" (PM, 29). Teilhard assembles a remarkable range of the then
known results from the researches of the modern sciences—physics, cosmology, chemistry, geology, paleontology, and biology—and weaves them into
his integral vision of unity.

### 1. Cosmogenesis

Teilhard uses the term "cosmogenesis" in two senses. First, it is his generic
term for the entirety of evolution; but second, it refers more specifically to the
evolution of the universe up to the emergence of the planet earth. He com-
bines the indeterminacy principle ($\Delta x \cdot \Delta \rho \geq h/2\pi$) from quantum mechanics
along with the discovery that the universe itself is bounded (from the general
theory of relativity), and concludes:

> We are bound to admit that this immensity represents the sphere of
> action common to all atoms. The volume of each of them is the vol-
> ume of the universe. (PM, 45)

Matter and energy, for him, are an "entirety of infinitesimal centers which
share the universal sphere among themselves" (PM, 46). The spatiotempo-
ral "tree" of the universe evolves through the interactions of these radiating
centers according to the "law of complexification" (PM, 48). Complexification produces diverse kinds of centered circulations at many different levels:
electrons in atoms, atoms in molecules, planets in star systems, and stars in
galaxies.

## 2. Geogenesis

According to Teilhard, "the earth was probably born by accident" as an especially stable part of the sun broke off, inaugurating the evolution of the earth (PM, 74, 67). But as soon as this accident happened, "it was immediately made use of and recast into something naturally directed," the process of geosynthesis (PM, 74). Initially this geogenesis organizes chemical elements (which originated in stars) by highly regular crystallization into "the rich variety of the 'mineral world'" (PM, 69). These processes of crystallization successively form the spherical layers of the earth: "barysphere [metallic core], lithosphere [rock layer], hydrosphere, atmosphere, and stratosphere." Crystallization entrapped great quantities of the chemical elements and "closed them prematurely in upon themselves . . . unfitted for growth." The "liberation" of energy during these processes complexified regular crystalline structures into larger and more widely diverse molecules—polymers and organic compounds (PM, 68–69).

## 3. Biogenesis

According to Teilhard, when the first cellular life-forms originated they "multiplied almost instantaneously" (PM, 92). He goes on to argue that "we are definitely forced to abandon the idea of explaining every case as simply as the survival of the fittest" (PM, 94–95, 150). According to Teilhard, "life would have spread and varied, but always on the same level" were it not for an additional factor that "acts as a vertical component" to accelerate diversification "*in a pre-determined direction*" that is "more and more improbable" (PM, 108–9). Teilhard acknowledges but minimizes the role played by "the struggle for existence" in the evolution of life. He argues that there is an orthogenesis as life "gropes" toward a goal with a kind of "directed chance" (PM, 110). This he claims is responsible for the organization of life forms into phyla, classes, orders, families, genera, and species that make up the "tree of life" (PM, 110–32).

The extensive proliferation, differentiation, and mutual interactions among biological species densely populate the earth. Because of its far greater volume, the physical body of the planet earth appears from without to be the much more significant body than the "negligible thickness" of the outer shell occupied by living organisms. But according to Teilhard, seeing the within of things makes it possible to recognize that this biosphere has evolutionary importance in inverse proportion to its size (PM, 148). The full force of cosmic evolution itself becomes concentrated in this biosphere.

## 4. Psychogenesis

Teilhard marks the transition from his discussion of biogenesis to psychogenesis with the following comment: "Asked whether life is going anywhere [whether evolution is directed] . . . nine biologists out of ten will today say no, even passionately" (PM, 141). Teilhard of course takes the opposite view. He presents as his evidence the increasing complexification of the nervous system as animal life evolves, which "could not be the result of chance . . . [and] proves that evolution has a direction" (PM, 146). Consciousness emerges along with the increasing complexity of the nervous system. Because the brain is "the sign and measure of consciousness" (PM, 146), therefore it is the rise of consciousness that confers upon life a sense of directedness. In fact, "the story of life is no more than a movement of consciousness veiled by morphology" (PM, 168). The vast diversity of animal species is a sign of "psychism seeking for itself through different [life] forms" (PM, 151).

## 5. Anthropogenesis (or Hominization)

Teilhard claims that the distinctive feature of human consciousness and thought is reflection.

> From our experimental point of view, reflection is, as the word indicates, the power acquired by a consciousness to turn in upon itself *as of an object* endowed with its own particular consistence and value: no longer merely to know, but to know oneself; no longer merely to know, but to know that one knows. By this individualization of himself in the depths of himself, the living element, which heretofore had been spread out and divided over a diffuse circle of perceptions and activities, was constituted for the first time as a *centre* in the form of a point at which all the impressions and experiences knit themselves together and fuse into a unity that is conscious of its own organization. (PM, 165)

According to Teilhard, this capacity for self-reflection provides the ground for the rise of art, logic, mathematics, science, reasoned choice, inventions, and so on (PM, 165, 218–20). Consciousness become self-consciousness—"the reflective psychic centre" (PM, 172). Because it is self-reflective, human consciousness explicitly recognizes its participation in the dynamism of the very same orthogenesis that brings everything (including itself) into existence. With the rise of the science of evolution humanity discovers that it *"is nothing other than evolution become conscious of itself"* (PM, 221).

While reflectiveness is in the first instance an individual achievement, it does not long remain merely an individual possession. Just as crystallization, polymerization, life, and animal consciousness all spread across the whole of the earth after initially arising at some one point on its spherical surface, so also human reflective thought spreads as it is shared through human communication. The spread and complexification of shared and communicated thoughts build up what Teilhard calls the "noosphere"—the penultimate in the series that began with cosmogenesis and continued onward to produce the baryspshere, lithosphere, hydrosphere, atmosphere, stratosphere, and biosphere.[7] Teilhard calls this process "hominization"—that is, the humanizing of the whole of the evolutionary process and the whole earth (PM, 181).

## 6. *The Omega Point and Christogenesis*

In Teilhard's view, if we wish to comprehend the *ultimate* meaning both of humanity and the whole of evolution we must look at what previous evolution "announces *ahead*" (PM, 190). This question of what lies ahead brings about a crisis. The next stages of evolution can only take place through the thoughtful and willing actions of human beings. But once human beings as reflective come to know the fact of evolution itself, such knowledge produces anxiety that can paralyze human action. The immensity of the spatial size, temporal age, and number of occupants of the evolving universe can make human effort seem futile (PM, 228; DM, 45). Yet, says Teilhard, our anxiety can be overcome if we form the conviction that we are "contributing infinitesimally . . . to the building of something definite" (DM, 56; PM, 229). In other words, if we reflectively recognize our own thought-guided actions as contributing to an evolving wholeness, then our own efforts would be understood as connected to, rather than alienated from, the immensities of the universe.

However, this is only half the battle. For even if we recognize and embrace the meaningfulness of our actions in the context of the wholeness of evolution thus far, this does not guarantee that evolution toward ultimate wholeness will continue. Uncertainty about the future produces "the truly cosmic gravity of the sickness that disquiets us" (PM, 232). We lose the conviction needed to act when we worry that evolution that may have no future. In particular, the inevitability of our own death raises, in a radical way, whether our efforts will have any lasting worth (PM, 270; DM, 81–2).

Teilhard proposes a solution to this existential crisis in the form of the "super-soul" or the "hyper-personal" Omega Point. The Omega functions like an "*x*" in an algebraic equation. Omega can be conceived on the analogy of taking the limit of a series in mathematics. A certain series of rational numbers can have a nonrational limit (such as $\pi$ or $e$) (PM, 247). So also, Teilhard conceives of Omega as the limit point, the unification toward which all of evolution has been moving and which, with human cooperation, will continue to move. The Omega Point would be the harmonious continuation of the various unifications that have occurred at every prior level of evolution and would "fulfil the ambitions aroused in the reflective being by the newly acquired consciousness" (PM, 246).

Given this limit definition, Teilhard argues that Omega would have certain properties. Because it is the absolute limit of evolution, it is the fullest meaning of evolution to which human actions contribute. In addition, it would also itself be a *personal* center that is completely universal, and thereby would effect a unification of individually centered human personalities in itself without annihilating those centers (PM, 261–62). Finally, Teilhard proclaims that this "synthesis of centers, center to center" is love (PM, 263). Only love "is capable of uniting living beings in such a way as to complete and fulfill them, for it alone takes them and joins them by what is deepest in themselves" (PM, 265). And what is deepest in the center of every human being is the very thrust of evolution toward ultimate fulfillment that produces every evolved being.

In this way Teilhard postulates an Omega, knowledge of whose existence would empower humanity to gain the confidence it needs in order to take up its role in continuing evolution toward the future. In order for Omega to perform its function of motivating human continuation of evolution, therefore, it *cannot* be merely the point that would eventually be reached by the process of evolution itself. Rather, Omega would have to exist and be accepted as *"already in existence* and operative at the very core" of the noosphere (PM, 291).

While Teilhard as a scientist and philosopher can specify that this Omega would be needed for evolution to reach its culmination, he cannot prove its existence by the same means that he has traced cosmogenesis up to this point. The existence of the Omega is, therefore, a matter of faith. But Teilhard argues that faith is not at all alien to science, as Enlightenment thinkers had assumed. The very pursuit of scientific investigations itself requires a certain kind of faith because scientists cannot know scientifically that their efforts can yield intelligible results. Still, faith in the existence of the Omega is an even further, distinct kind of faith. This kind of faith in the existence of Omega is needed to "give each and every element [in evolution] its final value by grouping them in the unity of an organized whole" (PM, 250).

In Teilhard's view, science and philosophy can take us only this far—that the evolutionary process of the entire universe culminates in human reflective consciousness, in the crisis that results from human self-awareness of its place in evolution, and the need for an actually existing Omega to overcome that crisis. But in the epilogue to *The Human Phenomenon*, Teilhard takes a further step as a Christian and professes faith that the Omega is Christ. He deliberately avoided using the term Christ (or God for that matter) in the main body of his book in order to show that the existence of Omega is essential to the wholeness of evolution strictly in scientific (or at least in philosophical) terms. But in the epilogue he explains why the Christ professed in his faith is exactly what is anticipated in the argument about the nature and future of evolution.

## 7. Tangential and Radial Energy

Teilhard postulates what for him is a most important point—that there "must be a single energy" differentiated into two interconnected forms: tangential (or physical) energy and radial (or spiritual) energy. He introduces these two interconnected forms of energy for two reasons, and criticizes science for having ignored the relationship between them. On the one hand he thinks this distinction is needed to make sense of certain elements of human experience (PM, 63–65). On the other hand, Teilhard thinks this distinction between tangential and radial energy is necessary in order to provide a complete explanation for all of the phenomena of evolution. Tangential energy links emerging entities with "all others of the same order" (PM, 65), and is responsible for the diffusions and associations that form the level of each of his successive spheres. Radial energy, on the other hand, is required to adequately account for the orthogenetic direction of evolution (PM, 88). Some transformation of tangential energy into radial energy, albeit an "extremely small amount" (PM, 65), is required, therefore, to account fully for the novelties and complexity of evolution.

Although the book traces the evolution of the universe from the earliest stages of matter and energy, it is entitled *The Human Phenomenon*. In Teilhard's view it is impossible to understand either the universe or the human phenomenon correctly and fully unless one understands humanity as intrinsic to the wholeness of evolution within which humans emerged. Teilhard may have had his first real epiphany of this unity of humanity when he was saying Mass for soldiers during the First World War.[8] That original epiphany gradually unfolded to incorporate a remarkable synthesis of the many things modern science had come to understand about nature and human beings with the fundamental tenets of Christian faith.

## Symbolism in Teilhard's Communication of Unity

The preceding section relied mainly upon *The Human Phenomenon* for two reasons. First, that is the book where Teilhard sets forth the most detailed articulation of his vision of the wholeness of evolution. And second, that wealth of detail facilitates the comparison with Lonergan's understanding of the wholeness of evolution. However, Teilhard's other writings and his charismatic personal conversations were at least as important for the widespread reception of his vision of the unity of nature and humanity with God in Christ. Indeed in the last month of his life he wrote that *The Human Phenomenon* contained "still exactly the same fundamental vision" that he set forth decades earlier in his prayer "The Mass on the World" and in *The Divine*

*Milieu.*[9] At the culmination of "The Mass on the World" he wrote: "the very purpose of my being and all my love of life, all depend on this one basic union between yourself [my God] and the universe" (HU, 36–37).

Teilhard's was a mystical vision of unity (DM, 116). Yet as Harvey Egan and Bernard McGinn have rightly pointed out, mysticism does not arise within a vacuum. Mysticism is the culmination of prolonged prayer and reflection within a religious tradition.[10] Teilhard's mystical apprehension of unity arose out of his Roman Catholic tradition which nourished his prayer and reflections. In particular, the epistles of St. Paul and the Gospel of John were rich sources for his prayerful reflections concerning "the Cosmic Christ."[11] His vision of the unity of the universe of modern science with Christ grew from these origins. *The Human Phenomenon* was intended to clarify, expand, and answer some misunderstandings that arose in reaction to his earlier writings. Hence it is important to bear in mind that *The Human Phenomenon* is a grand elaboration of the original vision of unity expressed compactly in that early prayer, and must be read in that spirit.

Arising out of such meditations, *The Human Phenomenon* and Teilhard's other communications were enormously successful forms of communication because they speak so strongly to people's desire for some meaning to the universe and their own lives. Teilhard was explicit about his intention to offer his readers an answer to the question "what is the *meaning* of this movement of expansion" of the universe, of life on Earth, and of human thought? (PM, 141, emphasis added). The emergence of the human species, he insists, is not just another "genus or family . . . one more pigeon-hole in the edifice of our systematization." In place of just "an additional order or branch," Teilhard offers the symbol of the noosphere, which supervenes upon and "crowns" the spheres symbolizing the previous stages of evolution. The noosphere manifests the penultimate meaning of the rise of those previous spheres, while the Omega reveals the ultimate meaning (PM, 182–83).

Teilhard embeds his account of evolution and its major stages within a rich and complex matrix of symbolism that comprises many dimensions. Ilia Delio, for example, draws attention to his use of the symbolism of heart and fire.[12] Again, Teilhard frequently draws upon music and its rhythms as symbolic of the dynamic unity of evolution (PM, 148). Likewise, the symbolism of return, doubling back, folding in upon itself permeates his writings (PM, 46, 70, 73, 130, 165, 206, 290).[13] The richness of Teilhard's symbolism deserves a thorough study unto itself. Here however I will focus only on his use of the symbolism of radiation, which is one of the most significant and pervasive symbols that Teilhard employs in communicating his vision of the unity of the evolving universe. Radiation in his sense is a compact symbolism integrating the symbols of light, orientation, and centering.

Radiation is, first of all, a symbol of light, illumination, and enlighten-ment. The symbol of illumination is already present in the title, *The Human Phenomenon*. Deriving from its Greek roots, "phenomenon" is what appears, what shines forth. In his very first sentence Teilhard explains that the purpose of the book is to *"make others see"* (PM, 31, emphasis added) or we might say "to illuminate appearances so as to enlighten others." *The Human Phenom-enon* abounds with the language of the symbolism of the radiance of light. The universe is "luminous in nature" (PM, 47), and the kinship of all living organisms "shines through" (PM, 99–100). As life spreads it is "diffracted and becomes iridescent" (PM, 105); mammalia reach "full florescence" in the Tertiary geological period (PM, 122); the rise of sophisticated consciousness "glows" and burns to "a point of incandescence" (PM, 160); there is a "phos-phorescence of [human] thought" (PM, 183). Throughout the world religions, light abounds as a symbol of sacred reality and the divine intelligence, and it is especially central in the Christian Johannine literature that had such a profound influence upon Teilhard.

Radiation is also a symbol of orientation. What radiates is sent out along a path or a mission toward something. Teilhard characterizes evolution in terms of its goals. The process of evolution is "convergent." It is heading *toward* greater complexity and consciousness (as he understood it). Cosmo-genesis, biogenesis, and Christogenesis are for him different stages of one single process that is unified from beginning to its ultimate culmination.

> Since, in concrete fact, only one singe process of synthesis is going on *from top to bottom* of the whole universe, no element, and no movement, can exist at any level of the world outside the "inform-ing" action of the principal center of things. (CE, 88)

Finally, radiation also contains the symbolism of the center. Radii radi-ate from a center, and symbolic centers abound in *The Human Phenomenon*. Teilhard traces the whole arc of evolution through the symbolism of suc-cessively unfolding series of spheres—space as a whole, then the geosphere (barysphere, lithosphere, hydrosphere, atmosphere, and stratosphere), bio-sphere, noosphere, and Christosphere. He repeatedly draws attention to the centers of these spheres, to each of which in succession is transferred the real meaning of evolution.

Mircea Eliade analyzed the importance of the religious symbolism of the center and its role in forming a unified cosmos for religious people.[14] The cen-ter is the place of the sacred. Only that which is connected with the sacred center has meaning and genuine reality. Nothing that is cut off from the cen-ter has reality; all that is cut off from the center is chaos, profane, without meaning. Eliade also draws attention to how religious symbolism accommo-dates a multiplicity of centers as epiphanies of the primordial center, which in turn functions as a kind of "Center to centers," to use Teilhard's phrase: "The universe fulfilling itself in a synthesis of centres. . . . God, the Centre of centres" (PM, 294).

In various places, these several dimensions of radiation symbolism come together in a single passage, for example:

> The elemental ripple of life that emerges from each individual unit does not spread outwards in a monotonous circle formed of individual units exactly like itself. It is diffracted and becomes iridescent [light symbolism], with an indefinite scale of variegated tonalities. The living unit is a center [symbolism] of irresistible multiplication, and *ipso facto* an equally irresistible focus of diversification [orientation symbolism]. (PM, 105)

The power and success of Teilhard's communication of the unity of the universe in Christ, therefore, is heavily dependent upon his richly symbolic expressions. It is this symbolism that carries the passion, faith, hope, love, and joy with which he beheld that unity. His work received an enthusiastic reception, and it was probably the symbolic richness, more so even than the force of his philosophical arguments, that was responsible for that reception.

## Limitations of Teilhard's Symbolic Communication

While a great many people were deeply inspired by Teilhard's writings, not everyone was so enamored. Nobel Prize–winning biologist Peter Medawar, for example, published a scathing review of *The Human Phenomenon*.[15] He wrote that much of the book "is nonsense, tricked out with a variety of metaphysical conceits, and its author can be excused of dishonesty only on the grounds that before deceiving others he has taken great pains to deceive himself." Medawar complained specifically about the exuberance of Teilhard's "tipsy, euphoristic prose-poetry" style that "creates the illusion of content." His criticisms of Teilhard's science were even more damaging. He disputed Teilhard's most fundamental claim that evolution is oriented toward the emergence of humanity and the growth of human culture (hominization). In opposition to Teilhard's claim, Medawar wrote

> that evolution flouts or foils the second law of thermodynamics is based on a confusion of thought; and the idea that evolution has a main track or privileged axis is unsupported by scientific evidence.[16]

In his contribution to this volume, Donald Wayne Viney disputes Medawar's claim that Teilhard "flouts" the second law of thermodynamics. However, Medawar did state the prevailing view among biologists that there is no scientific support for the idea of evolutionary directedness, a claim that Teilhard himself challenged. He was also critical of the way Teilhard used radial energy to characterize consciousness. Although Medawar does not say so explicitly, Teilhard's claim that some amount of tangential energy must be converted into radial energy contradicts one of the most fundamental laws in all of physics.[17] The hypothesis that energy is conserved only statistically has been proposed and refuted numerous times.[18]

Teilhard opened himself to exactly these sorts of criticisms. He insisted that *The Human Phenomenon* must be taken as a "scientific treatise," and that it was neither a theological nor a metaphysical work. He believed that he was simply drawing logical conclusions from the wealth of scientific discoveries that he wove together. But in spite of his protestations, *The Human Phenomenon* and almost all of his other influential writings were *not* in fact merely scientific. They were symbolic expressions of theological, philosophical, and metaphysical positions, after all. In fact, his metaphysics was heavily indebted to that of Henri Bergson, whose *Creative Evolution* was a major influence on the young Teilhard.[19] Viney also explains in his contribution to this volume that Teilhard had understandable reasons for wishing to avoid the term "metaphysics" itself. Elsewhere he preferred the phrase "hyperphysics" for the kind of thinking and writing he was doing. Be that as it may, his emphatic claim that *The Human Phenomenon* should be regarded as a scientific work opened him to unnecessary criticisms.

Teilhard's mystical vision of unity and its symbolic expressions also led him into difficulties on other fronts, especially regarding sin and evil. Gabriel Marcel in particular was shocked when, in the face of atrocities at Dachau, Teilhard persisted in his faith in the *inevitability* of human progress.[20] And of course his censure by Catholic and Jesuit authorities grew out of the way he seemed to be articulating a form of pantheism, along with his attempts to rethink the doctrine of original sin. Quite legitimately he puzzled about how to reconcile the findings of paleontology and evolutionary biology with the biblical claims that the human race emerged from a single couple (monogenesis), and that death came about because of the sin of that first human couple. But more problematic was his claim in 1920 that original sin did not begin with particular acts of particular human beings, but instead "symbolizes the inevitable chance of evil" that is built into the very structure of the whole universe. This would seem to carry the implication that God is responsible for sin and evil. While Teilhard modified this position in *The Divine Milieu*, still as late as 1947 he proposed that the primordial state of the universe ("the multiple" as he called it) was structured in such a way that "*Statistically . . .* it is absolutely inevitable" that suffering and sin would evolve (CE, 40, 195). Finally, his emphasis on the Cosmic Christ as Omega seemed to minimize the role of Christ as redeemer.

## Lonergan's Systematics:
## From Emergent Probability to
## the Mystical Body of Christ

Although Teilhard communicated his vision of the unity of the universe and humanity in Christ with passion, even ecstasy, his ways of using symbolism led to implications that could not be easily reconciled with some of the most basic affirmations of the scientific or Catholic communities. With his careful scholarship, however, Henri de Lubac performed the great service in defending and rehabilitating Teilhard's thought from the most severe and unfair criticisms on matters of faith.[21] Yet even de Lubac admitted that "his thought is still incomplete" and that "Teilhard was a little too hasty in his search for 'coherence' and increasingly looked for it along roads that were rather too direct."[22] Karl Rahner also adopted a positive though qualified view of Teilhard's work:

> Let us agree that even if Teilhard de Chardin has not in every respect succeeded in doing justice to dogma, then I would say *in magnis voulisse sat est*. That it isn't as bad as when we teachers of theology give forth with a very orthodox but sterile theology that is of interest to no one.[23]

On the other hand, Medawar accused Teilhard of using "in metaphor words like energy, tension, force, impetus and dimension *as if* they retained the weight and thrust of their specific scientific usages." This comment goes right to the heart of the issue. Teilhard was successful as a communicator precisely because he testified to the religious meaningfulness of scientific findings by his use of symbolism.[24] But Teilhard's compact symbols fused scientific, explanatory meanings with symbolic meanings in ways that caused confusion and seemed to legitimate untenable inferences. These were significant limitations to Teilhard's work. They are the sorts of limitation that were of great concern to Bernard Lonergan. He dedicated much of his career to developing methods that would preserve authentic meanings but also refine them so as to remove unintended negative implications.

Key to Lonergan's approach is his conception of a method of theology that comprises eight interdependent functional specialties. Of particular interest for present purposes are the relationships between the functional specialties of systematics and communications. The task of systematics according to Lonergan is "to work out appropriate systems of conceptualization, to remove apparent inconsistencies, to move toward some grasp of spiritual matters both from their own inner coherence and from the analogies offered by more familiar human experiences."[25] Communications on the other hand "induces in the hearer some share in the . . . meaning of the speaker."[26] These two functions are mutually interdependent. On the one hand the work of systematics and the six other functional specialties upon which it relies would "be in vain" unless they issued in a communication of the meanings so painstakingly discerned.[27] On the other hand, "To communicate one has to understand what one has to communicate. No mere repetition of formulas can take the place of understanding."[28]

The need for a specialized form of systematics arises because of what Lonergan calls the problem of the differentiation of consciousness.[29] Undifferentiated consciousness does not distinguish between dramatically different kinds of meanings. For example,

> doctrinal expression may be figurative or symbolic. It may, if pressed, quickly become vague and indefinite. It may seem, when examined, to be involved in inconsistency and fallacy.[30]

This problem, clearly, is not unique to Teilhard. Systematics seeks to hold on to what is normative in symbolic and other expressions while resolving inconsistencies and fallacies such as those that Teilhard ran up against.

In Lonergan's view, systematics can best perform this service when it uses categories that are derived from the structures of the acts of human consciousness.[31] In particular, he mentions that his treatment of "generalized emergent probability" in *Insight* is a prime example of the derivation of such categories. In the next section I will show how generalized emergent probability runs parallel to Teilhard's account of evolution while avoiding the many difficulties encountered by his way of expressing his vision.[32]

# Lonergan's Vision of Unity:
## The Method of Metaphysics and
## Generalized Emergent Probability

The vision of unity is central to Teilhard's project. Hence, a systematics approach to the question of unity is crucial to the task of reconciling scientific and religious affirmations. Teilhard approached the question of unity primarily in terms of the symbolism of radiation and the Center of centers. Lonergan, on the other hand, systematically worked out different meanings of unity in stages through almost the entirety of *Insight*. I first offer a succinct overview of Lonergan's account of unity in *Insight*. This is followed by a fuller elaboration of each stage. I will then conclude by drawing out connections with the issues and concerns that arose from Teilhard's work.

## 1. Overview: Unity and Intelligibility

The key to unity for Lonergan is intelligibility.[33] His precise definition of intelligibility is in terms of an act of consciousness: "By intelligibility is meant what is to be known in understanding," that is, in insights.[34] Insights understand intelligible connections among experiences, connections that were previously unnoticed. For this reason intelligibility is the key to the meaning of unity.

The unity most relevant to Teilhard's work is the unity of the universe. Lonergan understands the universe to be a dynamic, intelligible process. He arrives at his account of the intelligibility of this process by carefully probing the methods of empirical sciences, and identifying the distinct kinds of intelligibilities that they pursue. He then argues that the natural universe has a unity that synthesizes these distinct kinds of intelligibilities into a more unified intelligibility, which he calls "generalized emergent probability." Generalized emergent probability is Lonergan's way of envisioning the evolving universe. It is therefore what Lonergan means by the intelligible unity of the universe.

Yet even this finite unity of generalized emergent probability is not in itself fully intelligible. It is somehow lacking in the fullness of unity. We can ask, for example, why the universe has this kind of dynamic intelligibility, rather than some other. The answer to this question according to Lonergan lies beyond our merely contingent universe. Hence the methods of the empirical sciences alone are not adequate to provide an answer. Lonergan therefore extended his philosophical method to offer a merely "imperfect, analogous" understanding of God.[35] By means of this analogical understanding, Lonergan could claim that the answer to why the universe has the kind of intelligibility it does have resides in God's unrestricted understanding and valuing, which "is the ultimate cause of causes for it overcomes contingence at its deepest level."[36] In addition, because human beings and their actions are riddled with the fragmentations of irrationality and sin, the value of the universe as God creates it includes a kind of intelligibility that goes beyond anything envisioned by all the combined methods of the natural or human sciences (i.e., generalized emergent probability). That further intelligibility is the unity of a divine-human collaboration that draws a further unity and goodness out of the brokenness of human evil and sin. Although that unity is effected by God's supernatural initiative, it is nonetheless "a harmonious continuation of the actual order of this universe," that is, generalized emergent probability.[37] Such is the overview. The following sections explain its components in greater detail.

## 2. Science as Heuristic

In *The Human Phenomenon,* Teilhard synthesized a vast range of the scientific facts already known up to the time he wrote that book. By way of contrast, Lonergan did not rest his account of unity upon any provisional results of scientific research reached in the past. Instead, he based his argument upon the *methods* that scientists actually use, methods that anticipate future discoveries. In this way, his account of unity does not depend upon specific scientific findings that might be overturned. Rather it is open to *any* findings that will eventually be arrived at by using these methods. Lonergan did not offer his work for evaluation as a "scientific treatise," as Teilhard did. Rather, he set forth a heuristics, a framework of unity, so as to integrate any future contributions arising out of practicing the scientific methods.

While acknowledging the great variety and many differences among the methods employed in different branches of science and by individual scientists, Lonergan proposed that there are two basic kinds of heuristic methods, classical and statistical, used by all natural sciences, a third kind, genetic, added to the first two, which is employed specifically in the biological sciences, and a fourth kind, dialectic, that is needed along with the others by the human sciences.[38]

### 3. Classical Heuristic Method and Conditioned Correlations

Lonergan argued that classical methods pursue insights into the intelligible laws or "correlations" among events and things. In physics, for example, these correlations are formulated in equations expressing the correlations of variables to one another. These correlations are highly *conditioned*. They manifest themselves quite differently, depending upon environmental conditions. The classic example is Newton's laws of motion and gravitation. The very same "laws" manifest themselves in very different and indeed incompatible ways under different conditions. Depending upon the relative energies, momenta, and positions even of just two celestial bodies, their orbital paths could be hyperbolic, parabolic, elliptical, or circular. If more than two bodies are involved, the concrete forms of their relationships yield even more complex orbital behaviors.

Contrary to the connotation of law as an unconditional imperative, the laws discovered by classical methods do not by themselves alone determine the concrete events of the universe. The actual, concrete events of the universe depend also upon the conditions under which the laws operate.

### 4. Complexity and Emergence

Lonergan relies upon these general features of classical correlations to show how scientists approach the explanation of emergence and complexity. He focuses upon the cycles or "schemes of recurrence" that permeate so much of the universe as well as the earth.[39] These cycles are repeating sequences of events. For purposes of illustration it will be helpful to consider one of the cycles that is fundamental to almost every form of life on earth: the adenosine triphosphate (ATP) cycle of using and replenishing biological energy. This cycle involves the sequential combination of two different chemical reactions. First the ATP molecule is transformed into an ADP molecule plus a phosphate molecule along with energy that is subsequently transferred to some other biochemical synthesis. Then energy is supplied from some outside source to resynthesize the ADP and phosphate molecules, thereby returning back to the ATP molecular state. Each of the chemical reactions in the ATP cycle occurs in accord with a chemical law. The cycle as a whole, therefore, is a very concrete and particular way of combining these classical laws. But this cycle as a whole emerges and recurs only under very specialized conditions, such as those provided in the interior of a cellular mitochondrion, for example.

These combinations of correlations, whether simple or complex, can arise and continue to repeat themselves only if the proper conditions happen to be fulfilled in some way. In other words, once the requisite conditions are fulfilled, the intelligibility of this cycle will *emerge* into reality.[40] In no way does the emergence of these complex cycles require some special intervention of an *élan vital* or a radial energy over and above the classical laws. What is required over and above the classical laws, however, is that special and sometimes highly unusual sets of conditions come to pass.

Lonergan noted further that throughout the universe, simpler cycles can and do provide the conditions for the emergence and recurrence of ever more complex cycles. For instance, simpler solar fusion cycles form conditions for the terrestrial hydrological cycles. The hydrological cycles distribute and replenish water supplies that form the conditions for the cycles for the growth, reproduction, and evolution of plants. Plant cycles in turn constantly replenish supplies of carbohydrates consumed by herbivorous animals. The consumed carbohydrates are broken down and provide the conditions for Krebs cycles in the interiors of animal cells, and the Krebs cycles provide conditions for the emergence and recurrence of ATP cycles. There is then a long, complex network or "*series* of conditioned schemes of recurrence"[41] reaching from the interior of the sun to the interior of animals' cellular functionings.

## 5. Statistical Heuristic Method

The idea of a series of conditioned cycles provokes an interesting question: Is the whole universe therefore just one big complex cycle, one immense, deterministic, totalizing system? Lonergan's answer is no. He argues instead that the universe has a vast, nonsystematic, random dimension to it.[42] Since cycles of complexity can only begin to function once their proper conditions have arisen, they must rely upon some source other than themselves to provide those conditions. In general, this means that these sets of conditions arise and fall away in random, nonsystematic fashions.[43]

Lonergan argues that the second major kind of scientific method, statistical method, arose in order to investigate the intrinsically nonsystematic and random dimensions of nature. Statistical methods seek to understand populations of events and things. Statistical methods use techniques of counting and sampling in order to determine the actual numbers of occurrences of various kinds of events and things. But statistical method goes beyond merely determining *actual* frequencies. It seeks to discover in them a distinctive kind of intelligibility—*ideal* relative frequencies (called probabilities). The actual frequencies of events in the universe fluctuate nonsystematically (randomly) around the intelligible norms of ideal frequencies (probabilities).[44] But this means that the intelligibility of these probabilities is just as much a constituent of the universe as is the intelligibility of the classical correlations (or "laws" of science).

## 6. Emergent Probability

Just as classical correlations can be intelligibly combined to produce the more complex intelligibilities of schemes of recurrence, so also classical correlations and statistical probabilities can be combined to produce even more complex forms of intelligibilities. As Lonergan puts it, "classical laws tell what would happen if conditions were fulfilled; statistical laws tell how often conditions are fulfilled."[45] This means that statistical methods also can be applied to determine the probabilities of emergence and survival of various kinds of schemes of recurrence. Since schemes emerge when complex arrangements of conditions are fulfilled, statistical investigators can therefore determine the probabilities of such arrangements. Lonergan goes on to argue that once the proper environmental conditions are in place, the probability of emergence of a scheme increases dramatically.[46]

Lonergan introduces the term "emergent probability" to denote this synthesis of the intelligibilities of classical and statistical investigations. Classical methods explain how and why organized complexity functions. Statistical methods analyze the probabilities of conditions coming together for the emergence and survival of complex cycles. Cycles arise when appropriate conditions are assembled in the same vicinity at the same time. This assembly occurs in relatively random and nonsystematic ways, and yet in ways that conform to the ideal frequencies of probabilities. In other words, there are probabilities of events coming together to make possible the emergence of new, organized schemes of recurrence. Emergent probability is Lonergan's first approximation to the intelligible unity of the evolving universe.

As Lonergan puts it, the universe has an "upwardly but indeterminately directed dynamism."[47] The process is upward because earlier schemes set the conditions for the emergence of later schemes. It is indeterminate because the sets of conditions are assembled nonsystematically. But the whole process is nevertheless directed, because probabilities mean that out of large numbers of random events over long periods of time, sets of conditions with nonzero probabilities will eventually appear and lead to the emergence of corresponding cycles. And once these cycles emerge, they in turn shift the probabilities for more complex cycles from zero to some finite fraction.

Hence the complex and ever-shifting combinations of classical correlations and probabilities is responsible for increasing complexity and diversity in the universe. There is no need to postulate any special superforce, radial energy, or constantly intervening intelligent designer that directs this process over and above what is discovered by classical and statistical methods. This upwardly but indeterminately directed pattern is a natural consequence of the kinds of intelligibilities that scientific investigators find in the course of their researches.[48]

## 7. Hierarchy in Science and Higher Orders in the Universe

Like Teilhard, Lonergan disagreed with the reductionism which holds that all realities can be adequately explained by laws of physics alone. Instead, he presented an argument showing the emergences of distinctly higher orders of more complex schemes are completely compatible with and need to be investigated by the methods of science. If there are regularities in nature that cannot be fully explained by systematic combinations of the laws of physics—if physics "has to regard as merely coincidental what in fact is regular"[49]— then there really are higher generic orders in the universe.

Lonergan proposed that there actually are at least five distinct kinds of intelligibilities (classical correlations) proper to each of five distinct and hierarchically arranged sciences—physics, chemistry, biology, sensitive or animal psychology, and rational or human psychology—in ascending order. So it follows that there are at least five real and distinct generic orders. In the context of emergent probability (evolution) this means that there was a long period in which various kinds of purely physical schemes of recurrence were emerging and setting conditions for the emergence of still other physical schemes. But at some point in time a sufficient concentration of physical events and schemes brought about a shift in the probabilities of emergences of the simplest kinds of chemical schemes. Chemical schemes functioned with a regularity that cannot be accounted for by the laws of physics alone. Likewise, after a considerable period of time when a diversity and complexity of chemical schemes proliferated and the physical conditions (such as temperature) reached the appropriate states, they dramatically increased the probabilities for the emergence of life forms. And likewise, bacterial and botanical life forms eventually set the conditions and shifted the probabilities for the emergence of animals with simple nervous systems. Then gradually ever-more-complicated nervous systems emerged, finally setting the conditions for the emergence of human beings.

## 8. *The Higher Human Order*

Lonergan would define human beings as those sensate animals that have the capacity for higher acts of consciousness such as insights, judgments of fact and value, acts of feeling and response to values, free decisions, and acts of love. Furthermore, what makes human beings distinctively human is the manner in which these acts of consciousness are organized into a recurrent and self-correcting structure by an unrestricted desire to ask questions about what is intelligent, reasonable, valuable, responsible, and loving.

People in turn use these activities to construct social and cultural patterns and institutions. With the advent of human beings, emergent probability begins to advance not only intelligibly but also intelligently. Lonergan remarks that human intelligence is an endless source of new intelligible, recurring schemes.[50] Pre-animal schemes emerge intelligibly as appropriate conditions are fulfilled nonsystematically in accord with ideal frequencies (probabilities). But these processes do not involve consciousness (here Lonergan differs from Teilhard). With the rise of intelligent consciousness in human beings, however, new schemes originate when individuals have insights and put them into action. Human insights make possible the production of new kinds of goods and services—new technologies. Human insights also discover ever-new ways of distributing those goods and services—new economic arrangements. Insights also make possible new forms of human cooperation—social and political orders—and new ways of evaluating the justice and goodness of the economic, social, and political arrangements— cultural institutions and practices. Human insights also devise new ways of teaching one another these innovations so that the intelligent achievements of a few can become widely available to many. This intellectual transformation of the world corresponds to what Teilhard calls hominization, or the noosphere.

## 9. *Generalized Emergent Probability*

Lonergan claimed that two additional types of scientific methods are needed to fully and adequately investigate the natural and human universe—genetic and dialectical methods. Genetic method is needed to understand the distinctive kind of intelligibility that characterizes embryological and other forms of development. Development is a distinctive kind of self-modifying process. Rather remarkably, a given stage in a developmental process modifies and replaces itself by creating conditions for the emergence of a new and more complex scheme of recurrence. This distinctively intelligible form of self-modification also pertains to the growth of self-correcting understanding in individual human beings and in human communities as well. This remarkable linkage among self-modifying stages is the kind of intelligibility that genetic methods seek to understand.[51]

Dialectical method on the other hand is needed to address a problem unique to human affairs, namely, that people do not always act intelligently. Human affairs are mixtures of intelligent actions as well as irrational deeds that Lonergan called "the social surd."[52] Biased, irrational actions set the conditions for increased misunderstanding, frustration, anger, resentment, and further biased actions both from the perpetrators as well as from others affected by these actions. In order to deal with the complex, conflicting ways in which human affairs unfold, Lonergan saw need for a fourth, dialectical method.

Both developments and dialectical conflicts complicate the sets of conditions from which successive stages of the evolving universe emerge. Just as the emergence of earlier schemes of recurrence change the probabilities of emergence for later ones, the same holds true for the emergence of earlier developmental and dialectical processes. They also shift the probabilities for the emergence of subsequent schemes of recurrence, developments, and irrational conflicts.

This conditioned series of emergent cycles, developments, and dialectical processes is more general than emergent probability based on classical and statistical methods alone. This generalization is Lonergan's way of speaking of the intelligible unity of the evolving universe. For this reason he claims that the actual unity of the universe is "an immanent intelligible order, which we have found reason to identify with a generalized emergent probability."[53]

## 10. A Transcendent Unity: Collaboration with God

However, the dialectical elements in generalized emergent probability pose a problem for the notion of unity. The unity of the universe accessible by scientific methods alone remains a fractured unity. The evil and sinful states of affairs that result from freely chosen human actions that are nonetheless unintelligent, irrational, or irresponsible raise the question of whether or not the dynamism of the evolving universe is capable of attaining true unity after all. Teilhard's optimism about *inevitable* progress is seriously called into question by this broken, dialectical state of human affairs. For Lonergan, this is the problem of evil. Given that God is all-good, all-understanding, and all-powerful, the problem is that there has to be something more to the unity of the universe than has been envisioned so far in generalized emergent probability.[54] Evil is a problem to which this "something more" is the solution.

Lonergan worked out a heuristic account of the sorts of things that would have to be true of this further component to the unity of the universe. It would be a "supernatural" component because it goes beyond what can be envisioned by the four scientific methods (and indeed beyond human cognition in general).[55] This further dimension does not emerge from earlier stages of evolution. It is not the work of human beings alone, but "principally the work of God."[56] Nevertheless, this further dimension is "a harmonious continuation of the actual order of the universe," which means that it involves the emergence of "a new and higher integration of human activity."[57] The higher integration is a collaboration of human beings with God in transforming the effects of evil into good.[58] Human beings are made capable of this collaboration by God's gratuitous bestowal of the supernatural virtues of faith, hope, and self-sacrificing love.[59]

From a Christian theological point of view, this collaboration with God in transforming evil into good is the work of the Mystical Body of Christ. To understand the ultimate unity of the universe, therefore, is to understand the wholeness of all evolution as the evolution of the Mystical Body of Christ.

## Communication of Systematics:
## Teilhard and Lonergan Compared

Lonergan's systematics has a certain advantage over Teilhard's symbolic mode of communication. He does not need to invoke radial energy but can work out issues strictly in terms of methods and findings that scientists agree upon. He does not have to maintain that sin is inevitable. Rather, Lonergan's account of human "essential freedom" conserves the traditional position that sin is a radically free choice, in no way predetermined by the original state of the universe.[60] Nevertheless, Lonergan does leave open the possibility that "statistical laws . . . indicate the probable frequencies" that subsequent human actions will be sinful responses to the conditions of the "social surd" generated from other human beings' previous sinful actions.[61] His approach to theological method enabled him "to remove apparent inconsistencies, to move toward some grasp of spiritual matters,"[62] in a way that is beyond the capacity of Teilhard's compact symbolic approach.

While for Teilhard affirmation of the existence of the Omega has to be a matter of faith, for Lonergan the matter is a bit more complicated. Because of the manifold distortions that creep into human consciousness through the propagation of sin, human intelligence and reasonableness is weakened almost to the point of extinction. Thus, in his account of the "something further," Lonergan argues that God's gift of faith will make it possible for humans to believe what they could in principle have thought out themselves were it not for the distortions of sin. These include believing that God exists, and believing that God could in principle be known analogically by human intelligence and reason. Again, the gift of faith would also make it possible to believe that God endows humanity with special gifts enabling it to enter into the higher collaboration and higher unity with God. Lonergan also adds still further that the gift of faith might make it possible to believe things about God and God's interactions with humanity that could not even in principle be known directly solely by "immanently generated" human knowledge. Hence, the gift of faith is needed even more in order to believe that God has offered the actual solution and higher unity in Christ and the Holy Spirit.

Teilhard died before *Insight* was published, so he had no opportunity to comment on Lonergan's thought. On the other hand, Lonergan did have that opportunity and used it to comment positively on Teilhard's efforts. He did so in several places. The most detailed came at the 1962 institute on "The Method of Theology" sponsored by the Regis College Jesuit Community at the University of Toronto.

There Lonergan responded to a question from the audience regarding Teilhard:

> There is no easy unification of theory and common sense. There are ultimate limitations, and we must recognize them and build on them. Is this the problem that Teilhard was working on? The fundamental problem today is that there are all sorts of people at the peak of human culture whose ideas on religion are most elementary. Teilhard was able to talk religion to such people. Such limited objectives are legitimate. But Catholic truth is not contained within the limits of these limited objectives. . . . [A fuller theological method] has to be mediated by the subject for fundamental concepts and operations and for the elimination of the influence of horizon and lack of conversion. These are the fundamental problems. Clearing them up is the only way to get beyond the overload on dogmatic theologians.[63]

Lonergan clearly endorsed the positive contributions Teilhard made to communicating a more mature vision of God to those who understood evolutionary science. Teilhard himself explicitly said that he wrote *The Divine Milieu* for "waverers," rather than for people of faith (DM, 43–45). It is noteworthy, however, that when Lonergan endorsed Teilhard's mission to people "whose ideas on religion are most elementary," he did *not* indicate that this mission was limited to non-Catholics. Teilhard's writings made an especially strong contribution among scientifically educated Catholics who also, it would seem, had not gotten beyond elementary ideas on religion from the kinds of Catholic religious instruction that had been in vogue just prior to the publication of Teilhard's works. Nevertheless, it is also true that Lonergan regarded Teilhard's work as only a partial contribution to the task of communicating the fullness of Catholic faith. He saw his own work in systematics as a necessary supplement to and refinement of the communicative strategies of thinkers such as Teilhard.

On the other hand, Teilhard has certain advantages over Lonergan. The removal of apparent inconsistencies of symbolic expressions is often achieved only through the use of the technical language and subtle distinctions that are required in the work of theory and systematics. Yet that work needs to be mediated to people who do not specialize in such work. Even though Lonergan assigned great importance to the work of systematics, he used the symbol of the "chasm" from Luke's Gospel (16:26) to emphasize how foreign and deeply separated this work would seem to most people.[64] Yet the consequences of failing to either do the work of systematics or to bridge that chasm are serious indeed. That failure is evident in the undifferentiated suppression of Teilhard's writings at exactly the time when there was such a tremendous hunger and thirst for the kind of communication of unity that he strove to achieve. This is what Lonergan meant when he said that this combination of systematics with communications was "the only way to get beyond the overload on dogmatic theologians. . . . The alternative is the magisterium simply takes over."[65]

Hence the kind of work in the systematics of unity that Lonergan envisioned needs to be followed up by work as rich in symbolism as was Teilhard's. Dante sought to give poetic expression to the systematic theology of Aquinas. Teilhard gave symbolic expression to the metaphysics of Bergson and the vision of St. Paul. Something comparable remains to be done for the kind of systematic theology that Lonergan began and others are completing regarding the unity of the universe and humanity with God in Christ. Teilhard offers an inspiring example for the kind of work in communications that lies ahead.

## Points to Ponder

◆ For Teilhard, humanity discovers that it *"is nothing other than evolution become conscious of itself."* For Lonergan, "the tension that is inherent in the finality of all proportionate being becomes in [humanity] a conscious tension."

◆ Seeing the within of things makes it possible to recognize that this biosphere has evolutionary importance in inverse proportion to its size.

◆ It is the rise of consciousness that confers upon life a sense of directedness.

◆ If we wish to comprehend the *ultimate* meaning both of humanity and the whole of evolution we must look at what previous evolution "announces *ahead.*"

◆ The next stages of evolution can only take place through the thoughtful and willing actions of human beings. But once human beings as reflective come to know the fact of evolution itself, such knowledge produces anxiety that can paralyze human action.

♦ Uncertainty about the future produces "the truly cosmic gravity of the sickness that disquiets us." We lose the conviction needed to act when we worry that evolution may have no future.

♦ The Omega would be the harmonious continuation of the various unifications that have occurred at every prior level of evolution and would "fulfill the ambitions aroused in the reflective being by the newly acquired consciousness."

♦ Only love "is capable of uniting living beings in such a way as to complete and fulfill them, for it alone takes them and joins them by what is deepest in themselves."

♦ In order for Omega to perform its function of motivating human continuation of evolution, therefore, it *cannot* be merely the point that would eventually be reached by the process of evolution itself. Rather, Omega would have to exist and be accepted as "*already in existence* and operative at the very core" of the noosphere.

♦ In Teilhard's view it is impossible to understand either the universe or the human phenomenon correctly and fully unless one understands humanity as intrinsic to the wholeness of evolution within which humans emerged.

## Questions for Discussion

1.  The author draws a cogent comparison between Teilhard de Chardin and Bernard Lonergan. What is the unique contribution of each to the human phenomenon?

2.  In your view, are Teilhard's insights a corrective to modern science, an elucidation of modern science, or an embarrassment, as Peter Medawar suggested?

3.  What is Omega for Teilhard? How do you understand the relationship between Omega, consciousness, and the direction of evolution?

4.  What Gospel passages correlate to Teilhard's principal ideas on evolution and the human phenomenon?

# Notes

1. Referenced in PM, 294. See also 1 Corinthians 15:28, "When all things are subjected to him, then the Son himself will [also] be subjected to the one who put all things in subjection under him, so that God may be all in all." See Henri de Lubac, *Teilhard de Chardin: The Man and His Meaning* (New York: New American Library, 1965), 35–44; cited hereafter as *The Man and His Meaning*.

2. Bernard Lonergan, unpublished essay of 1935, *"Panton Anakephalaiosis* [The Restoration of All Things]—a Theory of Human Solidarity," later published in *Method: Journal of Lonergan Studies* 9, no. 2 (October 1991): 134–72.

3. Bernard Lonergan, *Insight: A Study of Human Understanding*, Collected Works of Bernard Lonergan, vol. 3, ed. Frederick E. Crowe and Robert M. Doran (Toronto: University of Toronto Press, 1992), 497; cited hereafter as *Insight*.

4. *Insight*, 498.

5. *Insight*, 498.

6. Pierre Teilhard de Chardin, *The Human Phenomenon*, trans. Sarah Appleton-Weber (Portland, OR: Sussex Academic, 2003). Originally published as *Le Phénomene Humain* in 1955. Teilhard apparently completed the original text in May of 1940 when he was at the Institute of Geobiology in Peking. He revised it in hopes of securing permission to publish it from his Jesuit superiors, and the preface of that revised edition is dated March 1948. See http://www.teilharddechardin.org. The title given the new translation more faithfully reflects Teilhard's French title and is also more respectful of gender-inclusive language. However, all citations in this article are taken from the earlier translation by Bernard Wall, *The Phenomenon of Man* (New York: Harper & Row, 1959), cited as PM.

7. Oddly, Teilhard does not mention a "psychosphere," which would seem to follow from his treatment of the rise of consciousness in animals.

8. Thomas M. King, SJ, *Teilhard's Mass: Approaches to "The Mass on the World"* (New York: Paulist, 2005), 8–11.

9. DM, 155, where it states that this book was composed in 1926–1927. Pierre Teillard de Chardin, "The Mass on the World," in HU, 19–37.

10. Harvey D. Egan, *Soundings in the Christian Mystical Tradition* (Collegeville, MN: Liturgical Press, 2011), xviii–xxi; 322–29. See also Bernard McGinn, *The Essential Writings of Christian Mysticism* (New York: Modern Library, 2006), xiv–xv, 303–4.

11. De Lubac, *The Man and His Meaning*, 35–44.

12. Ilia Delio, *Christ in Evolution* (Maryknoll, NY: Orbis Books, 2008), 74.

13. For the significance of the symbolism of return, see Mircea Eliade, *The Myth of the Eternal Return: Or Cosmos and History* (Princeton, NJ: Princeton University Press, 1971).

14. Mircea Eliade, *The Sacred and the Profane* (New York: Harcourt, Brace & World, 1959), 36–54. See also his *Patterns in Comparative Religion* (New York: Sheed & Ward, 1958), 367–88.

15. Peter Medawar, "The Phenomenon of Man," *Mind* 70 (1961): 99–106.

16. Ibid.

17. See Yehuda Elkana, *The Discovery of the Conservation of Energy* (Cambridge, MA: Harvard University Press, 1974).

18. See, for example, Max Jammer, *The Conceptual Development of Quantum Mechanics* (New York: McGraw-Hill, 1966), 183–86.

19. Teilhard read Bergson's *Creative Evolution* while he was in studies in Hastings, sometime between 1908–1911. See King, *Teilhard's Mass*, 3–4.

20. Mary Lukas and Ellen Lukas, *Teilhard* (New York: McGraw-Hill, 1981), 237.

21. See, for example, de Lubac, *The Man and His Meaning*, 46, 89, 103, 106.

22. De Lubac, *The Man and His Meaning*, 101, 46.

23. Quoted in Henri de Lubac, S.J., *Teilhard Explained*, trans. Antonoy Buono (New York: Paulist, 1966), 3. The Latin is taken from Sextus Propertius, *Elegies* II, x, 5 ["To simply have wanted is enough in great deeds"].

24. Medawar was condescending about Teilhard's success, and tried to explain it away, saying that the "spread of secondary and latterly tertiary education has created a large population of people, often with well-developed literary and scholarly tastes, who have been educated far beyond their capacity to undertake analytical thought." His criticisms of Teilhard for lack of differentiation seem to me legitimate. His haughty dismissal of the popular hunger for the symbolic mediation of modern science does not.

25. Bernard Lonergan, *Method in Theology* (New York: Herder and Herder, 1972), 132; cited hereafter as MT. In its fully mature form, systematics would "promote an understanding of what is affirmed in the previous specialty, doctrines" (MT, 335). Given the context of *Method in Theology*, one might assume that doctrines is concerned only with affirmations of religious truths. But I think Lonergan saw systematics as striving for a comprehensive and coherent understanding among both the affirmations of faith and the affirmations of "immanently generated knowledge" (*Insight*, 725). If this is correct, then Lonergan and Teilhard shared the ambtition to reconcile the positions of evolutionary science with the doctrines of Christian faith.

26. MT, 356.

27. MT, 355.

28. MT, 351.

29. See for example MT, 305–6.

30. MT, 132.

31. MT, 285–86.

32. MT, 287–88.

33. *Insight*, 543.

34. *Insight*, 523.

35. MT, 339.

36. *Insight*, 679–80.

37. *Insight*, 718.

38. *Insight*, 509.

39. *Insight*, 141.

40. *Insight*, 141.

41. *Insight*, 142, emphasis added.

42. *Insight*, 109–21.

43. *Insight*, 131; see also109ff. and 149–50.

44. *Insight*, 78–86.

45. *Insight*, 131.

46. *Insight*, 143–44.

47. *Insight*, 501.

48. This does not imply that there is no divine creator, however. See Patrick H. Byrne, "Lonergan, Evolutionary Science, and Intelligent Design," *Revista Portuguesa de Filosofia 63 (2007), Special Edition— Bernard Lonergan and Philosophy*: 893–913.

49. *Insight*, 281.

50. *Insight*, 291–92.

51. *Insight*, 476–92.

52. *Insight*, 255.

53. *Insight*, 533.

54. In the context of elaborating his analogical understanding of God, Lonergan presents a detailed argument for these traditional theistic attributes of God. See *Insight*, 680–84.

55. In fact Lonergan notes that there are several possible kinds of further components which are "in some sense supernatural." Each kind would be consistent with the nature of the problem of evil and would provide different kinds of solutions to it. See *Insight*, 746–50. Lonergan sketches these possibilities as aids to identifying the actual solution that God provides. I am grateful to Ivo Coelho for pointing this out to me. See his "'In Some Sense Supernatural': Making Sense of an Anomaly in Chapter 20 of *Insight*." Lonergan Workshop, forthcoming.

56. *Insight*, 741.

57. *Insight*, 719.

58. *Insight*, 741.

59. *Insight*, 720–35, 741–42.

60. *Insight*, 641–45, 689–91.

61. *Insight*, 767.

62. MT, 132.

63. Bernard Lonergan, "*The Method of Theology Discussion 3:2.*" Lonergan Archive Website, CD/mp3 326, second part of third discussion. See www.bernardlonergan.com.

64. Bernard Lonergan, "Understanding and Method," a typescript draft translation of *De Intellectu et Methodo*, by Michael G. Shields, SJ, 1959, 24–34.

65. See "The Mystical Body of Christ: A Domestic Exhortation at Regis College, Toronto, November 1951," unpublished mimeographed typescript.

*Chapter 7*

# METAPHYSICS, MORALITY, AND POLITICS

## DAVID GRUMETT

Among most theologians and people of faith, metaphysics does not currently enjoy the respect it deserves. In the wake of secularism, two paths to belief have gained prominence at its expense. On the one hand, there is a pervasive biblicism in which faith and theology are seen as founded on scripture alone. On the other, widely accepted experiential understandings of belief posit belief and doctrine as outcomes of personal, interior faith. Reason and observation, the classic building blocks of metaphysics and of natural theology, are generally thought redundant in a postmodern world of personal subjectivity. Many practice their religion within the interior castles of text or experience, unconcerned to give a rational account of that religion or to relate it to any larger reality.

This sidelining of metaphysics in religion and faith finds parallels in the natural sciences and philosophy, where it is even more advanced. Big-picture discourses are out of favor. Experiments focus on highly specific contexts, with the classic presumption that natural phenomena reveal something of divine power or activity in nature deemed laughably implausible by the large majority of natural scientists. Similarly in philosophy, reasoning is focused on an immanent plane, with analytical methods usually employed to predispose against religious claims. The discussion of fundamental metaphysical topics like being, power, causation, reason, and motion is foreclosed in ways that refuse any theological dimension.

In contrast with these trends, Teilhard made metaphysics central to his reflection. For him, metaphysics was the privileged discourse by which the person of faith might engage questions in cosmology and the natural sciences from the perspective of faith.[1] Teilhard regarded ongoing discussion of topics like being, cause, and so on as both a necessary human enterprise and a necessary theological enterprise. Moreover, he saw reflection on such topics as opening a path into faith.[2] Metaphysics was therefore central to his whole enterprise. That metaphysical topics are little discussed today is one of the reasons Teilhard's ideas can seem difficult.

In this chapter, I shall first talk about his view of metaphysics generally and its relation to morality. I shall then consider five specific aspects of his metaphysics and the moral and political principles that follow from these for today.

How does Teilhard conceive the relation of metaphysics to morality? In his 1945 essay "Can Moral Science Dispense with a Metaphysical Foundation?" he argues that the two are intimately linked. He writes:

> Moral science and metaphysics must inevitably be seen as, structurally, the two aspects (the intellectual and the practical) of one and the same system. A metaphysics is necessarily backed by a moral science, and vice versa. Every metaphysics entails its own moral science, and every moral science implies its own metaphysic. . . . In every case, we should note, *obligation* is a function of the solidarity and interdependence which the philosophical system establishes between individual freedom and the universe. The more an individual, as a consequence of his metaphysical convictions, recognizes that he is an *element* of a universe in which he finds his fulfilment, the more closely he feels that he is bound from within himself to the duty of conforming to the laws of the universe. (TF, 131–32)

The Christian idea of natural law is clearly in play here: the universe is governed by a God who gives it both physical order and moral order. Furthermore, Teilhard goes on to recognize that metaphysics is usually accepted implicitly rather than overtly. It is not as if we consult metaphysical texts and theories on a daily basis, or consider the fundamental nature of being before acting.

Yet if metaphysics has practical implications, such as grounding a sense of moral obligation, the question of which metaphysics I espouse is not one of disinterested speculation. In the same essay, Teilhard reminds us that our "intellectual adherence to a particular philosophy is a complex phenomenon, in which the operation of reason and will are intricately combined." He indicates clearly that coherence is needed between metaphysics and morality if either is to be credible.[3] But which is ultimately prior? Can a metaphysics be invoked to justify any moral action, or does morality trump metaphysics? The question is, at the ontological level, unjustified; within a single, divinely ordained system, metaphysics and morals do not ultimately conflict. But at the level of epistemology—that is, at the level of what we humans believe to be true on the basis of our limited knowledge—metaphysics and morals might well diverge. For example, I might believe on metaphysical grounds that humans should devote maximum energy to developing new communications technologies in order to advance the unification of global consciousness. But what if such technologies are unevenly accessible, being accessed relatively infrequently by poorer people and older people? Projects that formed part of a metaphysical vision of advancing human unity might in fact exclude some people and so contribute unwittingly to social fragmentation, which could evidently be called into question on moral grounds.

In response to this kind of possibility, Teilhard avers: "The test of a metaphysics is the moral system which is derived from it" (TF, 133). So it would seem that morality can sometimes trump metaphysics. Returning to the example of technological development just cited, my metaphysical notion of unification should not be framed in excessively abstract terms: unity is experienced tangibly by people as concrete, morally freighted interaction with their fellow humans. Tensions between metaphysics and morals should therefore cause us to rethink our metaphysics. Teilhard reiterates that metaphysics is a "structural complement" of morality, not simply a "fabricated justification." Metaphysics provides morality with its "necessary animating force" and "determines the modes and progressive developments of action." Without a vision of the larger ends to which my particular projects are contributing, I might not be sufficiently motivated to make any impact, positive or negative, on the wider world at all.

So metaphysics, because it impels and structures human action, has moral implications. Teilhard's own metaphysics is fundamentally a metaphysics of union (*unire*). He justifies this basic orientation in a 1945 essay, "Christianity and Evolution: Suggestions for a New Theology," as a reaction against the metaphysics of being (*esse*) that was, in his day, standard. In a metaphysics of being, he protests, pure act dominates being and thereby fails to account for the existence of participated being (CE, 178). A metaphysics of union, in contrast, leaves open the possibility of a further degree of unification beyond the merely immanent unity by which, within a metaphysics of being, created being is related to God. A metaphysics of union pictures being as "in tension towards a final state of maximum unification," and as possessing an "additional freedom." In a metaphysics of union, final unity is attained progressively in the realm of created being.

In "My Fundamental Vision," Teilhard presents the metaphysics of union in more detailed successive phases. The first phase is the "self-sufficient presence" of a First Being, subsisting in itself in splendid isolation. But a metaphysics of union must necessarily represent the Godhead as triune and as containing its own self-opposition. Teilhard states: "God exists only by *uniting himself*" (TF, 194). God's self-revelation as Trinity, by which God "unifies himself upon himself in order that he may exist," is thus the second phase of this metaphysics. The third phase comprises a different kind of opposition, this time occurring at the very opposite pole of being: that of the self-subsisting "unity" of multiplicity, bounded at its circumference by the pure multiple, or creatable *nihil*. This multiplicity is nothing, but because of its passive potentiality for arrangement nevertheless intimates a "possibility of being, a prayer for being . . . a prayer which it is just as though God had been unable to resist" (TF, 194–95). So there is some kind of natural orientation of being to God. The fourth phase of the metaphysics of union is participation. Teilhard contests presentations of participation as an arbitrary, indeterminate act of a first cause, "an 'act of God,' indeed, in the catastrophic sense of the term." In a metaphysics of union, by contrast, self-sufficiency and self-determination remain uncompromised and participated being is realized as a "sort of echo or symmetrical response" to God's Trinitarian self-unification. To create is, in this sense, to unite (TF, 196). A metaphysics of union portrays a relational and dynamic cosmos, not a cosmos in which one category of being is overpowered or annihilated by another.

Just as being and union are ontologically correlate, so other metaphysical entities may be paired and false conceptual dichotomies thereby overcome. Analogies for this "pairing" may be found in the natural sciences, such as mass-velocity and electricity-magnetism (TF, 208). Teilhard identifies being-in-itself and participated being as the "most mysterious of all those pairs." In other words, God (being-in-itself) is present in nature through sustaining action, while nature (participated being) is dependent on God for its continued existence. In his 1953 essay "The Contingence of the Universe," Teilhard reflects further on the implications of his metaphysics of union for understanding creation. Whereas in a metaphysics of being created being is an "entirely gratuitous supplement or addition" to a previously self-sufficient order, in a metaphysics of union, creation is seen as motivated by love. This is not to say that God creates out of need, unless such need is conceived as the "pleasure of giving for the sake of giving" (CE, 224, 226–27). Rather, to create is part of the character of God's mysterious being, and so the existence of the created order may rightly be regarded as a primordially accomplished fact (CE, 227). To account for the created order any other way would disvalue it by making it seem an arbitrary addition to a previous reality that would, as such, add nothing of value to what had preceded it.

This view of nature as intrinsically dependent on God controverts the view of nature as purely material that is dominant in modern science. Moreover, it is the underlying reason for many of the critiques of Teilhard's evolutionary theology by scientists. John Haught states perceptively of those critics:

> Something much more contentious is occurring here than merely scientific disagreement. What really repels them is Teilhard's suggestion that a metaphysically adequate explanation of any universe in which evolution occurs requires—at some point beyond the limits that science has set for itself—a transcendent force of attraction

to explain the *overarching* tendency of matter to evolve toward life, mind, and spirit.[4]

Teilhard's metaphysics is inevitably theological and profoundly political. It challenges the assumptions about how the world is and what it should become, assumptions that are held by most scientists and other powerful interest groups in society. It does not begin and end in abstract contemplation, but is a distillation and synthesis of insights emerging from a remarkable life lived at the intersection of science, philosophy, and theology.

Some critics have sought to present Teilhard's politics as Marxist because of his view of history, or even worse as tending toward fascism or nationalism, on the grounds that they possess a biological dimension. These appraisals of his commitments are false, as I have shown in detail elsewhere.[5] In a post-Marxist world order in which memories of fascism are, thankfully, fading fast, we are well placed to reappraise the moral and political principles that Teilhard espouses and their relation to his metaphysics. This task is especially important given the ongoing interest in his evolutionary theology: there is a danger that Teilhard will now be assumed to view human life as governed primarily by deterministic evolutionary mechanisms. In fact, Teilhard makes clear that in evolution's human phase, morality, religion, politics, and social issues take center stage. These are the new drivers of evolution and need to be considered in and for themselves.

I shall now consider five key aspects of Teilhard's metaphysics and how each informs his moral and political principles. As I progress through these, I shall outline Teilhard's concrete moral and political proposals and, just as important, develop a clearer understanding of his method of deriving practical principles for action from metaphysical reflection.

## Human Action and Divine Action

Opposed, with good reason, to any tendency toward sociobiology, the perceptive Dutch Jesuit interpreter of Teilhard, Piet Schoonenberg, complains that Teilhard did not "sufficiently bring out the essential element of . . . hominised evolution," namely, humankind's freedom and responsibility in human history, given by grace.[6] Schoonenberg is by no means alone in expressing a well-placed reservation about subsuming human initiative within impersonal biological mechanisms. He was writing at a time when not all of Teilhard's texts had been published and when *The Phenomenon of Man*, Teilhard's programmatic work on evolution, tended to provide the hermeneutic for the whole of his thought. Schoonenberg may therefore be excused for not giving full weight to key texts addressing human initiative, such as *The Divine Milieu*. But his recognition that human freedom and responsibility are vital moral and political corollaries of evolutionary theology, and that Teilhard needed to offer an account of them, is perspicuous. How might Teilhard in fact provide answers to the gaps that Schoonenberg perceived in his work? Teilhard does not picture human action as the mere result of being swept along in a vital current that we can do little to direct or resist. On the contrary, when humans truly act they participate in God's own action.[7] Of course, humans are often engaged in activity, but this is frequently unconscious or the result of habit. Such activity is not action according to the full meaning of the word. An action is something in which God is involved, acting in us by making us do in reality what we most deeply will. Action is a reflective movement of soul and body.[8] In *The Divine Milieu*, Teilhard affirms:

> It requires no less than the pull of what we call the Absolute—no less than you yourself—to set in motion the frail liberty which you have given us. And that being so, everything which diminishes my explicit faith in the heavenly value of the results of my effort, diminishes irremediably my power to act. (DM, 13)

Teilhard here presents a metaphysics of action different from the standard neo-Thomism of his day. Action is not, as Aristotle had supposed, the result of simple human deliberation. Teilhard shows that necessarily implicated in human action is divine action. Only when cooperating with divine action can human action generate a truly new beginning and humans really believe in their actions and their concrete results.

For Christians, social and political action that effects a real, material, and transformative difference in the world is not only a means of furthering God's justice. It is a sharing in God's creative action, drawing the world into greater unity, and thus into the unifying life of the Godhead, in a "communion through action" (DM, 20–22). Teilhard's high valuation of action, including political action, cannot, therefore, be attributed simply to a Marxist stream in Christian theology, with the human predicament viewed in primarily material terms. Understood properly and pursued faithfully, action does not estrange humans from God; on the contrary, it makes humans agents of the unfolding of God's providential plan for the world. Teilhard can help us articulate this theology of action and thereby show how social and political action, in their many different manifestations, are intrinsic to the Christian vocation. The forms that action will take, and the principles motivating it, will be considered in the following sections.

## Motion, Change, and Human Agency

In his 1948 essay "My Fundamental Vision," Teilhard presents his metaphysics of union, discussed in the opening section of this chapter, via the category of motion. This is, of course, an ancient way of understanding divine action, both immanently within the Trinity and in its external, economic processions. It has pre-Christian roots in Plato and Aristotle, who associated God with the heavens, which were believed to rotate.[9] But Teilhard finds a continuity with post-Einsteinian physics, in which motion is not independent of a body but physically engenders that body (TF, 193). Motion is also associated with unification, understood as a dynamic movement toward a unity not yet attained, and thereby remains intrinsically associated with bodies that have already been brought into being. In this phase it can be viewed both actively, as the uniting of created being by its own activity, and passively, as the uniting of created being by the activity of God. In each case, union is not a state already achieved, but a work in progress in which God impels the striving of created being toward its end. Because of this relation between God and beings, a kind of union is, paradoxically, already manifested in the striving for union. Teilhard sees union, thus, not in static terms but, literally, as movement.

In moral and political discourse, everyone nowadays seems aware of change. Many argue that change is happening more quickly, or across more dimensions of human life and society— gender, sexuality, technology, communications, global security, ecology—than ever before. But the conclusions that are typically drawn from such observations appear strange. It is frequently inferred that, in a changing world, God is no longer relevant, or that belief in the Christian God is no longer justified by the evidence. Aristotle believed in change, seeing the whole world as in motion. But his question was: What causes motion and change? Moreover, if I cause some movement or change, what is it that has moved or caused me to do so? In his *Metaphysics*, Aristotle traces a succession of causes, each due to an antecedent cause, and argues that at the origin of the succession of causes there must be an unmoved mover, an uncaused cause.[10] This is God, and Aristotle's argument, as developed by Thomas Aquinas, has joined the canon of arguments for God's existence.[11]

Teilhard protested that the neoscholastic view of God was indefensibly static. The major source of change and movement that he integrated into his theology but which most neoscholastics excluded was, of course, evolution. This fairly new theory of how human life, and indeed all life, had developed seemed to play havoc with classic fixed categories, essences, and natures. Embracing evolutionary theory in "The Movements of Life," Teilhard viewed the whole organic universe as predisposed to motion and change. Life is constantly on the move through chemical processes in phyla (that is, chains or lines of living beings) and their divisions and mutations, whether dispersions, radiations, or canalizations (VP, 143–50). Through these bifurcations and buddings life appears gradually, like a slowly growing tree.

By focusing on motion and change at this all-encompassing level, Teilhard provides an important corrective to that idea that change and narratives about change primarily concern individuals and local communities. We are familiar with the idea of an individual's "spiritual journey." But Teilhard sees the whole world as on a spiritual journey, telling the story of the cosmic journey of created being from its origins through to the present day—and, so far as he is able, into the future.

Motion and change are part of life. By travel, we keep in contact with family, friends, and colleagues, and experience new parts of our world, whether human communities or natural wonders. In his own life, Teilhard was frequently on the move, meeting new people and forging new relationships. Even if we stay put, our local communities are shaped by the arrivals of guests, visitors, and settlers. These movements of others also provide opportunities for new experiences and relationships that we would not otherwise have. They all reveal the creative, transformative function of motion in the world.

But, as already noted, Teilhard underlines the moral, and especially the political, implications of specifically biological change. Many are rightly wary of being drawn into sociobiology for fear that this will lead to the illegitimate transposition of Darwinian principles of species evolution into the political sphere. Indeed, in the United States, with its recent history of racial oppression and the dispossession of Native Americans, this concern might help account for the continuing wide acceptance of creationism in an otherwise scientifically advanced society. For Teilhard, however, the intellectual issues at stake are too great for serious interdisciplinary engagement to be avoided. Furthermore, where the technologies enabling genetic intervention exist, the reality of actual interventions is likely to follow, and moral discourse needs to anticipate this. In an important 1947 essay, "The Human Rebound of Evolution and Its Consequences," Teilhard addresses directly the biopolitics he sees emerging, while distancing himself explicitly from the "regrettable recrudescence of racialism and nationalism" (FM, 198). In his central discussion of "the moral ordering of invention," he makes clear that material pressures, whether biological, social, or economic, are by themselves insufficient motivators of human action. Morality is also needed. Some readers might be surprised at the character of the morality presented. Teilhard does not urge us to develop a new system of ethics for a new age, but to "recall and re-express, with a precise biological foundation, the broad lines of the empirical and traditional Ethics which has been evolved in some ten millennia of civilization" (FM, 203). Conscience and professional integrity, including the ability to tell the truth, will, he continues, be required if we are to bridge the "fast-growing gulf between technical and moral progress in the world today." Ongoing failure to foster moral capacity, Teilhard suggests, will impede future development. We see around us many areas of life, such as banking, commerce, politics, and sport, in which moral failures bring large costs. Teilhard shows that, because of their cumulative nature, these moral failures will ultimately endanger life as a whole. As he puts it, moral capacity will become a "condition of *survival* for the human race" (FM, 203).

## Complexity and Community

In the classic, hierarchical view of the created order, beings were ordered according to their status as matter, animal, human, or angel. Those with higher degrees of sentient, mental, or spiritual capacity were assigned to the superior levels of the order of being. At the summit of this order, informing and unifying everything, was God. This hierarchic ontology allowed for communication between beings that occupied different levels in the cosmic order. For instance, some angels came into the world on missions to humans, while animals were seen as embodying moral characteristics, both good and bad, from which humans might learn.

A hierarchic ontology could not, however, properly account for the interrelated nature of being. It could not explain why this particular order was in place, beyond stating that it was God's decree. Furthermore, it could not account for the emergence of some levels of being from others: for instance, the human from the animal. Teilhard saw that, in reality, the order of being that Aristotle and neo-Thomists thought had been in place eternally had in fact come into being gradually, with humans very relatively recent arrivals.

To aid our understanding of how, in a posthierarchic cosmos, beings are connected, both metaphysically and socially, Teilhard uses the idea of complexity. Complexity theory views reality as a set of systems, each characterized by points of connection within and between them. Furthermore, a system's degree of complexity can increase through time. As a system becomes more complex, its center gains depth and concentration, and its level of introspection and spontaneity increases (AE, 67).

Let us first consider complexity from a metaphysical standpoint, taking as an example its key application to the idea of the soul. From around the time of Aquinas, mainstream Christian theologians have viewed the soul as a discrete entity separable from the body, especially in purgatory.[12] It is the soul that gives humans identity and continuity through time. Moreover, only humans have a soul. But Teilhard, with his evolutionary view of the world, sees that it is not only humans that possess souls. In wider philosophical context, this approach was not entirely new. Aristotle, after all, had viewed every being as possessing some kind of soul in the sense of an identity and purpose, while before him Plato had, in his *Timaeus*, developed the idea of a world soul.[13] Teilhard does not, however, wish to present all beings as equivalently ensouled, as had Aristotle, nor the overarching world soul as static, as had Plato. Soul, for Teilhard, is not a discrete, abstract entity but a function of a being's degree of organization exhibited in the number of connections within it when viewed as a system (HP, 192-93). Different levels of the created order exhibit different levels of complexity. Moreover, like all other complex entities, soul is emergent, and develops through history in interaction with those entities.

Complexity necessarily extends beyond individual beings, because complex beings are themselves members of networks that stretch beyond them. In "Universalization and Union," Teilhard sees life's increasing complexification played out globally, with the world more interconnected economically, politically, and through more rapid and dispersed information flows (AE, 77-95). Elsewhere, he even prophesied the creation of the World Wide Web, referring to a "single gigantic network girdling the earth," which he terms the "Noosphere," emerging out of the acceleration and multiplication of mechanical and human complexity (FM, 171).[14]

I have so far presented complexity primarily in metaphysical terms—notwithstanding the obvious social implications of the rapid information transfer that the web has made possible. But complexity, as well as helping to account for the birth and growth of human consciousness, is a dynamic in the formation of human communities. It is not the case that, in our complex universe, humans are subject to deterministic fate. On the contrary, humans are constitutive of the universe and exercise agency within it.

Family, church, friendship groups, workplaces, shops, schools, and associations are all communities of complexity in which consciousness is focused. People are recognized, cared for, and loved. Ever attuned to the continuities between the scientific and the social, Teilhard describes the love that binds these communities together as a kind of energy.[15] This is communicated powerfully in his three published wedding addresses, in which a recurring theme is that love should not turn in upon itself (HM, 135-42, 150-51). Once love turns inward it loses its animating energy, which always lies beyond its immediate objects. Teilhard's vision of love, whether in marriage, church, the nation, or some other community, is therefore always one in which current boundaries are extending to encompass other people and communities. These networks of complex centers have intrinsic, indeed privileged, value. Teilhard writes: "Far from being impermanent and accidental, it is souls, and alliances of souls, it is the energies of souls, that alone progress infallibly, and it is they alone that will endure" (HM, 138).

Nurturing these "alliances of souls" should be a primary goal of political policy. Family life should be actively promoted. The economic, social, and educational barriers that perpetuate de facto racial segregation should be broken down. The penal system should be reformed to replace practices that dehumanize and criminalize prisoners with those that educate and reconcile. On the international stage, every possible opportunity for peace should be pursued, with military intervention a defensive last resort rather than a preemptive, preferred option.

Taking complexity seriously also means taking democracy seriously. In his essay "The Essence of the Democratic Idea: A Biological Approach," Teilhard makes clear that, in a complex system, the uniqueness of each constituent element must be preserved; if it is not, then the system's level of complexity is reduced (FM, 238–43). The classic democratic values of liberty, equality, and fraternity should, he suggests, rightly be regarded as underpinned by this fundamental metaphysical reality of human life, and indeed of all life. These values are not, however, in tension with the values of socialism.[16] Democracy is not about privileging one above the other, aiming rather to balance an individual perspective with the group perspective.

## Participation, Analogy, and Discourse

Teilhard has a passion for unity; no part of the world is entirely separate from any other or can be understood or described in isolation from the rest. In a holistic world, each part of the world needs to be viewed with reference to the larger reality in which it participates.

In this view of the world, Teilhard is inspired by a mystical vision but also, in perhaps unexpected ways, by his inherited Thomist cosmology. For Aquinas, God cannot be understood using pure reason. Rather, God is first known through God's effects in the world, which are known to us.[17] I might observe that natural things, even though they lack intelligence, nevertheless exhibit purposes. For example, trees convert carbon dioxide into oxygen and provide fuel for human use. For Aquinas, because such purposes are not due to the exercise of intelligence by natural beings—trees, after all, do not possess reason—they must be the result of design by a higher being. This being we call God.

So things in the world exhibit at least traces of the activity of a higher being. It might well be argued that this higher being is not necessarily the classic God of Christian theism, who is after all considerably more than a mere designer God. This is not a problem for the current discussion, however, which is not about proving God's existence but, rather, concerned with the implications of the theory of participation, considered as part of a theistic metaphysics, for moral and political theory.

Linked with participation is analogy. When I employ analogy, I invoke an ontology that is participatory, that is, an understanding of the world's different elements as really and truly related to each other and to God. Analogical language points to a relatedness and degree of similarity that really exists. Schoonenberg rightly views analogy as central to Teilhard's cosmology, noting that without analogy it is difficult to express how beings manifest their "being-in-itself." To overcome polarized metaphysical representations of the world—whether based on the oppositions of matter and spirit, creationism and evolution, or some other—analogy is needed.[18] Analogy enables descriptions of the "within" (*le dedans*) of things, especially their purpose and tendency to pursue their purpose, alongside the "outside" (*le dehors*) of things that natural scientists are so adept at measuring and classifying (HP, 22–32).

The political implications of participation and analogy are considerable. Instrumentalist views of the world, its people, and its resources are increasingly common, with large negative consequences for people and their natural environments. The alternative, participatory view of the world, however, is necessarily noninstrumentalist, because it relates beings in the world to a source and purpose that is greater than their immediate context. For instance, from an analogical perspective workers cannot be understood as mere units of labor, but as purposive producers engaged in an enterprise that is at once both material and spiritual, and which shares in divine creativity. The failure to regard workers in this way is, Teilhard avers, the result of the loss of an awareness of the final end toward which human effort should be directed, with energy being "dissipated in restless, undisciplined activity" (SC, 101–2). As well as being noninstrumentalist, analogy embraces ambiguity and imperfection, being founded in the intuition that God vastly exceeds humans' capacity to imagine.[19] Frequently combative and polarized political discourse would be tempered if the larger, cosmic reality of which it is but a small part were recognized, and if participants recognized more frequently that their positions are necessarily incomplete.

Before leaving this topic, let us be clear that Teilhard's analogy of being is situated within a universe with Christ at its head as its "Omega," or end, point.[20] Christ, by drawing the world into ever greater unity, establishes by his action and self-revelation the conditions in which analogy can rightly be employed to describe that world. For the Christian, there can be no better approach to political discernment than to recognize that all actions will ultimately be judged by how much they cooperate with, or detract from, Christ's own providential activity on and in the world, and by how much they conform with Christ's will for the world. Nevertheless, let those of us within the church not forget that, in a participatory world, traces of theological meaning are widely present and that concepts employed in one reality inevitably reveal something of the truth about another reality. Truth may be gained in strange places and from unlikely people, once these are related to God as part of a single universe in process of unification.

## A Finite World

It is sometimes supposed that Teilhard posits an open universe with no boundaries and an infinite range of future possibilities. This is untrue. As just discussed, Teilhard's universe is governed by the unifying action of Christ and is not free to determine its own ends. But neither is evolution preordained. A range of possible, convergent paths into God's future remains open. Teilhard describes these paths using the images of radiation, in which life follows a "limited but progressive number of directions, clearly determined by precise conditions of existence and surroundings," and canalization, when "very strongly 'polarized' changes of form converge, and move all together in a common direction" (VP, 145–46).

Convergence, long out of fashion, has recently been given renewed impetus by Simon Conway Morris, who has been gathering evidence of common selection outcomes in unconnected branches of descent in order to demonstrate that a convergence mechanism is, in fact, at work in evolution.[21] Convergence theory suggests that the choices open to us are necessarily finite in number. We should not, of course, view convergence as due to some form of divine intervention. Rather, convergence is based on the limitation of the range of possible developmental paths available to forms of life in evolution.

A useful contrast may be drawn here with the concept of "singularity" developed by the transhumanist Ray Kurzweil.[22] He sees humankind as now evolved close to a point at which, due to accelerating technological change, we will be able to transcend all previous limitations, even bodily death. But for Teilhard, despite his prescient understanding of technology's transforming power on society, current and future technological change is an analogical repetition of evolutionary developments in the past. He deploys the image of a "breakthrough of reflection" at the birth of humanity as a model for the growth of new global reflectivity in the twentieth century (TF, 174, 183). Although the notion of breakthrough is similar to Kurzweil's singularity concept, Teilhard does not understand this to signal an event entirely unlike anything preceding it. Rather, he sees present-day shifts in the nature of consciousness as intensified repetitions of the evolutionary shift that occurred with the original emergence of reflection in *Homo sapiens*. This continuity suggests that our future will be not as cyborgs, but as humans.

In a patterned, materially finite universe, moral and political discernment are vital. It is not the case that simply anything is in reality desirable or in principle attainable. Political programs must work with the grain of the world, advancing proximate goals that progress at least one step toward an ultimate end. Although many commentators have regarded Teilhard's view of humans' capacity for progress as optimistic, he in fact identifies boundaries to future human achievement and evolution. For example, in "Life and the

Planets" he believes that humans will not successfully colonize other planets (FM, 97–123). Moreover, he does not expect that humans will evolve materially into a higher species. The future of human development will, for Teilhard, be spiritual.

Although Teilhard did sometimes express optimism about the future of the world and of human life, this optimism was, as has just been shown, based on a belief that there exist appropriate pathways into the future, and that humankind is following those pathways. If, however, we humans seek to progress along paths not laid out for us, the result will be not development but regression. In the present day, if we are to remain alive in an ecologically habitable world, we will need to acknowledge the finitude of that world in its multiple dimensions and learn to live within the boundaries it imposes. Teilhard's belief in the oneness of the created order brings with it an acceptance that, morally, there are right paths and wrong paths of technological, economic, and social development. The range of possible options open to us is finite, and the range of morally desirable options even more limited.

Teilhard perceives an urgent need to reinvigorate moral discourse and apply it to the powerful political ideas, institutions, and movements of our day. In his metaphysics, he affirms the real, spiritual value of action in the world and the need to nurture the bonds of interconnectedness that constitute human community in its multiple dimensions. He helps us counter technological and economic instrumentalism with a view of the material world as participating in a higher, spiritual reality. He urges us to recognize the finitude of wealth, resources, and human ingenuity, and to be prepared to live contentedly, even joyously, within the boundaries these impose.

Teilhard's fusion of metaphysics, morality, and political principles is bold yet opportune. By tracing the connections between these three different components of our view of the world, which are usually disconnected, he shows how they are in truth mutually reinforcing, whether for good or ill. By bringing these connections into the open, he encourages all of us, as we face new questions and challenges in all three fields, to consider the connections anew for the present day. In so doing, let us hope that tendencies toward negative mutual reinforcement of metaphysics, morality, and political principles, such as in sociobiology and social segregation, will be countered as more profitable connections long hidden from view are given fresh consideration.

## Points to Ponder

♦ If metaphysics has practical implications, such as grounding a sense of moral obligation, the question of which metaphysics is not one of disinterested speculation.

- Metaphysics, because it impels and structures human action, has moral implications.

- Teilhard makes clear that in evolution's human phase morality, religion, politics, and social issues take center stage. These are the new drivers of evolution.

- When humans truly act they participate in God's own action.

- Action is not, as Aristotle had supposed, the result of simple human deliberation. Teilhard shows that necessarily implicated in human action is divine action. Only when cooperating with divine action can human action generate a truly new beginning.

- Social and political action that effects a real, material, and transformative difference in the world is not only a means of furthering God's justice. It is a sharing in God's creative action, drawing the world into greater unity, and thus into the unifying life of the Godhead, in a "communion through action."

## Questions for Discussion

1. What is the relationship between metaphysics, morality, and political principles? How do you see these principles at work in your own life?

2. How do you understand Teilhard's insight "God exists only by *uniting himself*"? What does this say about God? The physical world?

3. How does metaphysics affect our social and political decision making? What difference does evolution make to the future of our earth community?

4. Do you understand Teilhard as a naïve optimist or a critical realist?

## Notes

1. Piet Schoonenberg, *God's World in the Making* (Dublin: Gill, 1965), 12.

2. David Grumett, "Teilhard de Chardin's Evolutionary Natural Theology," *Zygon* 42 (2007): 519–34.

3. Joseph A. Grau, *Morality and the Human Future in the Thought of Teilhard de Chardin: A Critical Study* (Rutherford, NJ: Fairleigh Dickinson University Press, 1976), 62–68.

4. John F. Haught, *God after Darwin: A Theology of Evolution* (Boulder, CO: Westview, 2000), 83.

5. David Grumett, *Teilhard de Chardin: Theology, Humanity and Cosmos* (Leuven: Peeters, 2006), 237–60. See also the excellent study by Pierre-Louis Mathieu, *La Pensée*

*politique et économique de Teilhard de Chardin,* new ed. (Saint Étienne: Aubin, 2000), 21–117.

6. Piet Schoonenberg, *Covenant and Creation* (London: Sydney, Sheed & Ward, 1968), 202.

7. Phillipe Bergeron, *L'Action humaine dans l'oeuvre de Teilhard de Chardin* (Montreal: Fides, 1969), 88–98.

8. Beatrice Bruteau, "Sri Aurobindo and Teilhard de Chardin on the Problem of Action," *International Philosophical Quarterly* 12 (1972): 194.

9. For more detailed discussion, see Simon Oliver, *Philosophy, God and Motion* (London: Routledge, 2005).

10. Aristotle, *Metaphysics* XII.6, 18.138–45; see also *Physics* 8.12, 5.266–91. See especially Jonathan Lear, *Aristotle: The Desire to Understand* (Cambridge: Cambridge University Press, 1988), 293–306.

11. Aquinas, *Summa theologiae* Ia, q. 2, a. 3 (61 vols.; London: Blackfriars, 1964–81), 2.12–19.

12. Theologians have not always held this view of the soul. Prior to Aquinas, leading figures like Peter Lombard instead saw a quasi-physical "seminal core" as constituting bodily identity. See *The Sentences* bk 2, dist. 30, ch. 15, n. 6, trans. Giulio Silano (4 vols.; Toronto, ON: Pontifical Institute of Medieval Studies, 2008), 2.153; and, for background, Walter H. Principe, " 'The Truth of Human Nature' according to Thomas Aquinas: Theology and Science in Interaction," in *Philosophy and the God of Abraham: Essays in Memory of James A. Weisheipl,* ed. R. James Long (Toronto, ON: Pontifical Institute of Medieval Studies, 1991), 161–77.

13. Aristotle, *Metaphysics* XII.6, trans. Hugh Tredennick (2 vols.; Cambridge, MA: Harvard University Press, 1933–35), 2.138–45; see also idem, *Physics* 8.12, trans. Philip H. Wicksteed and Francis M. Cornford (2 vols.; Cambridge, MA: Harvard University Press, 1952–57), 2.266–91; Plato, *Timaeus* 34b–37c, 7.64–75.

14. See Eric Steinhart, "Teilhard de Chardin and Transhumanism," *Journal of Evolution and Technology* 20, no. 1 (2008): 1–22.

15. Ursula King, "Love—A Higher Form of Human Energy in the Work of Teilhard de Chardin and Sorokin," *Zygon* 39 (2004): 85–89; Joseph A. Grau, "The Creative Union of Person and Community: A Geo-humanist Ethic," in *Teilhard in the 21st Century: The Emerging Spirit of Earth,* ed. Arthur Fabel and Donald St. John (Maryknoll, NY: Orbis Books, 2003), 209–21.

16. On balancing socialization and personalization, see Ursula King, *The Spirit of One Earth: Reflections on Teilhard de Chardin and Global Spirituality* (New York: Paragon, 1989), 29–43.

17. Aquinas, *Summa theologiae* Ia, q. 2, a. 2, 2.8–11.

18. Schoonenberg, *God's World in the Making,* 23–40.

19. John F. Haught, *God and the New Atheism: A Critical Response to Dawkins, Harris, and Hitchens* (Louisville: Westminster John Knox, 2008), 99–101.

20. Christopher F. Mooney, *Teilhard de Chardin and the Mystery of Christ* (London: Collins, 1966), 48–66.

21. Simon Conway Morris, *Life's Solution: Inevitable Humans in a Lonely Universe* (Cambridge: Cambridge University Press, 2003). See www.mapoflife.org.

22. David Grumett, "Transformation and the End of Enhancement," in *Transhumanism and Transcendence: Christian Hope in an Age of Technological Enhancement,* ed. Ronald Cole-Turner (Washington, DC: Georgetown University Press, 2011), 37–49.

*Chapter 8*

# TEILHARD, MEDAWAR, AND THE NEW ATHEISM

*Between Science and Metaphysics*

## DONALD WAYNE VINEY

> I will have against me the pure scientists as well as the pure disciples of metaphysics. But . . . I do not see that one could say otherwise once one tries to work out to its conclusion a coherent place for man in our universe.
>
> —Teilhard to Max and Simone Bégouën
> concerning *Le phénomène humain*[1]

The movement commonly known as "the new atheism" is led by persons whose vocations range from science to philosophy to journalism. Richard Dawkins (biology), Daniel Dennett (philosophy), Sam Harris (philosophy and neuroscience), Victor Stenger (physics), and the late Christopher Hitchens (journalism) are the vanguard, but there are many others. The new atheists are united on at least two points. First, they criticize traditional forms of theistic religion for being irrational and dangerous. Second, they promote enthusiasm for the methods, the deliverances, and the promise of empirical science for the good of humanity. The new atheists consider their support of science to be an essential element in their attack upon theism. In their view, to be serious about promoting the rigors of scientific thinking is to be serious about censuring theistic religion. They are fond of noting that scientists more often than not express skepticism about God.[2] When it comes to addressing the arguments of theistic scientists, the new atheists typically claim that such scientists are confused about religion or about science. It is not simply a question of attacking theists who reject evolution (like young-earth creationists) or who wish to supplement it with supernatural explanations (like proponents of intelligent design). The new atheists are equally critical of theists who are as enthusiastic about evolution as they are. Francis Collins, for example, is respected as the head of the Human Genome Project, but his Christian apologetic, drawn from C. S. Lewis, is ridiculed.[3] Kenneth Miller, a professor at Brown University, has been in the thick of the cultural battles, fighting *against* intelligent design and *for* neo-Darwinian evolution. His credentials

127

as a biologist are impeccable, but he has been scolded by the new atheists for his adherence to Catholicism.[4]

Pierre Teilhard de Chardin (1881–1955), the famous Jesuit geologist and paleontologist, receives similar treatment. No one championed evolution more than Teilhard, and he would almost certainly not have supported intelligent design. He rejected interventionist metaphors for divine activity and he denied the claim that microevolution is insufficient to account for macro-evolution; indeed, he saw no use in this distinction (AM, 138, 218). When it comes to Teilhard, however, the new atheists, for the most part, allow Sir Peter Medawar (1915–1987) to be their spokesperson. Medawar is one of the best known of Teilhard's detractors. He was asked by his friend Gilbert Ryle, editor of the prestigious philosophy journal *Mind*, to review the first translation of Teilhard's *Le phénomène humain*. The review, which appeared in 1961, has achieved near legendary status among the new atheists.[5] Daniel Dennett and Richard Dawkins cite the review as, respectively, a "classic savaging" and "an annihilation" of Teilhard's views. Simon Blackburn, a philosopher sympathetic to the new atheism, says that the claims for the "rational respectability" of Teilhard's book were "exploded" by Medawar's review.[6] There can be no question that Medawar was a gifted scientist. He and Sir MacFarlane Burnet shared the Nobel Prize for medicine in 1969 for their work on tissue grafting. Moreover, Medawar's essays and books on the meaning of science are literary gems, thought provoking and entertaining. In what follows, however, I revisit Medawar's review to see if the assessments of it by the new atheists are justified. My conclusion is that Medawar's arguments are remarkably thin, marred by misrepresentations and elementary philosophical blunders—defects that are uncharacteristic of Medawar's writing.

I begin with some observations about Teilhard's standing in the scientific community, a preface made necessary by Medawar's comments on Teilhard's character and competence as a scientist. What can be conceded to Medawar is that Teilhard's work is not strictly scientific but belongs to a different genre. W. Henry Kenney suggested that *Le phénomène humain* might be a genuinely new genre of literature, as Augustine's *Confessions* and James Joyce's *Finnegan's Wake* were in their day.[7] That is a hypothesis worth exploring, but for the purposes of this paper I register my agreement with Robert O'Connell that Medawar did not read carefully enough what Teilhard said about the character of his own work as "hyperphysics," a word that does not appear in Medawar's review.[8] Specifically, I argue that Teilhard's work in *Le phénomène humain* should be located at the boundary between traditional science and classical metaphysics; it finds a near parallel in what Alfred North Whitehead called speculative philosophy.

## Teilhard's Standing in Science

In his preface to the ten-volume collection of Teilhard's scientific works, Jean Piveteau avers that Teilhard's popularity as a visionary based on the works that appeared only after his death—like *Le phénomène humain*—obscured the fact that during his lifetime he was widely recognized for his contributions to geology and paleontology (OS, xxi). Teilhard was probably best known for being one of the codiscoverers of Sinanthropos, commonly called Peking Man.[9] As Piveteau says, when Teilhard spoke of "fossil man" he had first-hand knowledge of the subject. The scientific establishment recognized his accomplishments in various ways. He was invited to accept the chair in paleontology at the Collège de France, left vacant by the retirement of L'Abbé Brueil. As Sir Julian Huxley says in his introduction to *The Phenomenon of Man*, this was "the highest academic position to which [Teilhard] could aspire . . ." (PM, 25). The résumé that Teilhard submitted to the Collège documents an impressive career (HM, 157–164). He might have taken the appointment had his religious superiors not barred the way. He was later made a member of the French Académie des Sciences. Those who worked with the man admired him not only for his attention to detailed scientific study but for his intelligence, humility, and creativity—as a typical example, see George Barbour's chronicle *In the Field with Teilhard de Chardin*.[10]

All the while that Teilhard worked as a scientist, he was developing a metaphysical framework to understand evolutionary development. His religious order repeatedly denied his requests to publish this work and they encouraged him to stick to science and to avoid philosophy and theology. He found it "psychologically unviable" and "directly opposed to the greater glory of God" to avoid philosophy and theology, but he did not disobey their prohibition on publishing his work (SC, 214). After a canon lawyer had been consulted, he left his writings to his secretary, Jeanne Mortier. She saw to their publication after he died. This is not to say that Teilhard's more religious and philosophical writings were unknown during his lifetime. He sent mimeographed copies of some of the manuscripts to friends and colleagues. These *clandestins*, as Teilhard called them, gained wide enough distribution to give him a reputation as someone who was pioneering new ways of conceiving the relation between science and spirituality. In August 1950 André Billy of the Academy Goncourt wrote an article for *Figaro Littéraire* praising the literary and farseeing qualities of Teilhard's work.[11] About the same time, two books were published in France that used the clandestins to launch a volley of criticisms at Teilhard's metaphysical appropriation of evolution.[12] The first book, published anonymously, was probably written by L'Abbé Luc Lefèvre, founder of *Pensée Catholique*.[13] Teilhard wrote a paragraph in response indicating that he did not recognize his thought in the book (OS, v. 10, 4290).

Teilhard did not publish a reply to the second book, but he wrote to his friend and colleague Père Pierre Leroy concerning the brittleness of the theology that it contained.[14]

The controversy that was brewing in France moved to the international stage after Teilhard's death when the clandestins were published and translated. The first of the thirteen volumes of Teilhard's œuvres to appear and to be translated into English was *Le phénomène humain* (1955), originally rendered as *The Phenomenon of Man* (1959) and later as *The Human Phenomenon* (1999). The French edition announces that the book is published, in part, under the patronage of a scientific committee—thirty-two eminent scientists from around the world whose names and credentials are listed. Of course, the list in no way consists of an endorsement by the committee of the ideas in Teilhard's book. However, as the note from the editors says, the list is "far from exhausting the number of friends and eminent admirers of Teilhard de Chardin."[15] The list verifies Piveteau's observation of the esteem in which Teilhard was held by his fellow scientists. One of those listed was Sir Julian Huxley. His introduction to *The Phenomenon of Man* is an enthusiastic recommendation of the book whose author he calls "a distinguished paleontologist" (PM, 11).

It may seem as though I am belaboring the obvious: Teilhard was admired by his peers. I believe, however, that Teilhard's reputation as a first-rate scientist should be kept in mind in assessing Medawar's review, for Medawar seems as keen on belittling Teilhard as a scientist as he does in assessing his ideas. Teilhard, we are told, "practiced a comparatively humble and unexacting kind of science."[16] Just to remind the reader of his opinion, he repeats it several pages later in almost the same words, adding a comment about Teilhard's level of skill: "Teilhard practiced an intellectually unexacting kind of science in which he achieved a moderate proficiency."[17] Perhaps enough has been said to show that this judgment is as unfounded as it is uncharitable.

Medawar does not stop with a criticism of Teilhard's competence but also attacks his character. He says that Teilhard "can be excused of dishonesty only on the grounds that before deceiving others he has taken great pains to deceive himself."[18] In Medawar's view, Teilhard is either dishonest with his readers or dishonest with himself. Another well-known scientist who charged Teilhard with dishonesty is Stephen Jay Gould (1941–2002). Gould concluded from circumstantial evidence that Teilhard was complicit in the Piltdown hoax and that the burden of proof is on Teilhard's defenders.[19] Dawkins' verdict on Gould's case is "a Scottish 'non-proven.'"[20] Others who give a more detailed account of the evidence pronounce a stronger verdict of "not guilty."[21] Medawar apparently thought Teilhard innocent, both in the sense that he was not guilty but also in the sense that Teilhard would not suspect someone of deceiving him by planting a doctored tooth.[22] In this context, Medawar seems to use "innocence"—which is really a kind of *trust*—as a mild rebuke; elsewhere, however, Medawar recognizes that the practice of science requires "a basis of confidence" so that "scientists do not suspect each other of dishonesty or sharp practice, and believe each other unless there is very good reason to do otherwise."[23] Perhaps, after all, Medawar's shrill tone in the review is hyperbole meant only to accuse Teilhard of overestimating the value and truth of his own ideas.

## Medawar's Critique

Medawar announces that the greater part of *The Phenomenon of Man* is "nonsense, tricked out with a variety of metaphysical conceits" and he sets about the task of unmasking what he regards as Teilhard's "tipsy, euphoristic prose-poetry which is one of the more tiresome manifestations of the French spirit."[24] In Medawar's view, Teilhard is given to oversimplification and exaggeration, also to "nothing-buttery"—by which Medawar seems to intend crude reductionism.[25] One may agree that Teilhard takes poetic license in describing his vision of a grand design of evolution. As Huxley says, he saw a need for "a broad sweep and a comprehensive treatment" (PM, 21). Huxley speaks of Teilhard's "genius for fruitful analogy" (PM, 20). In an essay on science and literature, Medawar expressed the view that literary flourishes should be kept at a minimum in scientific writing. According to Medawar, "In science the imaginative element lies in the conception, and not in the language by which the conception is made explicit or conveyed."[26] This is, however, largely a matter of personal preference so that Medawar is simply expressing his distaste for Teilhard's prose. Medawar comes close to admitting that he is dwelling on inessentials and matters of style when he says, "These are trivialities, revealing though they are, and perhaps I make too much of them."[27]

There follows Medawar's summary of the argument of Teilhard's book. In view of the denunciations with which Medawar set the stage, one expects an account of where exactly he believes Teilhard went wrong. Surprisingly, he does not do this. Medawar says that he does "not propose to criticize the fatuous argument," but says only that, in this case, "to expound is to expose."[28] For those who find genuine insights in Teilhard, Medawar reserves the barb that they are "educated far beyond their capacity to undertake analytical thought."[29] In other words, if they do not see, without Medawar explaining it to them, the flaws in Teilhard's views, then they are as greatly foolish as Medawar takes Teilhard to have been; or alternatively, if Teilhard's admirers had Medawar's level of learning, such reviews would be unnecessary. Since scientists themselves are divided on the value of Teilhard's theories, some finding valuable perspectives in them—not uncritically, but with qualifications and reservations—Medawar's assertion "to expound is to expose" is a non sequitur. Huxley's introduction is enthusiastic but not uncritical, not unlike other appraisals of Teilhard's work by scientists.[30] It is a clever rhetorical trick to offer insults in place of arguments, but even those who lack Medawar's credentials should understand the difference.

Medawar misses the central problem that *Le phénomène humain* addresses when Teilhard talks about consciousness, radial energy, and "the Within of Things." He understands that Teilhard criticizes science for not doing justice to "the human phenomenon" and for not showing how it makes sense in terms of evolution. Unhappily, he caricatures Teilhard's complaint thus: "[scientists] are shallow superficial fellows, unable to see into the inwardness of things. . . ."[31] This leads Medawar to the curious conclusion that Teilhard's book is "anti-scientific in temper."[32] Teilhard's point, however, is not that scientists are superficial but that they have, as a rule, treated consciousness as an anomaly or an epiphenomenon and generally failed to show how it fits into an evolutionary scheme. He takes "consciousness" [*conscience*] in the widest sense as including "every kind of psyche [*psychisme*], from the most rudimentary forms of interior perception conceivable to the human phenomenon of reflective consciousness" (HP, 25; PM, 57). This idea of consciousness is anticipated in Leibniz's concept of perception (and apperception, its human form) and in Whitehead's concept of prehension. All three thinkers try to navigate between what they see as the extremes of Cartesian mind-body dualism and materialism. Teilhard goes further by explicitly situating mental phenomena in an evolutionary context. It is no criticism of science that it has not solved the mind-body problem, for it is a question—really a bundle of questions—with which scientifically minded philosophers and philosophically minded scientists have struggled. There is still no universally agreed upon answer. At a minimum, science should leave room in its explanations for the varieties of mentality; Teilhard's methodology abides by the ancient standards of science to "save the appearances," the phenomena, and not to ignore or deny them. For Teilhard, science should include a theoretical framework in which mentality, in all its variations, can be understood in evolutionary terms. Teilhard's law of complexity and consciousness is his proposal for addressing the issue (HP, 28; PM, 61).

In the years after Teilhard wrote *Le phénomène humain*—midway through the twentieth century—there was much discussion about whether mental processes could be identified with dispositions to behave (as in the logical behaviorism of Gilbert Ryle) or with brain processes (as in the versions of the mind-brain thesis of U. T. Place and Herbert Feigl). Most philosophers agree that these theories failed to give an adequate account of the mind, although admittedly they remain attractive to some thinkers. More generally, reductionist and functionalist accounts of mental phenomena, as well as eliminativist views of mind, have failed to gain consensus and have often been on the defensive. In this context, one may mention David Chalmers' book *The Conscious Mind* which is something of a watershed for pressing the argument that consciousness is not completely amenable to physicalist or functional explanation.[33] Also of interest is that theories in Teilhard's day that emphasized the intentionality of consciousness, as in Edmund Husserl's phenomenology, did nothing to address the place of consciousness in an evolutionary worldview. Teilhard wrote to Claude Cuénot in 1953: "I do not understand how anyone can call himself a 'phenomenologist' and write whole books without ever mentioning or touching on cosmogenesis and evolution."[34] Whitehead most closely anticipated the Teilhardian view in his objections to what he called the "bifurcation of nature" between the mental and the physical.[35] Teilhard makes the same complaint:

> The apparent restriction of the phenomenon of consciousness to the higher forms of life has long served science as a pretext for eliminating it from its constructions of the universe. To dismiss it, thought has been classed as a bizarre exception, an aberrant function, an epiphenomenon. (HP, 23–24; PM, 55)

Whitehead could have written those words, with no suggestion that scientists are "superficial fellows" or that his books were "anti-scientific in temper." Suffice it to say that the problem that Teilhard raises about the place of the Within of Things in an evolutionary world remains with us. It is true that some form of physicalism is now the dominant philosophy, but the question of how far down the evolutionary scale mind extends is very much an undecided issue.[36]

That Medawar was not tracking Teilhard's concerns or that he did not fully appreciate the problem that consciousness poses for science is evident when he says that Teilhard's notion of radial energy can be understood in terms of information content. According to Medawar

> Teilhard's radial, spiritual or psychic energy may be equated to "information" or "information content" in the sense that has been made reasonably precise by modern communication engineers. To equate it to consciousness, or to regard degree of consciousness as a measure of information content, is one of the silly little metaphysical conceits I mentioned in an earlier paragraph.[37]

Medawar elsewhere clarifies that "information" is a structure that "makes possible the transmission of a meaningful message or in the form of a communication that prescribes and confers specificity upon any structure or performance."[38] Information, in this sense, functions as a formal cause, like

DNA, for specifying that an organism develops one way rather than another. Medawar simply asserts that the equation of information and radial energy captures Teilhard's meaning. Teilhard might have viewed information in Medawar's sense as a necessary feature of radial energy, but would he have accepted a strict equation between the two? Teilhard posited radial energy as that which draws the elements of the universe "in the direction of an ever more complex and centered state, towards what is ahead" (HP, 30; PM, 65). He believed that evolution, and the becoming of the cosmos itself, has a direction toward greater complexity. If this is correct, it is legitimate to ask for an explanation for the tendency for the universe to organize itself into ever more complex wholes; radial energy is Teilhard's candidate for such an account. Of course, Medawar denies that evolution has a direction (more of this shortly). But this fact does not explain why he thinks that Teilhard's radial energy equates to information content. There is the further problem that information may exist whether or not it is consciously entertained or used by a sentient being. There is a great deal of information in a cookbook about how to prepare various dishes, but that information is, at best, the object of consciousness, not its substance. There may be a metaphysical conceit here, but it is not Teilhard's.

Medawar alleges two other mistakes in Teilhard's writings that could be considered major failings. First, he says that Teilhard believed that "evolution flouts or foils the second law of thermodynamics" which, as Medawar says, "is based on a confusion of thought."[39] While this is indeed a confusion of thought, I do not believe that Teilhard was guilty of it. Huxley's statement that Teilhard conceived evolution as "an anti-entropic process, running counter to the second law of thermodynamics with its degradation of energy and its tendency to uniformity," may have misled Medawar (PM, 27). Yet, Teilhard's discussion of thermodynamics and its relation to evolutionary processes is quite orthodox. Teilhard explains thermodynamics as teaching that "in the process of every physicochemical transformation, a fraction of the available energy is irremediably 'entropized,' lost, that is, in the form of heat." He goes on to say, "from the real evolutionary perspective, in the course of every synthesis something is definitively burned up to pay for it" (HP, 20; PM, 51). Thus, Teilhard understood that the second law of thermodynamics is not incompatible with evolutionary processes. He also understood, however, that the second law is not an explanation of the tendency of the universe to arrange itself into ever-more-complex wholes. As noted above, Teilhard speculates that there is a countervailing agency directed toward increased complexity and consciousness. This "radial energy" would account for the tendency of matter to become more complex in the course of evolution.[40]

Teilhard's speculations about a radial form of energy are controversial but they are neither unheard of nor unreasonable. Again, a comparison with Whitehead is in order. In 1929, Whitehead wrote

> The material universe has contained in itself, and perhaps still contains, some mysterious impulse for its energy to run upwards. This impulse is veiled from our observation, so far as concerns its general operation. But there must have been some epoch in which the dominant trend was the formation of protons, electrons, molecules, the stars. Today, so far as our observations go, they are decaying.[41]

Paul Davies, a physicist and popular science writer, proposes, in a similar vein, a "law of increasing complexity" that stands alongside of the laws of thermodynamics.[42] Neither Whitehead nor Davies is guilty of claiming that thermodynamics is incompatible with evolution. It is difficult to understand Medawar's accusation against Teilhard concerning thermodynamics and evolution unless he conflated Teilhard's implication that thermodynamics does not explain the processes of complexification (which for Teilhard include the correlation between physical complexity and interiority) with the claim that thermodynamics is incompatible with these processes. This is on a par with arguing that the process of digestion does not explain thinking, so it must be incompatible with it. Again, the mistake is Medawar's rather than Teilhard's.

A second idea to which Medawar takes exception is the concept that evolution has a direction. According to Medawar, "the idea that evolution has a main track or privileged axis is unsupported by scientific evidence."[43] Medawar would have been more precise had he said that scientific evidence is open-ended on the question whether evolution has a main track or privileged axis. Teilhard's hypothesis is that the appearance through geologic time of increasingly complex organisms with increasingly rich inner lives is the clue to evolution's direction. Whatever one may think of Teilhard's hypothesis, the concept of convergent processes in evolution is not unreasonable, especially given similarities in environmental niches, optimal solutions to species survival, and design constraints. There are no creatures with wheels, but there are many with wings, ears, and eyes. Moreover, design constraints on the requirements of flight, audition, and vision permit of limited numbers of solutions—no elephant can use its ears to fly like Dumbo. In a much discussed book, Simon Conway Morris presents a powerful case from examples of evolutionary convergence that the emergence of sentient creatures, and perhaps even creatures with our kind of intelligence, was a near inevitability.[44] Medawar did not have the benefit of having read Morris, but Teilhard was more accurate, and more prescient, when he said, "uncertainty still prevails among biologists about the existence of a direction, and therefore even more, a definite axis, of evolution . . ." (HP, 110; PM, 164).

Daniel Dennett makes an argument that might lend support to a view of evolution as an aimless process by noting that the known mechanisms of evolutionary change are algorithmic. Dennett pinpoints what he takes to be Teilhard's basic mistake:

> The problem with Teilhard's vision is simple. He emphatically denied the fundamental idea: that evolution is a mindless, purposeless, algorithmic process. This was no constructive compromise; this was a betrayal of the central insight that had permitted Darwin to overthrow Locke's Mind-first vision.[45]

Teilhard anticipated this objection by addressing the assumption that the chance inherent in Darwinian mechanisms rules out a direction to evolution. He pointed out that the algorithmic mechanisms of Darwinian evolution may yet be directed to an end. By the play of large numbers working over vast time scales, evolution can move toward what was initially statistically improbable. This is what Teilhard calls *tâtonnement* (i.e., groping, or trial and error). "Trial and error [is] where the blind fantasy of large numbers and the precise orientation of a pursued goal are combined." For Teilhard, *tâtonnement* is "*directed Chance*" [*hasard dirigé*] (HP, 66; PM, 110). If evolution can have a direction, even supposing that it operates by algorithmic processes, then it is conceivable that the direction is divinely sanctioned or imposed. Of course, whether there is indeed an aim to evolution is an open question. But that question should not be begged, that is to say, closed, by talk of algorithmic processes. Put somewhat differently, evolution may or may not be purposive in the way that Teilhard believed, but the discovery of mindless evolutionary mechanisms does not show that he was wrong.

Dennett's mistake is similar to the one made by the National Association of Biology Teachers. In 1995, the NABT issued a statement saying that evolution is, among other things, an impersonal and unsupervised process. Two years later, at the urging of Alvin Plantinga (a theistic philosopher) and Huston Smith (a scholar of the world's religions), and with the help of Eugenie Scott (a nontheist and a science educator), the NABT dropped the adjectives describing evolution as "impersonal" and "unsupervised" on the grounds that they go beyond the evidence available to science.[46] One reply to this reasoning is that no "mind-first" explanations are necessary to explain evolutionary processes; if this is so, then perhaps Medawar and Dennett are right that science gives no support to the idea that evolution has a direction. There are, however, two problems with this line of reasoning. First, there is a difference between a process having a direction and a process being designed for the purpose of reaching a goal. A cat chasing a mouse is a process with a direction even if the cat's biological system was not specifically designed for that purpose. The evolutionary process itself may exhibit direction even if, contrary to many theistic evolutionists, it was not designed to do so. Second, to say that science "gives no support to X" is much different from saying "X is not true." Teilhard, it is true, accepted mind-first explanations; he was, after all, a theist. He did not, however, use them to *replace* known scientific findings about evolution. The question remains whether "mind-first" explanations can supplement the algorithmic explanations of science.

## Teilhard, Science, and Speculative Philosophy

Teilhard advises from the outset that his book is to be read "purely and simply as a scientific study" (HP, 1; PM, 29). He denies, moreover, that he addresses questions of "the essence of being," and for this reason he is not doing metaphysics. He explains, however, that his project has the *appearance* of philosophy because it tries to do justice to the *entire* phenomenon, which includes mind-like qualities as they are manifested throughout the evolutionary process. He speaks of his work as "Hyperphysics," extending beyond (*hyper*) physics or science but falling short of metaphysics (HP, 2; PM, 30). Medawar is blind to this nuance in Teilhard's approach, failing even to mention the expression "hyperphysics." Medawar appreciates that Teilhard attempts to build his case primarily on the deliverances of science. As we have seen, Medawar claims that Teilhard gets some of the major ideas in science wrong. Our examination thus far has shown that there are good reasons to mistrust Medawar's interpretation. In any event, Medawar says that the factual errors that he thinks he finds in Teilhard's work are not his "immediate concern."[47] He locates the book squarely in the tradition of *Naturphilosophie*, a tradition, he claims, that seems to have contributed nothing, even by accident, to the storehouse of human wisdom. He calls Teilhard's book "philosophy-fiction."[48] Medawar's fundamental complaint, therefore, is that Teilhard's book pretends to be scientific but that it doesn't measure up to the rigorous standards of a scientific treatise.

There is a truth in the vicinity of Medawar's accusation, but the reasoning is muddled. I leave others to address Medawar's complaint about the lack of wisdom in Fichte, Schelling, and Hegel—the *Naturphilosophen*. (They did have a habit of ascribing agency to abstractions.) There is little, however, to recommend Medawar's comparison between the Germans and Teilhard. It is true that Teilhard, like the German Idealists, sought a comprehensive vision of the world. But this is true of every metaphysically minded philosopher from Plato to Whitehead. There is certainly no question of intellectual influence from the Germans to Teilhard. Moreover, the German Idealists were responding to the unresolved dualities of Kant's transcendental philosophy.

Kant was never Teilhard's concern. Finally, the German Idealists, unlike Teilhard, were not practicing scientists and they were profoundly ignorant (as was everyone in their day) of humanity as a product of evolution. Evolution, however, is indispensible to Teilhard's conception of the cosmos, which he rightly described as a cosmogenesis. Teilhard says, "as far back as its most distant formulations, we discover that matter is in *a state of genesis . . .*" (HP, 18; PM, 49). Whatever missteps Teilhard may have made as to scientific details, he did not misunderstand the broad outlines of physics, chemistry, biology, geology, and paleontology as they bear on the question of evolution.

Medawar's comparison of Teilhard with the *Naturphilosophen* is unconvincing. A better comparison, as I have already suggested, is with Whitehead. Medawar was in a position to make such a comparison, but apparently he did not notice the parallels between Whitehead and Teilhard. In another essay Medawar quotes Whitehead's definition of "speculative philosophy."[49] In Whitehead's words, speculative philosophy is "the endeavour to frame a coherent, logical, necessary system of general ideas in terms of which every element of our experience can be interpreted."[50] Teilhard would have no quarrel with this definition, for he sought "to develop a *homogenous* and *coherent* perspective of our general experience as it extends to the human being" (HP, 6; PM, 35). To be sure, there are differences between the two thinkers. For example, Teilhard does not develop a detailed categoreal scheme as one finds in *Process and Reality*. On the other hand, both men were intent on preserving what is distinctive in "the human phenomenon" without making human beings alien to the natural world. On this planet, humans are unique in their use of symbols, in their capacity for self-reflection, and in their collective cultural and social lives; at the same time, they are continuous with and inseparable from the rest of nature, one type of organism among others. Neither Whitehead nor Teilhard could accept the idea of a mind (human or otherwise) that is not organically linked to a body. Nor could they accept what Charles Hartshorne called an "emergent dualism" of physical stuff animated by mind preceded by countless ages of mere matter in motion.[51] Both protested against what Whitehead called the "bifurcation of actualities." According to Whitehead, " . . . there are no concrete facts which are merely public, or merely private."[52] Arguably, Teilhard's expressions, "the Without of Things" and "the Within of Things," denote the same phenomena that Whitehead calls the public and the private. In a 1911 article titled "Homme" [Man] Teilhard denied a direct intuition into the nature of things. He noted, however, that things appear to us in two ways, from without (*du dehors*) and from within (*par le dedans*): in a word, we have a different access to our own experience or mental lives than we do of the mental lives of others, for whom we must rely on less direct evidence.[53] It became a centerpiece of Teilhard's project to generalize this point beyond the human and to conceive the Without (*le dehors*) and the Within (*le dedans*) as the two sides of every concrete particular.

Medawar's complaint that Teilhard strays beyond the usual boundaries of science gains traction when Teilhard speaks of evolution as something more than a theory. Teilhard says,

> Evolution is a general condition, which all theories, all hypotheses, all systems must submit to and satisfy from now on in order to be conceivable and true. Evolution is a light illuminating all facts, a curve that every line must follow (HP, 152; PM, 219).

This is an oft-repeated theme in Teilhard's writings (AM, 211; VP, 127; SC, 193; CE, 139). Teilhard seems to acknowledge that his views on evolution take one beyond a strictly scientific account. He is not speaking of Darwinian evolution—his references to Darwin are scarce—rather, he is extending the developmental categories of evolution to their widest generality. When Teilhard spoke of "evolution" he seems to have had in mind, at a minimum, the twin ideas that (a) nature's processes must be understood developmentally—what a thing is cannot be understood apart from the processes that gave rise to it, and (b) the order in which things appear in time throughout the cosmos are also the order in which they are created—hence, the cosmos is, in truth, a cosmogenesis. He realized that what he was doing might "look like philosophy," but he insisted that he was not "venturing into the profound domain of being" (HP, 1; PM, 29). Thus, in *Le phénomène humain*, Teilhard describes his project as limited to what is revealed by science, placing the "human phenomenon" front and center, but not as a treatise on the nature of existence such as would interest a metaphysician and such as his religious superiors had warned him against pursuing.

Teilhard refused to speak of the project of *Le phénomène humain* as metaphysical. He knew that Rome would never allow him to publish such a work. Moreover, he had little interest in presenting his own work as metaphysics in the traditional sense. He knew traditional metaphysics well, as is apparent in his 1911 article; there, he rehearses the arguments of the church for an immortal human soul that is not a product of natural processes but which exists unchanged from the moment of its creation by God.[54] Once Teilhard came under suspicion by church authorities, he became more circumspect in his approach to metaphysics. In 1935 he wrote to Mgr. Bruno de Solages concerning his essay "Comment je crois" [How I Believe], one of his many attempts to summarize his thought. He said in that letter that he sought "not to leave the plane of the experimental."[55] This sentiment is echoed and clarified in his 1954 letter to T. V. Fleming: "Personally, I believe in a 'phenomenology' (study of patterns and processes) more than in any 'metaphysics' seeking to deduce the Real from the laws of Thought."[56] Teilhard was careful to explain that his book fell short of metaphysics. Yet, as we have just seen, he realized that his project extended beyond the usual boundaries of scientific theorizing. In a September 1940 letter to George Barbour, Teilhard characterized *Le phénomène humain* as "half scientific, half philosophical."[57] Teilhard understood that his ideas about the Within of Things, radial energy, the Noosphere, and Omega were speculative and controversial and that they stretched the description of his work as "scientific" to its limits.

As we have seen, the expression that Teilhard uses in *Le phénomène humain* for the admittedly fuzzy frontier between classical science and classical metaphysics is "hyperphysics." This word had a certain flexibility in Teilhard's mind. In 1934, he wrote to Henri de Lubac:

> It seems to me, at present, that there are two types of "to know": an abstract, geometrical, extra-temporal, pseudo-absolute knowing (= "the world of ideas and principles"), which instinctively I do not trust;—and a "real" knowing, which consists in the conscious actualization (that is to say, in the prolonged creation) of the Universe around us. The first of these two knowings ends up in Geometry (and in Theology). The second, in the Physical and the Mystical. I mistrust metaphysics (in the usual sense of the word), because I smell a geometry in it. But I am ready to recognize another sort of metaphysics which would really be a hyper-Physics,—or a hyper-Biology.[58]

I suggest that it was precisely this other "sort of metaphysics" that Teilhard was developing in his *magnum opus*. This metaphysics, like Whitehead's speculative philosophy, does not derive truths *a priori* and it never leaves the "plane of the experimental." Neither Whitehead nor Teilhard viewed their task as deducing theorems from self-evident truths. Whitehead, himself a first-rate mathematician and logician, believed that philosophy had been mislead by the example of mathematics.[59] The rationalistic aspects of speculative philosophy—consistency and coherence—are balanced by the demands that philosophy be applicable to some experience and adequate to all experience. The word "experience"—like the word "consciousness" in Teilhard's lexicon—must have the widest possible meaning to include nonhuman forms of perception. Teilhard wrote in 1948 that his Weltanschauung "in no way represents a fixed and closed system" (TF, 164). In her explanation of Teilhard's views, Madeleine Barthélemy-Madaule cleverly says, "An incomplete world cannot give place to a complete system."[60] Within that open-ended horizon of inquiry Teilhard found a world buzzing with activity, a restless multitude in which novel layers of physical order and mental intensity continually emerge in a cumulative process. Extrapolating from this curve of development, Teilhard's bold speculative hypothesis is that the world is also converging toward greater complexity and interiority.

Teilhard's caution—perhaps "ambivalence" would be a better word— about whether his views were genuinely metaphysical is characteristic of all of his attempts to give a summary of his vision. The 1917 essay "Creative Union" promotes the idea that, "Creation is brought about by an act of uniting; and true union cannot be effected except by creating" (WTW, 156). Teilhard stresses that the order in which created things appear to us in history and in evolution is none other than the ontological order of creation (WTW, 162). This is in contrast to the usual habit of metaphysics—the word used by Teilhard—of constructing theories for "things that are completely made" (WTW, 167). In this essay, Teilhard is reticent to speak of "creative union" as a metaphysical idea; because he stays on the plane of the experiential he speaks of his project as "*infra*-metaphysics" (WTW, 167)—in other words, metaphysics that is "below" or "under" metaphysics per se. Yet, the same ideas as he had used in 1917 reappear in 1920, this time in a brief and tightly reasoned essay that ventures unabashedly into the metaphysical waters of Scholasticism:

> Beside "*creatio ex nihilo subjecti*" and "*transformatio ex potential subjecti*," there is room for an act *sui generis* which makes use of a pre-existent created being and builds it up into a completely new being. (CE, 22)

Four years later, in the lengthy essay "My Universe," the doctrine of creative union is said to be not exactly metaphysical (SC, 44). Nevertheless, in 1945 (CE, 178) and 1948 (TF, 193) Teilhard defended a "metaphysics of union." More precisely, he advocated in 1953 replacing a "metaphysics of *Esse* [to be] by a metaphysics of *Unire* [to unite] (or of *Uniri* [to be united])" (CE, 227). Teilhard's 1954 letter to T. V. Fleming, mentioned above, speaks of passing from "a metaphysics of Cosmos" to "a metaphysics of Cosmogenesis."[61]

Teilhard's caution or ambivalence about whether or not to call his ideas "metaphysics" was in part a product of his Jesuit training that identified metaphysics with a science of being that relegated the category of becoming to the status of "participated being" or of "secondary causes." However, Teilhard's equation of the order of creation with the order of evolution renders the idea of participated being at best problematic and at worse untenable. By identifying the temporal process with the order of creation, not only does Teilhard reject the idea of treating things as "completely made," he also calls into question the traditional idea of divine creation as an *eternal* act distinguishable from temporal processes. Another source of reticence was that, from July 1925 onward, Teilhard was explicitly warned by his religious superiors to steer clear of philosophy. In May 1950, Teilhard mentioned to Barbour that his clandestins were making the rounds "*sous le manteau*" (under the coat), that is to say, illicitly.[62] A month later, Teilhard wrote to Leroy that for thirty years he had been "going underground" to think freely in the church.[63]

Throughout this time, he never abandoned the project begun in his younger days of developing a worldview grounded in the doctrine of creative union. To label the doctrine metaphysical—which he sometimes did—represented not only a tension with the prohibitions put upon him by the church hierarchy, but also an extension of his work beyond the boundaries of what is usually identified as science. If he sometimes presented his ideas as scientific—though never without qualification that they were also *hyperphysics*—it was because he knew that his work was not metaphysics in a traditional sense. According to the view I am advocating, Teilhard's phenomenology, his hyperphysics, especially as it is expressed in *Le phénomène humain*, is a version of his metaphysics of cosmogenesis. If I am correct, then Teilhard's book is closer to what Whitehead called "speculative philosophy" than it is to a traditional scientific treatise.

## Conclusion

When Medawar republished his review of *The Phenomenon of Man* in *Pluto's Republic*, he said that he did not budge from his criticisms. He reports that his aged mother asked him how he could be so horrid to such a nice old man as Teilhard.[64] Medawar does not elaborate on whether his mother was talking about his personal attacks on Teilhard or his criticisms of Teilhard's ideas. In any event, he explained to her that Teilhard had presented his book as something it was not, namely a book of science, and that this misled the gullible. He suggested that the book would have been harmless had Teilhard only described it as "an imaginative rhapsody" based on science in the way that films are said to be based on books. In his memoirs he is more strident, speaking of Teilhard's "incoherent rhapsodies."[65] Medawar allowed that he had been "coarsely insensitive" in not interpreting the popularity of Teilhard's book as a symptom of a hunger for answers to questions that go beyond what science can provide.[66] Medawar considered that hunger to be legitimate, and he had no truck with the view of the logical positivists that these questions are mere pseudo-questions. The unhappy fact, however, is that Medawar did not respect Teilhard. In the same essay where he mentions Whitehead's definition of speculative philosophy, he says that Teilhard was "in no serious sense a thinker."[67] The problem is that Teilhard's thought never gets a fair hearing from Medawar. In light of his mishandling of Teilhard's ideas, it is unfortunate that his review has gained, among the new atheists, the status of a definitive refutation. A less aggressive and more magnanimous review might have allowed the new atheists to appreciate the problems that Teilhard was addressing as well as the fact that, never contradicting science, his theories are more in the nature of a hyperphysics, or in truth, a new understanding of metaphysics as speculative philosophy.

Had Medawar known more of Teilhard's metaphysics of union or even more about his struggles with Rome, it is possible that he would have written a more charitable review. Arguably, Medawar was not opposed in principle to the project that Teilhard set for himself, for he believed that science is capable of explaining only what is empirically verifiable or falsifiable. He spoke openly of "the limits of science"—the title of one of his books—making it clear that he believed that questions about "the origin, destiny, and purpose of man" are beyond the competence of science to adjudicate.[68] He maintained that *if* there are satisfactory answers—and he was skeptical that there are—they must be found in "myth, metaphysics, imaginative literature or religion."[69] Medawar allowed a place for metaphysics as long as its theories were "not outrageously incongruent" with experience and common sense.[70] He was also clear that he believed that reason is necessary, though not sufficient, to explain the human condition.[71] In this respect, Medawar was much more cautious about science than are the new atheists who, for example, usually treat the existence of God as a scientific question in defiance of the regnant traditions of philosophy from Plato and Aristotle until the present day. The new atheists parody the arguments of the great theistic philosophers but rarely is there any serious engagement.[72] Like the new atheists, Medawar comes to an atheistic conclusion, but not because he believed that science had done the job that philosophers had failed to do. It seems to have been the philosophical problem of evil that, for Medawar, posed the greatest obstacle to belief in God.[73] Interestingly, Medawar says nothing about Teilhard's reflections on the problem of evil at the close of *Le phénomène humain*.

Had Teilhard known more of Whitehead's thought, perhaps he would have recognized the affinities between the Englishman's speculative philosophy and his own hyperphysics. Although he admired Whitehead, his familiarity with his work was limited.[74] Teilhard says that *Le phénomène humain* is to be read not as metaphysics but as a scientific treatise. He realizes, however, that when science, philosophy, and religion express a "vision that extends to the whole" they tend to converge, analogous to meridians meeting at the pole of a sphere (HP, 1–2; PM, 30). Science thus extended beyond (*hyper*) its common field of inquiry becomes "hyperphysics" without quite being metaphysics defined as the study of "the profound domain of being" (HP, 1; PM, 29). In an early essay, as we have seen, Teilhard characterized this scientifically informed vision of the whole as being below (*infra*) metaphysics, "infra-metaphysics." Thus, Teilhard located his project in the interstice of science and traditional metaphysics. In the last decade of his life, Teilhard was more comfortable speaking of his views as metaphysical—thus, his "metaphysics of union"—but always anchored in the plane of experience and science. Like Medawar, he would accept no hypothesis that was incompatible with the deliverances of science or that was abhorrent to reason. On the other hand, Teilhard placed "the human phenomenon" in the center of his investigations, always endeavoring to preserve the integrity of the Within as something to be accounted for, not to be explained away. For this reason, he refused, as it were, to turn the Within *inside out* so as to make it a disguised form of the Without. Teilhard does not pretend to solve the problems of mind and body that so engage philosophers, but he insists, in good scientific fashion, to preserve "the phenomena" of the psychic as it appears across the full spectrum of the evolution of species. He believed that this developmental perspective, which was an essential element in his geological and paleontological research, and which is at the heart of evolutionary thinking, could not help but cast new light on the ancient question of the place of the human in nature.

## Points to Ponder

- ◆ While Teilhard worked as a scientist, he was developing a metaphysical framework to understand evolutionary development. His religious order repeatedly denied his requests to publish this work and they encouraged him to stick to science and to avoid philosophy and theology.

- ◆ Teilhard's reputation as a first-rate scientist should be kept in mind in assessing Medawar's review, for Medawar seems as keen on belittling Teilhard as a scientist as he does in assessing his ideas.

- ◆ Teilhard explains thermodynamics as teaching that "in the process of every physicochemical transformation, a fraction of the available energy is irremediably 'entropized,' lost, that is, in the form of heat." He goes on to say, "from the real evolutionary perspective, in the course of every synthesis something is definitively burned up to pay for it." He also understood, however, that the second law is not an explanation of the tendency of the universe to arrange itself into ever-more-complex wholes.

- ◆ Teilhard's hypothesis is that the appearance through geologic time of increasingly complex organisms with increasingly rich inner lives is the clue to evolution's direction.

- ◆ When Teilhard spoke of "evolution" he seems to have had in mind, at a minimum, the twin ideas that (a) nature's processes must be understood developmentally—what a thing is cannot be understood apart from the processes that gave rise to it, and (b) the order in which things appear in time throughout the cosmos are also the order in which they are created—hence, the cosmos is, in truth, a cosmogenesis.

- ◆ The world is also converging toward greater complexity and interiority.

◆ By identifying the temporal process with the order of creation, not only does Teilhard reject the idea of treating things as "completely made," he also calls into question the traditional idea of divine creation as an *eternal* act distinguishable from temporal processes.

## Questions for Discussion

1. How does this essay highlight Teilhard as a "mutational" thinker?

2. What is the relationship between science and metaphysics, as Teilhard perceived it?

3. Has Medawar's bias distorted Teilhard as a serious thinker? How can we move beyond this bias?

## Notes

1. Pierre Teilhard de Chardin, *Le rayonnement d'une amitié: Correspondance avec la famille Bégouën (1922–1955)*, ed. Michel Hermans and Pierre Sauvage (Brusseles: Lessius, 2011), 167; the letter is dated May 9, 1940.

2. Edward J. Larson and Larry Witham, "Leading Scientists Still Reject God," *Nature* 394 (1998): 313.

3. Sam Harris, "Science is in the Details," *New York Times*, July 26, 2009; see the expanded version at http://www.samharris.org.

4. David Scharfenberg, "Ken Miller Just Can't Win," *Boston Phoenix*, March 3, 2010. http://thephoenix.com.

5. Peter Medawar, *Memoir of a Thinking Radish* (New York: Oxford University Press, 1988), 141. Medawar's review is republished in his book *Pluto's Republic* (New York: Oxford University Press, 1982), 242–51.

6. Daniel Dennett, *Darwin's Dangerous Idea: Evolution and the Meanings of Life* (New York: Simon & Schuster, 1995), 32; Richard Dawkins, *A Devil's Chaplain: Reflections on Hope, Lies, Science, and Love* (Boston: Houghton Mifflin, 2003), 196; Simon Blackburn, *The Oxford Dictionary of Philosophy*, 2nd rev. ed. (New York: Oxford University Press, 2008), 359.

7. W. Henry Kenny, *A Path through Teilhard's Phenomenon* (Dayton, OH: Pflaum, 1970), 32.

8. Robert J. O'Connell, *Teilhard's Vision of the Past: The Making of a Method* (New York: Fordham University Press, 1982), 1.

9. Amir D. Aczel, *The Jesuit and the Skull: Teilhard de Chardin, Evolution, and the Search for Peking Man* (New York: Riverhead, 2007).

10. George B. Barbour, *In the Field with Teilhard de Chardin* (New York: Herder & Herder, 1965).

11. André Billy, "Un grand poète à demi clandestin," *Le Figaro Littéraire*, August 5, 1950.

12. *L'Evolution Rédemptrice du P. Teilhard de Chardin* (Paris: Cèdre, 1950); Louis Cognet, *Le Père Teilhard de Chardin, et la pensée contemporaine* (Paris: Au Portulan, chez Flammarion, 1952).

13. Donald W. Viney, "Teilhard: Le Philosophe malgré l'Église," in *Rediscovering Teilhard's Fire*, ed. Kathleen Duffy (Philadelphia: Saint Joseph's University Press, 2010), 86, n. 24.

14. Pierre Leroy, ed., *Letters from My Friend Teilhard de Chardin 1948–1955*, trans. Mary Lukas (New York: Paulist Press, 1980), 131.

15. P. Teilhard de Chardin, *Le phénomène humain* (Paris: Éditions du Seuil, 1955), 10.

16. Medawar, *Pluto's Republic*, 245.

17. Medawar, *Pluto's Republic*, 250.

18. Medawar, *Pluto's Republic*, 242.

19. Stephen Jay Gould, *Hen's Teeth and Horse's Toes* (New York: W. W. Norton, 1983), chaps. 16 and 17.

20. Dawkins, *A Devils's Chaplain*, 198.

21. See Thomas M. King, "Teilhard and Piltdown," in *Teilhard and the Unity of Knowledge*, ed. Thomas M. King and James F. Salmon (Ramsey, NJ: Paulist, 1983), 159–69; see also John Evangelist Walsh, *Unraveling Piltdown* (New York: Random House, 1996).

22. Medawar, *Pluto's Republic*, 210.

23. Peter Medawar, *The Limits of Science* (New York: Oxford University Press, 1984), 6.

24. Medawar, *Pluto's Republic*, 242, 243.

25. Medawar, *Pluto's Republic*, 244.

26. Peter Medawar, *The Hope of Progress: A Scientist Looks at Problems in Philosophy, Literature and Science* (Garden City, NY: Anchor, 1972), 20.

27. Medawar, *Pluto's Republic*, 244.

28. Medawar, *Pluto's Republic*, 247.

29. Medawar, *Pluto's Republic*, 249.

30. See Theodosius Dobzhansky, "The Teilhardian Synthesis," in his *The Biology of Ultimate Concern* (New York: New American Library, 1969), 108–37; see also Edward O. Dodson, *The Phenomenon of Man Revisited: A Biological Viewpoint on Teilhard de Chardin* (New York: Columbia University Press, 1984); see, finally, the essays by James F. Salmon, Daryl P. Domning, and Ludovicio Galleni in *Rediscovering Teilhard's Fire*.

31. Medawar, *Pluto's Republic*, 246.

32. Medawar, *Pluto's Republic*, 250.

33. David J. Chalmers, *The Conscious Mind: In Search of a Fundamental Theory* (New York: Oxford University Press, 1996). Chalmers is the subject editor for the philosophy of mind for the online *Stanford Encyclopedia of Philosophy*; he maintains a list of all *SEP* articles on the subject (http://consc.net). Currently, this is the most complete source on the Internet for following contemporary discussions in the philosophy of mind.

34. Claude Cuénot, *Teilhard de Chardin, A Biographical Study*, ed. René Hague, trans. Vincent Colimore (Baltimore: Helicon, 1965), 256.

35. Alfred North Whitehead, *Process and Reality: An Essay in Cosmology*, corrected edition, ed. David Ray Griffin and Donald W. Sherburne (New York: Free Press, 1978), 289.

36. For views of consciousness or sentience that are not unlike those of Teilhard see the following: Galen Strawson, *Consciousness and Its Place in Nature: Does Physicalism Entail Panpsychism?*, ed. Anthony Freeman (Charlottesville, VA: Imprint Academic, 2006); Charles Hartshorne, "Physics and Psychics: The Place of Mind in Nature," in *Mind*

*in Nature: Essays on the Interface of Science and Philosophy*, ed. John B. Cobb Jr. and David Ray Griffin (Washington, DC: University Press of America, 1977), 89–96; Charles Hartshorne, *Creative Experiencing: A Philosophy of Freedom*, ed. Donald Wayne Viney and Jincheol O (Albany: State University of New York Press, 2011), chap. 6; and Thomas Nagel, *Mind and Cosmos: Why the Materialist Neo-Darwinian Conception of Nature Is Almost Certainly False* (New York: Oxford University Press, 2012). Interestingly, Michael Ruse criticizes Nagel for being backward in his thinking about evolution (a point with which Teilhard would probably agree), but he is friendly to the idea that Darwinian evolution cannot give an adequate explanation of consciousness. See "Philosophy's Strain of Unevolved Thinking," *The Chronicle Review* (November 30, 2012): B 4–5.

37. Medawar, *Pluto's Republic*, 248.

38. Medawar, *The Limits of Science*, 79.

39. Medawar, *Pluto's Republic*, 248.

40. John O'Manique, *Energy in Evolution* (London: Garnstone, 1969). For a more recent assessment of Teilhard's views on thermodynamics see Harold J. Morowitz, Nicole Schmitz-Moormann, and James Salmon, "Teilhard's Two Energies," in *The Legacy of Pierre Teilhard de Chardin*, ed. James Salmon and John Farina (New York: Paulist, 2011), 150–66.

41. Alfred North Whitehead, *The Function of Reason* (Boston: Beacon Press, 1958), 24.

42. Paul Davies, *The Last Three Minutes: Conjectures about the Ultimate Fate of the Universe* (New York: Basic Books, 1994), 117.

43. Medawar, *Pluto's Republic*, 248.

44. Simon Conway Morris, *Life's Solution: Inevitable Humans in a Lonely Universe* (New York: Cambridge University Press, 2004).

45. Dennett, *Darwin's Dangerous Idea*, 320–32.

46. Eugenie Scott, acceptance speech for the American Humanist Association's 1998 Isaac Asimov Science Award: www://ncse.com.

47. Medawar, *Pluto's Republic*, 243.

48. Medawar, *Pluto's Republic*, 242, 249.

49. Medawar, *Pluto's Republic*, 209. Medawar took pride in reading the three volumes of *Principia Mathematica* of Whitehead and Russell and following its proofs (Medawar, *Thinking Radish*, 64–65). He elsewhere speaks of "the extreme length, leaden prose and general air of joyless learning characteristic of the principal writings of Alfred North Whitehead" (*Limits of Science*, xi). This is a truly singular judgment. Medawar's description fits the *Principia Mathematica* and the second chapter of *Process and Reality*. Otherwise, Whitehead's writing is of average length (as in *Science and the Modern World* and *Adventures of Ideas*) and often quite brief (as in the three books *Symbolism, Religion in the Making*, and *The Function of Reason*); A. H. Johnson's collection of Whitehead's sayings demonstrates that Whitehead's prose was very often neither leaden nor joyless. See A. H. Johnson, ed., *The Wit and Wisdom of Alfred North Whitehead* (Boston: Beacon Press, 1947).

50. Whitehead, *Process and Reality*, 3.

51. Hartshorne, *Creative Experiencing*, 50.

52. Whitehead, *Process and Reality*, 290.

53. Pierre Teilhard de Chardin, "Homme," in *Dictionnaire Apologétique de la Foi Catholique contenant les Preuves de la Vérité de la Religion et les Réponses aux Objections tirées des Sciences humaines*, 4th ed., ed. Adhémar d'Alès, vol. 2 (Paris: Gabriel Beauchesne, 1911), 505.

54. Teilhard de Chardin, "Homme," 506–8.

55. Pierre Teilhard de Chardin, *Lettres Intimes de Teilhard de Chardin à Auguste Valensin, Bruno de Solages, et Henri de Lubac 1919–1955,* ed. Henri de Lubac (Paris: Aubier Montaigne, 1972), 295.

56. T. V. Fleming, "Two Unpublished Letters of Teilhard," *Heythrop Journal* 6, no. 1 (1965): 42.

57. Barbour, *In the Field with Teilhard de Chardin,* 110.

58. Teilhard, *Lettres Intimes de Teilhard de Chardin,* 269.

59. Whitehead, *Process and Reality,* 8.

60. Madeleine Barthélemy-Madaule, *Bergson et Teilhard de Chardin* (Paris: Éditions du Seuil, 1963), 568.

61. Fleming, "Two Unpublished Letters of Teilhard," 41.

62. Barbour, *In the Field with Teilhard de Chardin,* 130.

63. Leroy, *Letters from My Friend,* 56.

64. Medawar, *Pluto's Republic,* 23.

65. Medawar, *Thinking Radish,* 97.

66. Medawar, *Pluto's Republic,* 22–23.

67. Medawar, *Pluto's Republic,* 210.

68. Medawar, *The Limits of Science,* 92.

69. Medawar, *The Limits of Science,* 88.

70. Medawar, *The Limits of Science,* 93.

71. Medawar, *The Limits of Science,* 98.

72. For my responses to the new atheists see Donald Wayne Viney, review of *The God Delusion* by Richard Dawkins, *The Midwest Quarterly* 48, no. 4 (2007): 602–5; "Atheism's New Prescription: The End of Faith *and* of Reason" (concerning Sam Harris's *The End of Faith* and *Letter to a Christian Nation*), *Vital Theology Newsletter* 4, no. 1 (February 2007): 3, 7; and "How Not to Be an Atheist: a Neoclassical Response to the New Atheism," *Concrescence, Australasian Journal of Process Thought* (2008): 7–22.

73. Medawar, *Pluto's Republic,* 93, 97.

74. Donald Wayne Viney, "Teilhard and Process Philosophy Redux," *Process Studies* 35, no. 1 (2006): 14–15.

*Part Three*

# SPIRITUALITY AND ETHICS FOR A NEW MILLENNIUM

To lose oneself in the unfathomable,
to plunge into the inexhaustible,
to find peace in the incorruptible,
to be absorbed in the definite immensity,
to offer oneself to the fire . . . and
to give one's deepest self to that
whose depth has no end.

—TEILHARD DE CHARDIN
*The Divine Milieu*

## Chapter 9

# AN EVOLVING CHRISTIAN MORALITY

*Eppur si muove*

## EDWARD VACEK, SJ

For Pierre Teilhard de Chardin, moral living is to live inspired by a mystical intuition of a grand historical synthesis in love. Teilhard's thought was unconstrained by any academic demands to fit in with the accepted canon of moral theology. Indeed, he proposes that morality itself should undergo an evolution because the nature of being human itself is undergoing substantial change (FM, 15, 17). As Teilhard reframed the ethical project, he stunningly turned natural law into Christian ethics, autonomous agency into responsive cooperation, the requirement of conformity into creativity, and a focus on self-fulfillment into building both the world and—most provocatively—God.

The strengths of Teilhard's reflections derive from thinking in terms of cosmic history. Teilhard reckons time in aeons, not days. His Google Earth view is set to find large forests, not trees. Rather than focusing on this or that Sally and Sam, he locates humanity within a vision of the cosmos. In the King James Version, Proverbs 29:18 tells us that without wisdom, the people perish; and Teilhard's provocative vision helps Christians to live in this new era. Most of us rarely focus on the big picture of evolution as we go about our days. We don't attend to the fact that our lives belong to an erratic continuum that began thirteen billion years ago and will end who knows how long from now, a time when the cosmos is destined to dissipate into cold death. In practice we have little need to know that evolutionary history when we make our beds, eat, work, talk, and in various ways go through our day. Still, we are reflective animals. We can ask large questions about the meaning of our lives in the cosmos. That is where Teilhard begins (SC, 42; CE, 78, 97, 11–12). His primary concern was to redeem the meaning of Christianity, and indeed human life, after science had exposed our insignificance relative to time and to space. Human and religious concepts have existential and pragmatic truth for us if they are coherent with the meaning of the evolving universe (CE, 99, 111–12, 154, 212–13, 218–19; AE, 231–43; FM, 49; HE, 141–42, 162). Post-Darwin, Christianity needed and still needs to be rethought. In particular, we have to ask, what changes does evolution require us to make in fundamental moral theology? Teilhard attempted an answer by interpreting scientific evidence in terms of religious experience. I will discuss the way this affected his views on seven major theological concerns: (1) God and creation; (2) divine causality; (3) cooperation with God; (4) building the world; (5) developing the self; (6) fulfilling God; and (7) in time for eternity.

## Christ Evolves the World

For Teilhard, as is well known, the overall meaning of evolution points to Omega which, in turn, he identifies with Christ (SC, 54). He postulates that evolution's Omega is leading an original chaotic multiple toward various unities such as particles, elements, and molecules, on to ever-more-complex unities such as carrots, cats, and Cubans (SC, 45, 58). As a unifying center, Teilhard thinks, Omega explains why, in spite of entropy, evolution has progressively produced higher and higher forms of life. What is important for this essay is not whether this final goal should be called Omega, but rather the challenging connection Teilhard makes between this evolutionary process and God.

Citing Colossians 3:11, Teilhard connected evolution with God in Christ. Waxing metaphysical, he holds that God is present in all things and is "the fundamental and substantial unity of the universe" (CE, 22–23). Through a random, protracted process, Christ attracts a primordial multiplicity into various "incomplete and hierarchically arranged substances linked together in sequence." The path to greater being and hence greater goodness is, for Teilhard, through unions. For example, hydrogen and oxygen can unite to make water. Teilhard focused on those cases where substances find "in this relationship the fullness of their individual differentiation and power to act." He then extended this insight to the God-world relationship, giving the name pantheism ("panentheism" better fits his thought) to describe a love union between God and creature that preserves and accentuates their differences (CE, 56–75, 171–72, 184–85). God is in all and all is in God (SC, 52–61).

It is helpful to understand the kind of religious thinking that goes on in Ignatian spirituality that influences Teilhard's theology. Religious people are those who see life in relation to God (HU, 124; CE, 29–30; DM, 65–67). That is, humans who are graced with a religious sensibility connect at least some things such as sacraments or certain persons or places with God. Humans who are deeply religious, that is, lovers of God, want to see all things in relation to God. Teilhard was such a religious person, inclined to "find God in all things," including evolution. He does not assume that we must somehow make ourselves become related to God. Rather, we are already really related to Christ, just as we are already really a part of the human community and already really part of the evolutionary process (SC, 75). These are not "voluntary associations," even though we can resist or reject our membership in them. These relationships, however, are only partially complete, and we must do our part to complete them. That is the central ethical task. Christian ethics is not at its base a matter of "Do good and avoid evil." Even less is it a matter of "Fulfill your human nature" or "Seek happiness" or "Respect human rights." Rather, it is a relational task: we are to contribute to our relationship with Christ who is building the universe (CE, 115). The most fundamental ethical norm then becomes fidelity to this religious relationship.

What is important in this understanding of creation is that God is involved with the evolution of the world. Far from being only a thirteen-billion-year prelude to humanity's arrival, the world is, as far as creation itself is concerned, the central activity of God. God's creative activity now leads humans toward unity and mutual influence, whereby "they become spiritualised" (SC, 52; HE, 145-60). Since Christ is at work in evolution, ordinary human activity itself has a vast religious significance. All our activities are part of God's grand project that is cosmic history. God's activity of fostering evolution continues in ourselves. Its movement toward ever-greater being takes place through our free engagement (HE, 105-6). Hence, our ethical life fits within the evolutionary framework that is directed by Christ toward a grand summation in Christ.

## God's Attractive Activity

The type of divine causality that Teilhard points to is intriguing. In the modern era, especially with the rise of science, we tend to think of causality as efficient causality. One body exerts force on another body. If, accordingly, we think of God's activity, then we will tend to look for God's activity as occasional interventions when God contravenes nature's laws. For example, the Catholic tradition held that organic life could not come from inorganic materials, and it still holds that the human soul cannot come from the evolution of an animal body. Hence God occasionally has to intervene first to introduce life into the evolutionary stream and later to create each human soul. (Outside of the evolutionary process, God is also thought to cause occasional "miracles" such as at Lourdes and innumerable daily interventions all over the globe in response to prayer). For Teilhard the history of evolution indicates that—without any special intervention by God—organic life and human thought and beneficial events arise naturally from the interactions of matter (CE, 19-24). The question then arises how God is involved in the actual process of evolution.

Teilhard did not envision God's causality in an interventionist way. The distinctive way he did depict God's actions is quite novel. He describes God as an attracting cause (HU, 84, 119; DM, 133-34). He speaks as if God were ahead of us in time. Let me propose one way we can understand his image.

God is ahead of us in the sense that, for a religiously sensitive person, a good possibility is felt to be an invitation from God. The possibility of, for example, a new child or a new kind of telephone exists as a possibility in the present, but it points to the future when it may become real. When we love God and have an ongoing historical relationship with God, such possibilities may be experienced as a next step to which God invites us. Process theologians sometimes describe this as an experience of God acting to lure us or as God's persuasive power.

Usually, ethics concerns itself with our own agency. Our autonomy means that we and not others, including God, are the origin of our actions. When Teilhard reflects on human experience, he discovers that this is not an accurate description (FM, 194). If we are attentive, we notice that whenever we act there is an aspect of response. For example, a new job opens up, and we apply. We are persons who are attracted to the good, whether that good is actual or only possible. As I have noted above, the religiously sensitive mind sees this responsive activity in relation to God. That is, when we reflect within our relation to God, we discover that God's invitation precedes our human autonomy. This point is not asserted as a way of protecting God's sovereignty or asserting a doctrine of the primacy of grace, which are the usual reasons for an anti-Pelagian claim of God's priority. Rather it is a reflection on ordinary moral experience, as experienced by a religiously attuned person. We experience ourselves responding to Christ (CE, 152; FM, 75, 93).

This depiction of the future as various inviting possibilities helps us to see how often human agency is directed to what is not yet real. Moral decisions are commonly about who we should become, what structures we should create, and so forth. In this sense, most moral choices are exercises of hope. Unlike efficient causality, the attractive power of future possibility leaves us free to assent. Our freedom consents or dissents to an opportunity that presents itself. Thus, if we are lovers of God, our experience is that God may be inviting us to take the next step. In this way, God's invitation activates rather than usurps our freedom. In every good decision we make, we are also consenting to God.

Within this kind of moral experience, it becomes clearer why love is central to Christian moral living. The primary love of our lives, insofar as we are religious, is the love of God. Within this love, we are moved to understand all things triadically: in relation to the God we love, to ourselves as lovers of God, and to our love relationship with God. Love of its nature is directed to the greater value. In Teilhard's language, it is directed to more being (PM, 249, 265; SC, 40). This being attracted to the real or potential good of the beloved is an aspect of love that is frequently overlooked. Love and emotions generally consist not only of an outgoing affirmation of the beloved, but also a receptive aspect in the lover. In older understandings of emotions, the receptive or being-attracted (or repulsed) aspect was better understood, and hence they were called passions. Teilhard recognized that good possibilities are in this sense attractive. These attractions, seen in relation to God, are experienced as invitations from God to love creation, that is, to enhance its good. God, as it were, is in the future beckoning us.

In this framework, moral experience is not a matter of an external obligation imposed on ourselves by an authority, not even by God as supreme authority. Neither is it, following Kant, an obligation we impose upon ourselves at the risk of being otherwise inconsistent. Experiences of obligation usually arise because of some resistance in ourselves to what is good. The experience of obligation likely indicates our lack of saintliness. For the good person, in contrast, moral experience is primarily one of welcomed opportunity. The commandments become invitations from a God who loves us, that is, invites us to what is good or discourages us from evil. More broadly, attraction toward the good is experienced as grace.

An invitation, of course, is usually much less clear or certain than a divine command. Thus, for Teilhard, morality took the form of much more open-ended daring than would have been possible if morality were for him a matter of obeying commandments or conforming to a pregiven nature. Instead, moral living involves consenting to attractive possibilities in the hope of creating something new and better. Of course, this morality of invitation also has more possibilities of failure, since the future cannot be known and a cascade of contingencies can frustrate the best plans.

Not every invitation or attraction should be pursued. The attraction of a possible good should not blind us to the evil which might be involved in achieving that good or which is collateral with its achievement. We should avoid a radical consequentialism or social Darwinism. Since evolution has reached a new reflective stage in us human beings, we ought not continue the brutal patterns of evolution. That is, our reflective love should welcome only opportunities that foster personalistic progress. Such progress will require attention to the details of actual moral living in addition to the big picture (cf. SC, 53). Similarly, we Christians as disciples will also want to be attentive to the Jesus who lived a distinctive life in Nazareth and Jerusalem (cf. CE, 53, 101, 181; DM, 117). Thus, in addition to adhering to the cosmic Christ named in some New Testament epistles, we will also learn from the Gospel accounts detailing Jesus's life.

## Moral Living Is Cooperating Out of Love

Teilhard's own approach to moral theory contrasts with three alternatives that have been standard in Western Christianity. The first, the juridical model of ethics, is that in which law plays the dominant role. More commonly, this style of ethical reflection is called divine command ethics: an action is right or wrong depending on what God commands, and obedience is the only morally relevant feature of an action (SC, 67–68). In an extreme example, Abraham is right to try to kill Isaac because God commands him to do so. That is, what would otherwise be wrong, namely, slaughter of one's own innocent son and with him the promise of endless future generations, is in fact right because God commands it. Both Augustine and Luther affirmed divine command ethics because of its strong biblical grounding. Teilhard rejected it.

A second kind of ethics, also rejected by Teilhard, focuses on human rights. This type of ethics springs up because our dignity as human beings is often violated, and so we need to be protected against each other (HE, 106). Thus we claim a right to life, a right to privacy, a right to free expression, and the like. These rights prevent others from encroaching on our space. Teilhard worried that highlighting such rights would put obstacles in the way of the most important part of moral living, namely, how we can love and support one another and how we must make sacrifices of our lives to build the future.

A third alternative has been classical natural law. This type of ethics insists that human beings must act in accordance with their own nature which was fixed by God at the time God created Adam and Eve. Since Teilhard understood human beings in light of the haphazard process of evolution, he was not disposed to think that human nature manifested some God-given perfect plan. Rather our nature is the product of chance and law, leading to new unities and open to ever further evolution. The process of nature instead points only in a direction toward ever-more-spiritual being. We need not detain ourselves with questions on the adequacy of Teilhard's view of these three kinds of ethics. What is important here is the ethic that Teilhard offers as an alternative: an ethic of loving cooperation directed at growth (HE, 106–7; AE, 51–53, 71, 119).

This new ethic, an ethics of love, might be called "natural law" where the term "natural" refers to the processes of evolution. Thus, it is natural that species evolve through synthesis or love of others. In this sense the traditional demand that we follow our supposedly fixed human nature could well be a failure to follow nature's law. That is, human morality must continue the evolutionary process and be open to further development. The criterion for whether a development is a positive development is whether the new is "more being" brought about by love. This is what God has been doing in evolution. It is our great dignity that we can continue God's activity of love. We do so when we cooperate with God in furthering this process (SC, 32). In terms of Christian ethics, the core insight Teilhard offers is this: What we human beings do to make a better world coheres with what Christ has been doing and is doing and will do. In other words, our ordinary and our extraordinary activities can be ways of cooperating in Christ's activity. This point becomes clearer when contrasted with two positions that Teilhard rightly considered insufficient. The first is that the only Christian parts of our day are those that are explicitly devoted to prayer or the sacraments. The second is that God cares only about our religious souls, so activities such as work and play are religiously valuable only to the degree they enhance our religious soul.

While the classical Protestant question asked whether (deeply sinful) Christians can be ethical, Teilhard asked whether ordinary ethical living can be (distinctly) Christian. Many Catholic theologians, following the natural-law tradition, had answered no. That is, there is nothing specifically Christian about our moral lives. Doing one's job is just a human activity, whether carried out by an atheist or by a believer. Normal ethical living is secular. It may be lived by persons who are Christian, but that does not make the work itself Christian. Teilhard's religious understanding rejects this split. The work that both believers and nonbelievers do is itself the work that Christ is doing. Therefore, objectively, all ethical living is Christian. In the Christian dispensation, all ethical activity is basically cooperating with God. This thesis has four implications which we will explore in the remainder of this essay. First, we enact our love for God by cooperating with God in the building up of the world around us, including especially the lives of other human beings. Second, we cooperate by developing ourselves. Third, we contribute by our actions to God's own development. Fourth, since our actions are related to God, whatever is good in them belongs to eternity.

## Building the World

Much of the Catholic tradition considered contemplation to be the highest human activity. Work had a much lower status and dealt largely with main-tenance activities that provide enough of life's necessities to get us to life's one truly crucial moment, namely, our death. Contrary to this view, Teilhard argued that the work we do throughout our lives to improve our world is the primary exercise of our Christianity. Our ethical life is a productive activity. Since God has been involved in evolution, our love for God requires cooperat-ing with God's activity in building up the world (DM, 60–62; HU, 92–93). This ethical activity of building the world is itself an enactment of grace since in it we are united with God. There is no need for a separate sphere called "super-natural" (SC, 17; CE, 127, 152–53; DM, 65–67; AE, 264). In an older spirituality, the supernatural was sought in certain practices such as receiving the sacra-ments or praying a novena. Life in this supernatural realm was soul building, and what we accomplished in daily life was in itself religiously irrelevant. To recall an old spirituality example, if we were being obedient, watering a dead stick was as good as planting a fruit-bearing tree. Our obedience, not what we accomplished, was all that religiously mattered. Our intentions decided heaven or hell; and heaven or hell, not the earth, was what mattered. Rather, for Teilhard, since God is active in building the world, it is religiously important that we cooperate in this project. Agnostics cooperate unknowingly. Believers cooperate as an act of adoration. For both, "The vital, organizing influence of the universe . . . is essentially grace" (SC, 57; DM, 65–66).

Although he continued to use the word "supernatural," Teilhard often did so in scare quotes. Indeed, the language of supernatural, like that of original sin, becomes superfluous, even counterproductive. Original sin implies that there once was some perfect human state from which we have fallen, whereas in fact evolution has been, overall, a matter of progressing toward, not away from, some mythic Garden of Eden. Similarly, supernatural seems to imply that God has not been involved in the natural processes of evolution and that God now intervenes. Instead, God's attractive invitation has been present from the first, leading creation by natural processes of continuity and discontinuity. According to evolution, if we want to understand humans, we must study first the activity of animals. According to Christianity, if we want to understand God, we must study the activity of good humans. God's activity is present whenever humans are enticed into committing themselves to improve the world. Sanctification, for Teilhard, means freely participating in this stream of life that is ascending toward fullness. Fullness is a relational term, meaning to be incorporated into God's evolving world. As Teilhard writes, "We are spiritualised by being carried along by the spiritualisation of all things. We are united to Christ by entering into communion with all men. We will be saved by an option that has chosen the whole" (SC, 77).

Because of his emphasis on the whole, Teilhard was a harbinger of ethical currents that are taking prominence in our time. Buzzwords are globalization, solidarity, ecology, and the common good. Each of these terms makes clear—in a way that older emphases on divine commands, natural law, or human rights did not—that the ethical task refers to building communities, the whole human race, and the earth itself. Teilhard promoted a "sense" of the human. The term sense refers to a feeling that we already belong to these groups and that through our actions we promote or retard their flourishing. We foster these groups not simply because doing so will help fulfill our own human nature, but because they belong to the evolving creation. As such they may even be worthy of losing ourselves or dying for.

We must exercise our own creativity if God is to achieve what God intends. Without our effort, God not only will not but cannot bring about "thy kingdom come." This is a crucial and, of course, controversial point. Whether one says with those who propose a kenotic Christology that God has chosen to humble God's own self and not intervene in the world, or whether one says in line with the direction of Teilhard's thought that creaturely activity can be done only by creatures and not by God independently of those creatures, the moral upshot is that human activity is now necessary for the building of the world. No carpenter, no house. Without human beings, God cannot accomplish what God wants to accomplish (CE, 28, 31–34, 179; DM, 62–64, 85).

The point can be extended. God not only needs human labor to build stable skyscrapers and dig deep oil wells. God also plans through us. That is, God uses and thereby depends on our thoughts and affections in figuring out how to build the earth (CE, 160; DM, 64). Put more sharply, the will of God is not an antecedent plan to be discovered by us, but rather a plan to be cocreated through the exercise of our own minds and hearts. Discerning the will of God essentially requires thinking our own best thoughts. God speaks to us in our own voice. In the best run of things, our thoughts are God's thoughts and our ways are God's ways. This claim is not as surprising as it may first seem. It has always been held, of course, that we can do nothing without God. As Teilhard occasionally noted, we are secondary causes who depend on God as primary cause (CE, 25–35). Even more, we cannot save ourselves. But what usually has not been said, perhaps out of reverence for the primacy of God, is that God cannot save us without our own activity. Our unwillingness to cooperate with God is the meaning of sin. Unless salvation is understood just juridically—the judge pronounces us innocent whether we are or not—we must freely cooperate with our own salvation (DM, 141; CE, 131–32). To be saved is to love God, and we cannot love God unwillingly. Our willing cooperation is our salvation.

## Developmental Ethics

Teilhard described his ethics as a *morale du mouvement*. This perspective powerfully jolts previous systems of ethics into the recognition that they have failed adequately to see that humanity, human beings, various groups, and indeed God develop in time (HE, 105–7; SC, 51, 69, 76–77; DM, 108). In this section, I focus on individual human development. Teilhard's proposal is an ethics for people who are in transit. It does not presuppose that any of our decisions could be perfect. One standard natural law position has been some version of a response to the question, What is my nature? The natural law ethicist describes the nature of sex or of speech or of religion, and that nature becomes the moral norm. The only relevant question, then, is whether people freely follow the norms. If they do not, they are morally at fault. They sin. Teilhard's thought modifies this pattern in two ways. His understanding of evolution as still in process implies that every human decision is incomplete, and his understanding of history means that norms may have to change as history develops. Let us briefly consider these two developmental points.

It was usually assumed by traditional natural law ethicists that persons could act with full knowledge and freedom. To be sure, it was admitted that sometimes people are less than fully knowledgeable or free, but the presumption was that this was a deviation from the normal pattern. Commonly, moral theology held that after the age of reason people usually have the full freedom that is required for a mortal sin. Excessive fear or passion might diminish this freedom on occasion, but in general we normally act with full freedom. By contrast, in a morality of movement, full freedom at best is rare. Indeed, our freedom and knowledge themselves develop over time, and in practice they are always incomplete. What is morally required, then, is not that we act in a fully autonomous and knowledgeable way. Rather, we are responsible for developing these capacities. We exercise them in a particular case to the degree we are able but also to the degree that is appropriate. We should not pretend we ever are fully free or knowledgeable, and we don't even have to try to be our full human selves when we engage in most daily acts, for example, brushing our teeth or shopping for groceries.

Secondly, the norms proposed by moral theology often admitted no change over time. For example, when a young boy pleasurably fondles his genitals, moral theory said that he was thereby committing what objectively was one of the gravest of sins. There was no place for saying that the act of the boy was age-appropriate behavior and not objectively sinful at all. In the older account, taking account of his immaturity might be approved as a pastoral accommodation, but it would not allow any change in what was objectively wrong in itself. The act was intrinsically wrong. In an evolution-sensitive ethics, only the next step in moral maturing is usually what is objectively required. The lad must develop in his sexuality.

Teilhard, of course, was especially concerned to show how history makes an enormous difference in the norms that guide our moral decisions, for example, in assessing the social-justice standards of a given society. If lack of primary schools was once morally acceptable, graduate schools are becoming necessary in more and more countries. If underpopulation once determined sexual ethics, it should do so no more. The use of some form of birth control, as even Vatican II acknowledged, might now be morally required. Pushed further, Teilhard was open to the possibility, indeed, the likelihood that we would have to develop through genetics better human beings, that is, human beings with either enhanced or new capabilities. His exuberant maxim was, "we must try *everything,*" and in his enthusiasm he could praise unlimited power (HE, 127, 108, 134–35; SC, 32; PM, 282). Thus, if a gene were to be discovered that enabled people to be more generous, that gene, all else being equal, should become not only available to all but required of all.

## Christogenesis

If we love God, we also want God to be enhanced. In the tradition, this enhancement was said to be impossible. Following Aristotle, it was thought that we should work for our own happiness and that we could contribute at best only to the external glory of God, that is, to God's fame. But if we can do nothing for God, our love is stunted. We cannot love God with our whole mind and strength. In the older tradition, moral living was necessarily self-centered, though not in the sense of being selfish. Rather, the only one we could ultimately help was ourselves, since building our souls could not be done by another. And so eudaimonistic ethics made our own happiness both the goal and norm of our ethical activity.

Lovers want to do something for the one they love, and that includes the God we love. But the older tradition insisted that we and our work could make no difference to God since God is incapable of enrichment. A perfect God cannot become more perfect. However, in the process theology that seems to be present in Teilhard's thought, we and what we do make a difference to God (SC, 180–81). God takes it all in. Hence our worldly successes make a difference to God. They are important to God and not just to us or to our posterity. Christ/Omega is both intimate to all things and leading them to maximal unity. There is, Teilhard adds, "one single physical reality developing in the cosmos, one single monad" (SC, 52; DM, 114). Teilhard's Omega fills the role of the "consequent" aspect of God described by process theologians. God receives into God's self the good that occurs in creation. This process theology likewise developed in response to the discovery of evolution. On the one hand, as the classical tradition insisted, God is or has a transcendent aspect, and so God is not the culminating result of evolution. On the other hand, God is immanent in all things. Put poetically, Teilhard says, God "penetrates everything" (SC, 57). God thereby is also changed by the activities of creation, so the traditional doctrine of the immutability of God is no longer appropriate. That is, when God relates to the world, a real relation in God is created. For Teilhard, this meant that Omega is being modified through Christ's ongoing relationship to creation. In Christ, God is modified in time.

The supreme dignity of work, then, is that it is Christogenic (AE, 279; SC, 17; CE, 71–75, 177–79; DM, 61–62, 138–40; FM, 22). Whereas most biological evolutionists see human activity as, fundamentally, serving the propagation of genes, Teilhard sees this activity as contributing religiously to Christ's evolution. That is, part of God's being is to be related to all that is good. Where relationships are seen to be a genuine perfection, God must be maximally involved with all creatures. If God could not be really related to what goes on in creation, God would be less than the fullness of being. Our lives and our work therefore fill out God's relational self (CE, 182, 226, 239). Teilhard regularly worried that we would stop working if we thought that our work had no lasting significance. The greatest significance of our work is that it affects God's own relational life. When we contribute to the building of the world and to developing ourselves, we make a positive difference to God's life. Teilhard rightly notes that we should love humanity and the world. But his supreme theological claim is to suggest that we contribute to Christogenesis.

## Toward the Future, Out of the Past, in the Present's Eternity

Teilhard reversed the standard time frame used in Christian ethics. Most Catholic and Protestant moral theology has been in principle retrospective, harkening back to a primordial revelation given in the past. Catholics especially looked to Genesis, the story of the creation of Adam and Eve in the image and likeness of God. Or the practice has been to look to the historical Jesus to see in him the model of perfect humanity. Or the more philosophically inclined studied the book of human nature, assuming that, since our nature was created by God, we could discover God's own design for us in this book. Accordingly, it would be sacrilegious to presume that we could improve on the past since that would imply that our design would be better than God's. "Back to the past" is the watchword.

"Whatever it takes to get to the future" is Teilhard's maxim. Teilhard's emphasis on the future has the salutary feature of making us responsible for the future (AE, 210–13; FM, 18). It refutes the cynicism of "Why should I do something for posterity? What has posterity ever done for me?" In his holistic view, we are responsible for the future. Obviously, Teilhard's ethic is well suited for dealing with the environmental and resource issues that have become prominent in our time. Our responsibility for evolution requires more than passing on a world no worse than the one we have inherited. Rather, a morality of movement requires that we improve the world.

Evolution has given us an ever-better world, and we are responsible for continuing that creative enhancement. Of course, this better world will consist not primarily in more things and more material resources, but rather in increased personal capacities, greater religious devotion, and closer cooperation. Teilhard proposes an ethic based on evolving to the future. He sees human life as a drama whose glory is in its completion. Even in the midst of terrible tragedy, Teilhard was ever hopeful (SC, 82; FM, 140–48). Past evils can be turned into "happy faults," to use a theme of the Exultet sung at Easter. There remains to be considered a near-fatal twist in Teilhard's program, however. The unavoidable problem is that, for us individuals and for the rest of creation, the future is death (DM, 87–90). Teilhard acknowledged this problem when he wrote, "the whole task of the interior moral and mystical life may be reduced to two essential and complementary processes: to conquer the world, and to escape from it" (SC, 66). I have spoken at length here of the first. Now we must consider the second.

We should not live only in the present or, worse, only in some primordial past. We should also not live just from or for the future. We also need to be ethical for eternity. By this I do not mean that we should act ethically so that we can go to heaven. Rather, I refer to the eternal significance of what we do. The God ahead of us, inviting us to build our selves, one another, and the whole earth, is also the God above us, transcendent of time. Religious people have a sense of eternity that accompanies doing intrinsically good acts (HU, 130–31, 152). This includes doing good acts that may turn out to fail. What Tennyson wrote of human development, namely, "It is better to have loved and lost than never to have loved at all," also suggests to a religious mind the hope that all of our good actions will themselves be preserved in God who enables them.

Teilhard's profound theology of diminishment addresses this sense that we are with God, even when everything falls apart. Eternity here is not simply a Platonic realm of unchanging essences or ideal forms. Rather, like all human terms for God, the word "eternal" contains a negation of our earthly way of living. It connotes that God is not in time as we are in time (PM, 270; DM, 103). What happens in time to and through us does not disappear into a past that is no more. Rather, it is preserved in God. The experience that the God we meet in prayer and in history actually loves us indicates, as we have seen, that we make a difference to the eternal God. The hope, then, is that nothing good is lost. Even though each and every accomplishment we achieve will eventually become space dust, and that dust may itself dissipate into cold cosmic darkness, we hope that God will not let our efforts turn to nothing. We hope and we sense that all is preserved in God (PM, 270–75, 305; SC, 40–41; DM, 92; HE, 141–42, 162).

In conclusion, the big-picture issue introduced by the discovery of evolution presents a major challenge to Christian ethics. Teilhard rose to meet that challenge. He saw how evolution altered the meaning of what we are doing. Teilhard's cosmic synthesis offers a breathtaking response to scientific discoveries that perplex us still and demand a revision in the ultimate meaning of Christianity. His approach shows that our ordinary ethical life is Christian, that individual autonomy develops as it develops human history, that love leads not only to unity but to cooperative creativity, and that beyond self-fulfillment we are responsible for building both the world and God in eternity.

# Points to Ponder

♦ As a unifying center . . . Omega explains why, in spite of entropy, evolution has progressively produced higher and higher forms of life.

♦ Christian ethics is not at its base a matter of "Do good and avoid evil. . . ." Rather, it is a relational task: we are to contribute to our relationship with Christ who is building the universe.

♦ Far from being only a thirteen-billion-year prelude to humanity's arrival, the world is, as far as creation itself is concerned, the central activity of God.

♦ All our activities are part of God's grand project that is cosmic history. God's activity of fostering evolution continues in ourselves. Its movement toward ever-greater being takes place through our free engagement.

♦ Love . . . is directed to more being. This too is the story of evolution. This being attracted to the real or potential good of the beloved is an aspect of love that is frequently overlooked.

♦ Since evolution has reached a new reflective stage in us human beings, we ought not continue the brutal patterns of evolution. That is, our reflective love should welcome only opportunities that foster personalistic progress.

♦ What we human beings do to make a better world coheres with what Christ has been doing and is doing and will do. In other words, our ordinary and our extraordinary activities can be ways of cooperating in Christ's activity.

♦ The work that both believers and nonbelievers do is itself the work that Christ is doing. Therefore . . . all ethical activity is basically cooperating with God.

♦ Without human beings, God cannot accomplish what God wants to accomplish.

♦ God cannot save us without our own activity. Our unwillingness to cooperate with God is the meaning of sin.

♦ Our lives and our work therefore fill out God's relational self. . . . We make a difference to the eternal God.

## Questions for Discussion

1. What new insights on Christian ethics are discussed here? How do these insights make a difference in the current condition of humankind?

2. Discuss the importance of "future" for an evolutionary-based ethics. What are some Gospel passages that support Teilhard's insights in this respect?

3. Discuss Teilhard's ethic of divine-human cooperation and its import for Christogenesis. How does this ethic of cooperation change our understanding of God and our relationship to God?

*Chapter 10*

# TEILHARD DE CHARDIN AND THE NEW SPIRITUALITY

WILLIAM D. DINGES AND ILIA DELIO, OSF

Do not be conformed to this world.                      *—Romans 12:2*

*Salve Regina, mater misericordiae* . . . From this foreign land . . . so lost, so full of fear, we mourn, we grieve, we sigh from this tearful vale of exile. . . .                      *—Salve Regina*

Thou shalt love God in and through the genesis of the universe and of mankind.                      —Pierre Teilhard de Chardin

Paul Tillich once suggested that the adjective *spiritual* is "lost beyond hope." Whether the word is "lost" is debatable; that its meaning has changed in profound ways over the last century is not. In what follows we move in these directions: We first sketch the broad parameters of what has come to be known as the "new spirituality," a hybridization of traditions of the past, beliefs and practices of the present, and innovative ideas surrounding a new scientific synthesis and cosmology. Second, we briefly contrast core themes of the new spirituality with a pre-Vatican II current of Catholic spirituality that accentuated otherworldliness and that fostered a deep sense of human alienation from world and nature. Third, we situate Teilhard de Chardin's visionary thought on the spiritual efficacy of world and nature within both the paradigm of the new spirituality and that of pre-Vatican II Catholic spirituality. In so doing we contextualize his ideas in a broader cultural framework.

Teilhard's thought did not occur in a vacuum. It occurred in the context of a historic Zeitgeist, in relation to various modes of theological and scientific discourse of his day, to a cultural mechanism of legitimation, and to multiple social exigencies and orientations. Within Catholicism, Teilhard's thinking offered a more this-worldly spirituality, a creative revitalization of the tradition's sacramental sensibility, along with a rearticulation of its relationship to secularism, science, and evolution—central to all of which was the actualization of the "new Christ" in and through the world.

## On the New Spirituality

In the latter half of the twentieth century a new spirituality (also referred to as alternative spirituality, new spiritual synthesis, progressive religion, a new paradigm of spirituality, the New Age movement) has emerged. This new spirituality is not a homogenous phenomenon. It is diverse, eclectic, multi-cultural, diffused, decentered, and often uncoupled from traditional religious sources, particularly from more hierarchical, orthodox, and theistic ones.[1]

The emergence of the new spirituality affirms a rejection of secularization theories and assumptions. It reinforces the insight that individuals do not respond to new social and cultural problems by abandoning religion or spirituality as much as by developing new directions or new syntheses, often on the pathways of the old. In the context of modernity and postmodernity, the relationship between religion and spirituality is changing rather than disappearing.[2] Secularization is not a zero-sum game necessitating the demise of supernaturalism. Nor does the new spirituality reject science. What it rejects is *scientism* in which the methodology and data of natural science *alone* are allowed to contribute to our understanding of the world and the human condition in it. The new spirituality also calls on natural science itself as a witness against the inadequacies of a purely secularized worldview.[3]

The new spirituality emerges from a complex array of historical, social, and cultural sources. Some elements are new in an innovative and creative sense; others are quite old, but reappropriated and reinterpreted in the new historical setting.[4] In general terms, the new spirituality is derivative of what Paul Heelas and Linda Woodhead describe as the distinction between "life-as" and "subjective-life" orientations, a distinction that reflects the broader Western cultural turn toward the subject. While the life-as orientation focuses on a transcendent source of significance and authority to which individuals must conform at the expense of the cultivation of their unique subjective lives, the subjective-life orientation, in contrast, idealizes a life lived in a full awareness of one's state of being, in enriching one's experience, and in actualizing in maximum ways the quality of one's life. This "subjectivization thesis" shift means that contemporary spirituality is less located in authoritative structures and institutions and more located within the internal control and consciousness of individuals.[5] It is an orientation that has historical roots in the spirit of the Reformation, and contemporary ones in the dynamics of market economy logic that accentuate the priority of individual choice.

Other dynamics surrounding the new spirituality have sources outside Western culture. In this regard, the new spirituality is one element of a contemporary global religious megasynthesis that includes a colonization of the Western mind by Eastern esoteric psychologies, philosophies, and religious traditions.

In the West in general, the new spirituality is a response to the contra-dictions of late capitalism's commodity culture and to the spiritual poverty of techno-industrial societies marked by massive bureaucracies, depersonal-ization, and aesthetic sterility. In the American context, the new spirituality inherits a long-standing utopian tradition and the quintessential American dream of transcending one's background by reinventing one's self.[6] In the world context, currents of the new spirituality reflect the cultural influences of globalization and the information-technology revolution, both of which are progenitors of democratization in multiple settings (social, cultural, com-mercial, political, etc.) and of expectations relating to how individuals should participate in shaping their own lives, careers, citizenship—and spirituality.

In terms of its social location, the new spirituality is associated with progressive religious thinkers and organizations, but not confined to them. Demographic and class dynamics are evident where opportunities for spiri-tual experimentation occur more readily among the affluent and social elite who have the resources (power, time, and finances) for such activity.[7] The growing number of religious "nones" (nonaffiliated), especially among younger age cohorts who increasingly identify themselves as "spiritual but not religious," is another social dynamic of the new spirituality.[8]

The new spirituality has also emerged in the context of a widespread cul-tural malaise within mainstream Christianity.[9] Forms of traditional religion have increasingly lost their authority and their monopoly on the sacred, in part because of their failure to respond creatively to the "signs of the times" and to the unparalleled advances of a new historical, cultural, and cosmolog-ical situation. The new spirituality is often uncoupled from these traditions and their symbol systems.[10] As such the horizon of the new spirituality sug-gests the liberation of the human psyche from aspects of traditional revela-tion and points to the ascendance of subjective ("mystical") experience as the primary datum of religion, to the widening cultural democratization of the sacred, and to the tendency to reject vertical transcendence—all of which are linked with spiritual experimenting and a quest for the sacred *within* the secular. This horizon is also an aspect of the emergence of a post patriarchal paradigm and a new rapprochement between science (à la "the new physics," evolutionary theory, the new cosmology) and religion—including the alleged "reenchantment" of the former.[11] In conjunction with the emergent ecologi-cal age, the new spirWEUalty is deeply holistic; it fosters solidarity both within the human framework and within a more expansive biocentric one.[12]

Although holistic and not a narrow expression of atomistic individual-ism, the new spirituality, especially in relation to the subjective turn noted earlier, also harbors individualist strains. This is primarily by way of its focus within, its emphasis on the autonomy of conscience and choice, and with its shift of authority away from traditional and outside sources.[13] The "higher consciousness" and "divine within" animating much of the new spirituality suggest less of an imitative spirituality in the traditional Christian sense, and more of a reflexive one expressing the dynamics of contemporary identity work.

What is reflexive identity work? As its social basis and ascribed status wane, religious identity in the postmodern context increasingly becomes an individual and reflexive project in keeping with the previously described subjective turn. The British sociologist Anthony Giddens has observed that in the context of pluralism, the fragmented milieus of postmodernism, the radical openness to social life, the synthesis of global culture, and the eclectic mixing and diversity of various "authorities," achievement and autonomy have become primary determinants of individual identity. The construction of the self is increasingly a deliberative and reflexive project, a constant monitoring and revision of beliefs and practices in the light of changing circumstances. Individuals try to negotiate and sustain a coherent yet continuously revived biographical narrative within a context of multiple choices filtered through various abstractions and social systems. In the contemporary context, we find that identities are increasingly adopted, exchanged, and shed. Individuals lay claim to multiple identities with varying degrees of commitment to each, depending on their needs relative to evolving circumstances.[14]

Within this postmodern identity-as-self-construction-project paradigm, spirituality (as with religious identity in general) readily transforms into a more subjective and private affair, one segment of identity work in which the individual selects spiritual meaning and significance from an ever-proliferating variety of choices and wares. As religious identity becomes less connected with ethnicity or class, with obedience or obligation, or with the acquisition of a cumulative tradition that is handed on, it takes on the character of a more deliberated or reflexive exercise of choice, a micro and potentially ever-changing project of the individual. The key point here is that religio-spiritual identity derives increasingly from internal agency by virtue of the individual's own authority and cultural (lifestyle) preferences, rather than those of traditional institutional or external norms.[15] The prevalence of choice and a multiplicity of the lifestyle options available in the postmodern context foster the weakening of traditional normativity—religious and otherwise.[16] It is this reflexive quality of modern religious identity that drives much of the spiritual-seeker syndrome associated with the new spirituality.

In its multiple realizations, the new spirituality is profoundly this-worldly. As such, it challenges the older, dualistic, apolitical, sex-negative, and world-denying spirituality as it also opposes systems of economic, military, and ecological violence that threaten the integrity of the planet. The new spirituality reveres the grandeur of nature in an unfolding universe. It celebrates an embodied spirituality and repudiates any impulse to reject, abuse, or trivialize the body—which is renowned as our first spiritual encounter with the mystery of creation.[17] The new spirituality is also this-worldly in its postmillennial, progressive-looking agenda for the transformation of individuals and societies. This agenda accentuates values of connection, communion, and subjectivity that are foundational to the transition from a techno-industrial into an ecological age.[18]

The new spirituality also contains elements that privilege the role of reason (or mind/consciousness, intellect, awareness, imagination) in spiritual-life questions, along with hopes for a scientifically assisted evolutionary progress. In the new spirituality, nature is reanimated, and teleological motifs (spiritual evolution and evolution, itself, as a spiritual process) are accentuated—with tantalizing suggestions regarding the human future.[19]

In summary, the new spirituality is one element of a paradigmatic cultural transition. It is eclectic, pluralistic, and holistic. It reflects the subjective turn of modernity and postmodernity; emphasizes feelings, experience and the quest for human authenticity; accentuates human fulfillment in this world; reveres and affirms the cosmos and our belonging to it; finds the sacred in the secular; promotes a recomposed and embodied spirituality; and recognizes the infusion of nature and matter with spirit, consciousness, or life force.

## Teilhard and Pre-Vatican II Catholic Spirituality

Catholicism has a rich and variegated history of spiritual traditions illustrating continuity and change. Teilhard's thought needs to be situated within this history, as well as within the parameters of the new spirituality. Both perspectives stand out against the gestalt of a hegemonic form of pre-Vatican II Catholic spirituality that accentuated a stark otherworldliness and a penchant for a deep-seated alienation from nature, world, and cosmos.

Accordingly, the world itself was a spiritually dangerous place. God created humans not for this "vale of tears," but for his kingdom in the next. Just reward came in the next world, not this one. The existential choice was between a blissful heaven and a sinful world.[20] The salvation of souls and the world hereafter trumped all other concerns. Aspirations for human (or spiritual) fulfillment in the world were vain, misguided, and fleeting. The brevity of life and fallen nature of humanity were emphasized, as were the vanity of earthly things, the harshness of God's punishment, the precariousness of eternal life, the importance of sacrifice, the necessity of choosing between heaven and a sinful world, and the imperative for order, regularity, control, penance, self-discipline, self-denial, and self-mortification. Personal moral weaknesses, the necessity of moral rigor, and reparation for sin were dominant motifs. The impetus to mortify the flesh and control the passions, notably sexual ones, was paramount. Through ubiquitous reminders of death, divine retribution, punishment, and themes of calamity, pre-Vatican II Catholic culture reinforced this otherworldly sensibility that pitted an empire of grace against an empire of nature.[21]

The sources of Catholicism's tendency to downplay human fulfillment in the secular world and to accentuate a negative conception of the spiritual life reflected a long-standing historical ambivalence within the Christian tradition regarding the world and humanity's place in it. This ambivalence derived in part from an undercurrent of neo-Platonic influences promoting liberation from embodiment and an emphasis on ascending into the transcendent and eternal.[22] It was also reflected in the role of religious life and the monastic contemplative ideal as models of a higher striving for spiritual perfection and holier calling than available to laity in the world. Christ's kingdom was not of this world; suffering and death were ever-present realities; the greatest glories lay in the world to come. Although various apostolic orders had enshrined active service (charity, almsgiving) on a somewhat equal plane with interior spiritual exercises, the purely contemplative life was seen as the superior one.[23] A spiritually threatening world fed the impetus to withdraw in both literal and symbolic ways.[24] The religious monastic ideal represented the more perfect response to this imperative.

Aside from the theological presuppositions animating nineteenth- and early twentieth-century Catholicism's negative spirituality, the view was also a reaction to a world characterized by Protestant apostasy, dramatic political upheavals, the corrosive influence of materialistic science, the social disruptions of urbanization and industrialization, a worldwide Great Depression, two catastrophic World Wars, the global spread of "atheistic communism," and the emergence of historical consciousness. These collective traumas psychologically reinforced a deep sense of sin, alienation, and estrangement, along with an apocalyptic sense of living in a sinful world facing the last days. Little wonder that so much of the church's pronouncements and theological reflection at the time, especially on the errors of modernism, accentuated the rhetoric of calamity, unbelief, avarice, ungodliness, libidinous passions, and so forth. A corrupt and unwieldy world of sin, pride, materialism, and incredulity necessarily faced an imminent eternal judgment by God.

## Teilhard de Chardin and Sacred Secularity

Inherent to the new spirituality and in Teilhard de Chardin's thought is a fundamental shift in our understanding of the world and relationship to it. Modern science has ushered in an understanding of the cosmos as one of change and complexity. We no longer live in a three-tiered universe of heaven, earth, and underworld but an expanding universe of unfolding space-time, open to a future of unlimited possibilities. Teilhard de Chardin was a trained pale-ontologist who understood evolution as the starting point for Christian faith. His synthesis of evolution and Christianity aimed to illumine a new under-standing of God in the secular world. In his foreword to Teilhard's book *Christianity and Evolution*, N. Max Wildiers states that the core problem of Teilhard's thought is that of secularization and the values inherent in earthly and human activity.[25] Teilhard saw an inability to resolve the conflict between the traditional God of revelation and the "new" God of evolution. Wildiers states, "the conflict we are suffering today does indeed consist in the conflict between a religion of transcendence and a secularized world, between the 'God of the Above' and the 'God of the Ahead,' between a 'religion of heaven' and a 'religion of the earth.'"[26]

Evolution marks a significant change in cosmology, from a fixed, stable order to a dynamic order of change. Teilhard saw that evolution freed Chris-tianity from its Greek philosophical framework and brought about a new understanding of God in a way that invigorated core doctrine. To grasp the dynamism of Christianity, one must accept evolution as the explanation for unfolding life. Evolution is not background to the human story; it *is* the human story. In his *Human Phenomenon* he wrote:

> For many, evolution still means only transformism, and transform-ism itself is an old Darwinian hypothesis as localized and obsolete as the Laplacean concept of the solar system or the Wegnerean theory of continental drift. They truly are blind who do not see the scope of a movement whose orbit, infinitely transcending that of the natural sciences, has successively overtaken and invaded the surrounding fields of chemistry, physics, sociology, and even mathematics and history of religions. Drawn along together by a single fundamental current, one after the other all the domains of human knowledge have set off toward the study of some kind of *development*. . . . Evo-lution is a general condition, which all theories, all hypotheses, all systems must submit to and satisfy from now on in order to be con-ceivable and true. (HP, 152)

Teilhard's approach to the problem of secularity begins with accepting evolution as the process of unfolding life, whereby new life emerges over deep time. The key to secularity is found at the very center of Christian faith, in a Christology relevant to the world in which we live, since the universe is organically linked to Christ. It is precisely because our world is in evolution that human activity takes on new meaning and importance: human work is integral to evolution. The zeal of the Christian for the transformation of soci-ety, or the revolution in which the Christian is engaged to change the struc-tures of society, is nothing less than evolution toward the fullness of Christ.

Wildiers writes: "He [Teilhard] put the theological problem of secularity in an extremely original and illuminating form and at the same time provided a truly Christian solution that fits in completely with the faith handed down by tradition."[27] Teilhard's solution to the problem of secularity is to rid ourselves of the old God of the starry heavens and embrace the God of evolution.

To appreciate Teilhard's in-secularization of the divine is to understand his synthesis of God and evolution. He understood the science of evolution as the explanation for the physical world and viewed Christian life within the context of evolution.[28] In his *Science and Christ* he wrote that "Christians should have no need to be afraid or shocked by the results of scientific research, whether in physics, biology or history. . . . Science should not disturb our faith by its analyses. Rather it should help us to know God better" (SC, 35–36).[29] To reject evolution, in Teilhard's view, is to reject God. Until we come to know God in light of evolution, we shall find the world a problem.

Teilhard recognized that there is a unifying influence in the whole evolutionary process, a centrating factor that continues to hold the entire process together and move it forward toward greater complexity and unity. His faith in Christ led him to posit Christ as the future fullness of the whole evolutionary process. Christ is the centrating principle, the pleroma, and the Omega Point where the individual and collective adventure of humanity finds its end and fulfillment. Through his penetrating view of the universe, he found Christ present within the entire cosmos, from the least particle of matter to the convergent human community. The whole cosmos is incarnational. This opening in Teilhard's thought to an embodied perspective both echoes the influences on his thinking from Henri Bergson and Maurice Blondel and as projects forward into the phenomenological thought of Martin Heidegger and especially Maurice Merleau-Ponty. While these thought streams are now pervasive in Christian theology, there have been few Christian theologians who have been able to move from an incarnational theology that is wholly anthropocentric to a theology of the universe story that does not collapse simply into the biocentric move. Teilhard's position opens that possibility for an embodied perspective that sees human flourishing as embedded in the flourishing of the Earth community in which both are manifestations of the emergent universe story. In *The Divine Milieu* he wrote, "there is nothing profane here below for those who know how to see" (DM, 66). Christ invests himself organically with all of creation, immersing himself in things, in the heart of matter and thus unifying the world.[30] By taking on human form, Christ has given the world its definitive form: he has been consecrated for a cosmic function. The Pauline phrase *Omnia in ipso constant* (In him all things consist; cf. Col 1:17) dominated Teilhard's thought. "It is impossible for me," he wrote in 1924, "to read St. Paul without seeing the universal and cosmic domination of the Incarnate Word emerging from his words with dazzling clarity" (SC, 57). It became increasingly evident to Teilhard that if Christ is to remain at the center of our faith in an evolutionary universe, then this cosmic Christ must begin to offer himself for our adoration as the "evolutive" Christ—Christ the evolver (CE, 181). The *one who is in evolution* is himself the *cause and center* of evolution and its goal. This evolutive Christ is not distinct from Jesus but is indeed "Jesus, the center towards whom all moves."[31] As evolver, Christ is the one who is coming to be in evolution through the process of creative union, which is the term Teilhard used to talk about divine creative action as relatedness and union. As Omega, Christ is the one who fills all things and who animates and gathers up all the biological and spiritual energies developed by the universe.[32] Since Christ is Omega, the universe is physically impregnated to the very core of its matter by the influence of his superhuman nature.[33] The material world is holy and sacred. Through grace, the presence of the incarnate Word penetrates everything as a universal element. Everything—every leaf, flower, tree rabbit, fish, star—is physically "christified," gathered up by the incarnate Word as nourishment that assimilates, transforms, and divinizes (SC, 59). The world is like a crystal lamp illumined from within by the light of Christ. For those who can see, Christ shines in this diaphanous universe, through the cosmos and in matter (SC, 53–60).

## A Participatory World

Teilhard coined the term "Christogenesis" to describe evolution as the genesis of the total Christ, "the triumph of the personal at the summit of the mind" (PM, 297). He envisioned the evolutionary process as one moving toward evolution of consciousness and ultimately toward evolution of spirit, from the birth of mind to the birth of the whole Christ (FM, 309).[34] He urged Christians to participate in the process of Christogenesis, to risk, get involved, aim toward union with others, for the entire creation is longing for its fulfillment in God. He opposed a static Christianity that isolates its followers instead of merging them with the masses, imposes on them a burden of observances and obligations, and causes them to lose interest in the common task. "Do we realize that if we are to influence the world it is essential that we share in its drive, in its anxieties and its hopes?"[35] We are not only to recognize evolution but make it continue in ourselves.[36] Teilhard emphasized that our role as Christians is to "christify" the world by our actions, by immersing ourselves in the world, plunging our hands into the soil of the earth and touching the roots of life. His deep secular humanism reaches the core of Christian life which is a "mysticism of action," involvement in the world compenetrated by God.[37] He held that union with God is not withdrawal or separation from the activity of the world but a dedicated, integrated, and subliminated absorption into it.[38]

Before, he said, the Christian thought that he or she could attain God only by abandoning everything. One now discovers that one cannot be saved except through the universe and as a continuation of the universe. We must make our way to heaven *through* earth. Teilhard's spirituality is one of deep secularity. The world in its physical roots is permeated with Christ (CE, 93).

By bringing together evolution and incarnation in a single vision, Teilhard reshaped the meaning of Gospel life. The Gospel call to "leave all and follow me" no longer means leaving the world but returning to the world with new vision and a deeper conviction to take hold of Christ in the heart of matter and to further Christ in the universality of Christ's Incarnation (CE, 170). We humans are evolution made conscious; hence, our choices for and in the world shape the future of the world. What we have to do, Teilhard said, "is not simply to forward a human task but to bring Christ to completion . . . to cultivate the world. The world is still being created and it is Christ who is reaching his fulfillment through it" (CE, 49). The Christian of today must gather from the body all the spiritual power it contains, and not only from the personal body but from the whole immense cosmic body which is the world stuff in evolution. We are to harness the energies of love for the forward movement of evolution toward the fullness of Christ. This means to live from the center of the heart where love grows and to reach out to the world with faith, hope, and trust in God's incarnate presence.

The greatness of Teilhard's insight to the question of secularity lies in the organic nature of Christ as the heart of change in the universe. Teilhard offers a new vision of the God-world relationship, beginning with evolution, whereby secular and earthly activity are integrated into the future of the world lying ahead of us (TF, 95). The religious person must be truly secular because it is only an embrace of secularity that discloses God. Teilhard's incarnational doctrine offers three new perspectives on the problem of secularism: First, his love of matter and spirit is a dual commitment to God and to the world; second, his inclusion of suffering and evil in the forward movement of evolution offers a realistic approach to evil as part of unfolding life; and third, the participation of humans is essential to the process of Christogenesis, that is, the evolution of Christ in the world and the world in Christ. "If we are to remain faithful to the gospel," he says, "we have to adjust its spiritual code to the new shape of the universe. . . . It has become the great work in process of completion which we have to save by saving ourselves" (CE, 91–92). The Christian response to secularity, therefore, is not to escape or reject the world, nor is it to live with a double standard of values, spiritual and worldly. Rather, the secular is the realm of incarnation, which means the Christian must see the world in its divine depth which is shown precisely in the worldliness of human activities and earthly affairs.

In *The Divine Milieu* Teilhard confronted the problem of a twofold spirituality, namely love of God and love of the world. He observed how many people have become divided in their religious beliefs and practices, seeing their activity in the world as only something to be endured until the next life. Yet the question of human action is central to the whole spiritual venture. The world is the place sanctified by the presence of God (DM, 66). Thus he urges us to be conscious of the larger dimension of our efforts, which means laboring in the midst of the world so that our activities become part of the unfolding of the earth process itself. This includes tending to nonhuman creation by recognizing the inherent dignity of all creatures and our mutual relatedness to all created things.

Teilhard was passionately in love with the world because he saw God at the heart of it. God is not to be sought in some distant heaven. Rather, God reveals Godself everywhere, beneath our groping efforts, as a universal milieu, only because God is the ultimate point upon which all realities converge. The world, therefore, is not the problem. Rather, the problem is we do not see the world correctly; we do not contemplate the world. The Incarnation speaks to us of a world filled with God, but only a heart in love with matter can see this God-filled world. Teilhard's secular mysticism calls for oneness of heart with God: "I merge myself through my heart with the very heart of God" (CE, 75). This heart-centered being-in-the-world is a penetrating vision that sees the divine depth of worldly things, as Teilhard wrote: "God is, in a sense, at the point of my pen, my pick, my paint-brush, my needle—and my heart and my thought. It is by carrying to its natural completion the stroke, the line, the stitch I am working on that I shall lay hold on that ultimate end towards which my will at its deepest levels tends."[39] God is the ultimate point upon which all realities converge so that in every action we must adhere to the creative power of God, to coincide with it and become its living extension.

For Teilhard, God evolves in the universe and brings it to its completion through the cooperative cocreative "great work" of human beings. Living from a deeper center within, the Christian is to go about urging all reality toward the Omega, to the final synthesis which is constantly growing within him or herself. What we seek is not the appearance of God in the world but the shining of God through creation, a "diaphany" of God radiating through a world that becomes transparent. The diaphanous appearance of Christ in and through every creature of the universe is encountered in a loving act of surrender in which Christ becomes the "Thou" complementing our "I." Each Christian, now awakened to a new consciousness of Christ's universal presence, discovers his or her own self-realization and full maturity in "being-with-Christ." Christ becomes the unifying and integrating center in creation, as each person seeks his or her self in Christ and thus in one another. Therefore, "it *does* matter what the human person does, for only through his/her action can one encounter God."[40] Human action is to help evolution advance in every field of enterprise—business, science, education, law, agriculture, social sciences, cultural, and artistic pursuits—all of which are involved in a transforming process much greater than ourselves. We are not called to relate to a God without a world. To love God we must also love what God loves. We are called to love this created world as God loves it. We are to help transform this universe in Christ by seeing Christ in the universe and loving Christ in the heart of the universe.

Teilhard provides a thoughtful position from which to engage the problem of secularity by including the values of earth in a Christocentric vision of the universe. The world is not the place of evil or ungodliness to be renounced nor is it the place of human flourishing at the expense of God. Rather, it is the place of divine presence in the midst of multiplicity and a complexity of forces. His spiritual vision is one that brings us an expanded sense of perspective and a new sense of purpose. He believed in love as the personal energy of evolution: "Love is the most universal, the most tremendous and the most mysterious of the cosmic forces" (HE, 32). Divine love is evolutionary—it changes, grows, complexifies—and this growth and complexification is the basis of unity. What Teilhard tried to show is that evolution in all its materiality is not only the universe coming to be but it is *God* who is coming to be. Thus he states, "God is entirely self-sufficient; and yet the universe contributes *something that is vitally necessary to* God" (CE, 177). Evolution, he claimed, requires a divine source located not in the past or "up above" in a timeless present but "up ahead" in the future.

Teilhard dispensed with the classical, static God-world relationship where the end returns to the beginning (*Omega revolvit ad alpha*) by reframing the God-world relationship in terms of evolution. "The organic vastness of the universe," he states, "obliges us to rethink the notion of divine *omnisufficiency*: God fulfills himself, he in some way completes Godself, in the pleroma" (CE, 178). Evolution is the genesis of God in space-time; yet, the God who is coming to be is the divine, transcendent source of love that energizes evolution and is the future horizon "that draws an entire universe, and not just human history, toward an unfathomable fulfillment yet to be realized."[41] He posited a dynamic view of God and the world in the process of becoming something more than what it is because the universe is grounded in the personal *center of Christ*. He wrote: "It is . . . not merely a vague, cold *something* but a warm and well-defined s*omeone*" who holds together the plurality of elements in a personalizing center (CE, 156).

It is this personal Christic center that distinguishes Teilhard's theology of evolution and sets him apart from postsecular theorists. The whole evolutionary process is secular, that is, the community of life-as-world, including organic and inorganic matter which are mutually interrelated and interdependent. The progression of evolution toward greater unity discloses the cosmic secular as the realm of divine transcendence. The key to deep secularity for Teilhard is to see God within the whole evolutionary process and as the future of this process.[42] By identifying incarnation with evolution, Teilhard forged a new path for Christian life. He moved beyond the classical God of Hellenic influence that distinguished being over the world (and hence contributed to the God-world problem) to an understanding of God that is both consonant with evolution and thoroughly incarnational. Matter is holy, the cosmos is holy, and evolution is holy because God is empowering evolution from within.

Christians are called to love God by engaging the secular as the place where God is alive and active; to risk, get involved, and to realize that the whole evolutionary movement is eager to give birth to Christ: "Thou shalt love God in and through the genesis of the universe and of mankind" (CE, 184). Christian love is not directed to an other-worldly end or to an other-worldly God. Rather, to love God in and through evolution is to love the cosmos, the earth, the body, materiality—the stuff of life—which is one with God without being identical to God. Followers of Christ are baptized into a new divine action of raising up the world, seeing the world with new vision, loving the world with a new depth of heart and embracing the earth with a new zest for life. Such a following of Christ trusts in the power of love to build one's soul by creative engagement with the world, helping to unite that which is separate, overcoming disunity through bonds of selfless love. With God at the heart of the cosmos, we cannot be saved "except through the universe and as a continuation of the universe" (CE, 128).

## Conclusion

Teilhard's visionary thought, like various currents of the new spirituality, stands as a necessary corrective to an alienating otherworldliness and the God-world problem. The affinities of his thought with the new spirituality include his this-worldly focus ("deep secularity"), his belief in progress and celebration of the human role in building the earth, his affirmation of holism and human potential—especially in relationship to the centrality of the process of evolution—and his rejection of otherworldly and life-denying asceticism as a norm of spiritual virtuosi.[43] Other affinities include his rejection (via a redefinition) of secularism and his deep embrace of science and the evolutionary process.[44] His spiritual code was profoundly Christocentric and focused on the immanence of God, accentuating the power of love and communion with others. In this respect, his vision was at a distance from some of the nontheistic dimensions of the new spirituality and from some of the more excessive expressions of hyperindividualism and subjectivity found in it.

In terms of his own Catholicism, Teilhard's corrective is in keeping with the Second Vatican Council's emphasis in *Sacrosanctum Concilium* on Word and sacrament (especially the latter); with the theological turn toward the subject associated with the primacy of the individual's experience of the divine; with a praxis-oriented and this-worldly engagement; and with a creative embrace of the signs of the times (evolutionary biology) that has brought Catholicism into a more congruent and plausible relationship with its social and intellectual environments.

Like much of the new spirituality of our day, Teilhard found the sacred within the secular. He rejected the categorical antipodes of spirit/matter, body/soul, and sacred/profane distinctions. The world is not the problem, according to Teilhard. Our resistance to science and to the reality of evolution is the problem. To embrace this world is to enter into its conflicts, struggles, hopes, and dreams and thus to be attentive to God who is the center of all life and the power of the future. We are to harness the energies of love for the forward movement of evolution toward Christ Omega.

> Let us establish ourselves in the divine *milieu*. There we shall find ourselves where the soul is most deep and where matter is most dense. There we shall discover, where all its beauties flow together, the ultra-vital, the ultra-sensitive, the ultra-active point of the universe. And, at the same time, we shall feel the *plenitude* of our powers of action and adoration effortlessly ordered within our deepest selves (DM, 115).

## Points to Ponder

- Individuals do not respond to new social and cultural problems by abandoning religion or spirituality as much as by developing new directions or new syntheses, often on the pathways of the old.

- The new religio-spiritual identity derives increasingly from internal agency by virtue of the individual's own authority and cultural (lifestyle) preferences, rather than those of traditional institutional or external norms. . . . It celebrates an embodied spirituality and repudiates any impulse to reject, abuse, or trivialize the body—which is renowned as our first spiritual encounter with the mystery of creation.

- The new spirituality also contains elements that privilege the role of reason (or mind/consciousness, intellect, awareness, imagination) in spiritual-life questions, along with hopes for a scientifically assisted evolutionary progress.

- To reject evolution is to reject God. Until we come to know God in light of evolution, we shall find the world a problem.

- The *one who is in evolution* is himself the *cause and center* of evolution and its goal.

- The question of secularity lies in the organic nature of Christ as the heart of change in the universe. Teilhard offers a new vision of the God-world relationship, beginning with evolution, whereby secular and earthly activity are integrated into the future of the world lying ahead of us.

- God evolves in the universe and brings it to its completion through the cooperative cocreative "great work" of human beings.

- The Christian is to go about urging all reality toward the Omega, to the final synthesis which is constantly growing within him or herself.

## Questions for Discussion:

1. How does the new spirituality complement the new cosmology?

2 What is Teilhard's contribution to the new spirituality?

3 What challenges does Teilhard's vision offer to Christian spirituality?

## Notes

1. The description of the new spirituality here is an aggregate and general one. More in-depth and select treatments include James A. Herrick, *The Making of the New Spirituality: The Eclipse of the Western Religious Tradition* (Downers Grove, IL: InterVarsit, 2003); Gordon Lynch, *The New Spirituality: An Introduction to Progressive Belief in the Twenty-first Century* (London: I. B. Tauris, 2007); Paul Heelas and Linda Woodhead, *The Spiritual Revolution: Why Religion is Giving Way to Spirituality* (Malden, MA: Blackwell, 2005); Carol P. Christ, *Rebirth of the Goddess: Finding Meaning in Feminist Spirituality* (New York: Addison Wesley, 1997); Marilyn Ferguson, *The Aquarian Conspiracy: Person and Social Transformation in the 1980s* (Los Angeles: J. P. Tarcher, 1980); and Daren Kemp, *New Age, A Guide: Alternative Spiritualties from Aquarian Conspiracy to Next Age* (Edinburgh: Edinburgh University Press, 2004). Sociological treatments include Phillip E. Hammond, *Religion and Personal Autonomy: The Third Disestablishment in America* (Columbia University of South Carolina Press, 1992); Charles Y. Glock and Robert N. Bellah, eds., *The New Religious Consciousness* (Berkeley: University of California Press, 1976); Robert Wuthnow, *After Heaven: Spirituality in American since the 1950s* (Berkeley: University of California Press, 1998) and *Rediscovering the Sacred* (Grand Rapids, MI: Eerdmans, 1992); and Wade Clark Roof, *Spiritual Marketplace: Baby Boomers and the Remaking of American Religion* (Princeton, NJ: Princeton University Press, 1990). For an analysis of the Vatican assessment of the new spirituality primarily via the New Age movement, see William D. Dinges, "The New (Old) Age Movement: Assessing a Vatican Assessment," *Journal of Contemporary Religion* 19, no. 3 (2004): 273–88.

2. Danièle Hervieu-Léger, *Religion as a Chain of Memory* (New Brunswick, NJ: Rutgers University Press, 2000), 68.

3. See David Ray Griffin, ed., *Spirituality and Society: Postmodern Visions* (Albany: State University of New York Press, 1988).

4. Consider, for example, the popularity of the Joseph Campbell (with Bill Moyers) reworking of mythological themes in *The Power of Myth* (New York: Doubleday, 1988).

5. Heelas and Woodhead, *The Spiritual Revolution*. Heelas and Woodhead's study of the impact of the subjective turn on spirituality is focused primarily on Britain and the United States. Other works exploring multiple aspects of the "subjective turn" include Charles Taylor's *Sources of the Self: The Making of the Modern Identity* (Cambridge: Cambridge University Press, 1989) and, more recently, *A Secular Age* (Cambridge, MA: Belknap, 2007); Robert Bellah et al., *Habits of the Heart: Individualism and Commitment in American Life* (Berkeley: University of California Press, 1985); Anthony Giddens, *The Transformation of Intimacy* (Stanford, CA: Stanford University Press, 1993); and Philip Rieff, *The Triumph of the Therapeutic* (New York: Harper & Row, 1966).

6. James R. Lewis and J. Gordon Melton, eds., *Perspectives on the New Age* (Albany: State University of New York Press, 1992).

7. Attention has been drawn to the large number of middle-aged, middle-class women involved in holistic spirituality pursuits. See, for example, Linda Woodhead, "Why So Many Women in Holistic Spirituality? A Puzzle Revisited," in Kieran Flanagan and Peter C. Jupp, eds., *A Sociology of Spirituality* (Hampshire, England: Ashgate, 2007), 115–27; also Heelas and Woodhead, *The Spiritual Revolution*, 94–107.

8. Danièle Hervieu-Léger calls this the "spiritualization" of traditional religion in her *Religion as a Chain of Memory*, 68. In the United States, "nones" now constitute approximately 20 percent of the population. See " 'Nones' on the Rise: One in Five Adults Have No Religious Affiliation" (Washington, DC: Pew Research Center Forum on Religion & Public Life, 2012).

9. This malaise has been less evident regarding evangelicalism or Pentecostalism. Both traditions, but especially the latter, have remained somewhat adverse toward aspects of the new spirituality. See John A. Saliba, *Christian Responses to the New Age Movement: A Critical Assessment* (New York: Geoffrey Chapman, 1999).

10. Roof, *Spiritual Marketplace*.

11. David Ray Griffin, ed., *The Reenchantment of Science: Postmodern Proposals* (Albany: State University of New York Press, 1988).

12. Tom Berry, *The Dream of the Earth* (San Francisco: Sierra Club, 1988).

13. José Casanova sees much of the New Age spirituality as having become normalized in the modern world, but argues that this phenomenon is best classified as an expression of private, or what Thomas Luckmann called "invisible," religion. José Casanova, *Public Religions in the Modern World* (Chicago: University of Chicago Press, 1994), 5.

14. Anthony Giddens, *Modernity and Self-Identity* (Stanford, CA: Stanford University Press, 1991), 32–33; 195–201.

15. Charles Taylor argues that a more radical individualism with its ethic of identity authenticity and moral and spiritual instrumentalism means that in the context of religion, there is no "necessary embedding of our link to the sacred in any particular broader framework, whether 'church' or 'state.' " Today it is simply axiomatic that one should never conform to some external authority that does not ring true to the dictates of one's own inner sense of self. See Charles Taylor, *Varieties of Religion Today: William James Revisited* (Cambridge, MA: Harvard University Press, 2002), 80, 85, 101.

16. Giddens, *Modernity and Self-Identity*, 83.

17. Joe Holland, "A Postmodern Vision of Spirituality and Society," in Griffin, ed., *Spirituality and Society*, 51.

18. See Thomas Berry's "The Ecological Age," Riverdale Papers (photocopies) VI, 1–19.

19. Herrick, *The Making of the New Spirituality*, 257–61.

20. This composite summary of pre-Vatican II Catholic spirituality draws on Joseph P. Chinnici, O.F.M., "Organization of the Spiritual Life: American Catholic Devotional Works, 1791–1866," *Theological Studies* 40 (June 1979): 229–55, and his *Living Stones: The History and Structure of Catholic Spiritual Life in the United States* (New York: Orbis Books, 1996), along with Joseph P. Chinnici, Christopher J. Kauffman, Angelyn Dries, eds., *Prayer and Practice in the American Catholic Community* (New York: Orbis Books, 2000), 246, and Jay P. Dolan, *Catholic Revivalism: The American Experience: 1830–1900* (Notre Dame, IN: University of Notre Dame Press).

21. As Chinnici pointed out, the incarnation and with it the world and the individual lost their positive dimension as an act of creative love in the context of this emphasis on the corruption and nothingness of the human person and on the subsequent debasement and humility of Christ becoming a person like us. "Organization of the Spiritual Life," 240.

22. The lingering influences of Gnosticism, Manichaeism and, in the more modern European and American context, Jansenism, along other tendencies exaggerating the division between body and spirit accentuated the negative side of this world/nature ambiguity. An excellent summary and discussion of these influences can be found in Anna Peterson's "In and of the World," *Journal of Agricultural and Environmental Ethics* 12, no. 3 (2000): 237–61.

23. Patricia Wittberg, *From Piety to Professionalism—and Back? Transformations of Organized Religious Virtuosity* (New York: Rowman & Littlefield, 2006), 6–7.

24. Chinnici, "Organization of the Spiritual Life," 246.

25. N. Max Wildiers, foreword to Pierre Teilhard de Chardin, *Christianity and Evolution*, trans. René Hague (New York: Harcourt Brace Jovanovich, 1971), 9. The material in this section and following are based on my article Ilia Delio, "Is 'the World' a Problem? A Teilhardian Response," *Teilhard Studies* 60 (Spring 2010): 1–26.

26. Wildiers, foreword to Teilhard de Chardin, *Christianity and Evolution*, 10.

27. Wildiers, foreword to *Christianity and Evolution*, 12.

28. In *Christianity and Evolution* Teilhard writes: "I would say that man's origin by way of *evolution* is now an *indubitable* fact for science. There can be no two ways about it: the question is settled—so finally that to continue to debate it in the schools is as much a waste of time as it would be to go on arguing whether or not the revolution of the earth is an impossibility" (SC,139).

29. See also *Pierre Teilhard de Chardin: Writings Selected with an Introduction by Ursula King*, ed. Ursula King (Maryknoll, NY: Orbis, 2003), 92.

30. PM, 293–94; Timothy Jamison, "The Personalized Universe of Teilhard de Chardin," in *There Shall Be One Christ*, ed. Michael Meilach (New York: Franciscan Institute, 1968), 26.

31. De Lubac, *Pierre Teilhard de Chardin*, 37.

32. De Lubac, 94.

33. De Lubac, 96.

34. In the last entry in his journal, written three days before his death on Easter Sunday 1955, Teilhard brought together his principal thesis: *"Noogenesis=Christogenesis*

*(=Paul)"* summed up in Paul's First Letter to the Corinthians (15:28): "that God may be all in all" (e*n pasi panta Theos*).

35. De Lubac, 124.

36. Ursula King, *Christ in All Things* (Maryknoll, NY: Orbis Books, 1997), 80.

37. King, *Christ in All Things,* 93.

38. King, *Christ in All Things,* 93.

39. Teilhard de Chardin, *Hymn of the Universe.* http://www.religion-online.org.

40. George A. Maloney, *Cosmic Christ: From Paul to Teilhard* (New York: Sheed and Ward, 1968), 189; N. Max Wildiers, *The Theologian and His Universe: Theology and Cosmology from the Middle Ages to the Present,* trans. Paul Dunphy (New York: Seabury, 1982), 207. Wildiers writes: "The completion of the world in Christ is not imposed on us as a necessity but is offered to us as a possibility that will not be realized without our cooperation. The further evolution of humankind ought to be our main concern."

41. John F. Haught, *Deeper Than Darwin* (Cambridge, MA: Westview, 2003), 174.

42. CE,156, 184. Social and cultural theorists note today a return of religion to modern life and hence the arrival of a "postsecular" age. According to José Casanova, Peter Berger has described "the de-secularization of the world" as a sort of reversal of the secularization process. Casanova writes: "Becoming post-secular does not mean necessarily becoming religious again, but questioning our stadial consciousness, de-stabilizing if not our secular immanent frame, at least the possibilities of transcendence within the immanent frame, and being open, receptive, [or] at least curious to all the manifold forms of being religiously human." Casanova, "Are We Still Secular?" 25–26.

43. In the realm of sexuality, for example, this means that sexual intimacy is spiritually calibrated in a much more positive way as exemplified by John Paul II's theology of the body.

44. Some of the "new spirituality" is prefigured in the "New Piety" or "American spirituality" of the nineteenth century promoted by Isaac Hecker (1819–1888) and Orestes Brownson (1803–1876). See Joseph Chinnici, *Living Stones: The History and Structure of Catholic Spiritual Life in the United States* (Maryknoll, NY: Orbis Books, 1996); Patrick Carey, "American Catholic Romanticism, 1830–1888," *Catholic Historical Review* 64 (October 1988): 590–606.

*Chapter 11*

# THE ZEST FOR LIFE
*A Contemporary Exploration
of a Generative Theme
in Teilhard's Work*

## Ursula King

Teilhard de Chardin's writings represent a rich legacy of ideas for the twenty-first century. They contain many vital resources that can inspire and motivate countless human beings to move into new thinking and action. The many-layered elements of his work are closely interwoven with the texture of an unusual life marked by a deep religious, in fact mystical, commitment, and an equally passionate devotion to scientific research on geological, biological, and human evolution. More than fifty years after his death new interpretations of his daring scientific-philosophical synthesis continue to appear. Yet much of his legacy remains to be critically sifted and expanded in order to become more effective in our fast-changing world.

His corpus of writings offers a large, but unevenly developed, synthesis based on his double career as an internationally known evolutionary scientist and that of a gifted writer equally passionately devoted to expressing a powerful universal, and also deeply personal, vision of an evolving cosmos animated by a spiritual center. He returned to this vision again and again in a continuous stream of essays and books written over forty years, most of which he was prohibited from publishing during his lifetime.

Teilhard's ideas are intimately connected with many philosophical and theological concepts of the Western Christian tradition. Yet he radically transcends their boundaries by transforming them through novel expressions, unusual thought experiments, and innovative theories that open up new vistas and possibilities for human interaction, creativity, and collaboration. There exists the urgent task to develop his key ideas creatively and critically, since they are often more exploratory and suggestive than fully evolved.

What sometimes appears as an almost inchoate state of thinking or hesitant expression is to some extent due to his unusual working conditions during many parts of his life. These were shaped by an itinerant lifestyle, much travel, and a lack of dialogue and critical reactions to his work, due to its remaining unpublished. In addition, he experienced considerable insecurity because of geopolitical as well as administrative and personal difficulties with his own religious institution. But these difficulties of his personal situation were also affected by the unusual way in which his writings were largely disseminated privately during his lifetime and only published posthumously, after his death in 1955, without his being able to exercise any editorial control.

In what follows, I will reflect mainly on the meaning of one expression in his work—"the zest for life" (*"le goût de vivre"* or *"le goût de vie"*)—so often mentioned in Teilhard's letters and essays but, as far as I am aware, not discussed at any length by his commentators.[1] I consider the frequently mentioned idea about the zest for life as embodying one of those "generative themes" of which the Brazilian educationalist Paulo Freire speaks: a theme that touches people so deeply that it can stir them into effective action for creating profound social change.[2]

What does this "zest" mean in an increasingly globalized, or, what Teilhard often called it, "planetized" world? What is the special significance of this "zest for life" for individuals and communities, and how far can this important sense be considered a necessary, activating drive in the further evolution of the human species?

To find some answers to these questions, it will be helpful to look first at some of Teilhard's publications, and then expand the discussion by considering the significance of the zest for life for our contemporary world.

## Taking Off from an Important Correspondence

To select just one set of Teilhard's ideas out of many, one has to take off from somewhere, be it a particular context, a single idea chosen out of many, or a specific set of texts that can be analyzed, developed and commented upon. Before concentrating exclusively on the zest for life, I have chosen to begin my discussion with one of the latest publications, the hitherto unknown correspondence of Teilhard de Chardin with the French couple Max and Simone Bégouën, *Le rayonnement d'une amitié. Correspondance avec la famille Bégouën* (*1922–1955*), which was only published in 2011.[3] This correspondence provides an inspiring *practical* example of how Teilhard's own zest for life, and his reflections on the power of life, were life-giving and sustaining to his closest friends and to many other people who came in contact with him.

Teilhard first met Max Bégouën, twelve years his junior, in 1915, during the First World War. However, he had already made the acquaintance of his father, Count Henri de Bégouën, in 1913. Teilhard shared with both the father and his three sons (of whom Max was the eldest) their enthusiastic interest and researches in prehistory.[4] The friendship with Max took off after the Great War when Max and his wife, Simone, became some of his most intimate personal friends, so that Teilhard spoke more openly about his major intellectual and spiritual concerns to them than to many other correspondents. His first letter to Max dates from January 28, 1925. Their exchange of letters, lasting thirty years until Teilhard's death in 1955, demonstrates convincingly, and very powerfully, what an enormous influence Teilhard exercised from the 1920s onwards, first on particular individuals and small groups of friends, then increasingly on ever-larger groups of acquaintances and colleagues. This happened through both his personal presence and communications, and through diffusing his thought in an unusual way, as I explain below.

In the letters of his friend Max Bégouën, included in the same correspondence, one can see how Teilhard communicated a large vision of hope, a new understanding of the Christian faith and of a world in evolution, a passion for looking toward the future, and a conscious commitment to take on the responsibility of working toward the greater unification and higher evolution of the human species. The correspondence also includes many reflections that illuminate Teilhard's struggle in developing some major ideas for important essays and for his magnum opus, *The Human Phenomenon*.[5] All in all, the correspondence bears witness to the strong belief in life, and to Teilhard's efforts in animating and enlarging the zest for life among his friends and followers.

Teilhard had begun writing essays during the First World War, in 1916,[6] but subsequently his order withheld permission to get these and other writings published. Simone Bégouën suggested that she would type Teilhard's essays, and she did so from 1928 onward.[7] In this way he could distribute some of his texts to others. At first this happened on a somewhat irregular basis, until Simone made the further suggestion in early 1933 to cyclostyle Teilhard's texts so that they could be easily duplicated and distributed more effectively in larger numbers, an idea which had also occurred to Teilhard. He was delighted, and from then on all his texts were reproduced by this method in multiple, and sometimes very numerous, copies. Simone was in charge of this operation, but also had additional support from many of her friends. The first essay so reproduced was "How I Believe" (1934), of which several dozen, perhaps even several hundred copies were made.[8] Earlier writings, already typed, such as the book manuscript of *The Divine Milieu,* were now again reproduced by this method.

When analyzing human action in "How I Believe," Teilhard says that, in its present form, the zest for life in the world remains still emotional and weak. He is reflecting on his own zest and tries "to relate it to some structural feature of the world." He writes:

> I tell you, in all truth, that before the human mass sets out tomorrow
> on the great adventure from which its fulfilment is to emerge, it must

gather itself together, as one whole, and once and for all investigate the value of the drive which is urging it ahead. (CE, 111)

Through the private distribution of Teilhard's officially unpublished works he gained an increasing readership and following (augmented through additional translations into English, undertaken by Lucile Swan in Beijing from the early 1930s).[9] These privately circulated publications were later somewhat dismissively described as Teilhard's "secret writings." But they had nothing secret about them; they were dated and signed by him, and distributed to a wide range of friends and acquaintances as well as interested listeners of some of his public lectures. These so-called *"clandestins"* have sometimes been likened to Soviet samizdat literature, the self-published, secretly written, copied, and widely circulated underground literature of the former Soviet Union.

It is evident that the Bégouën couple played a central role in the initial diffusion of Teilhard's thought. When Max and Simone Bégouën moved in 1941 for personal and political reasons to Casablanca, the task of cyclostyling and distributing Teilhard's writings was handed over to Mademoiselle Jeanne Mortier who followed the same system.[10] She has recounted how she had first received *The Divine Milieu* from a friend in 1938, one of the many copies cyclostyled and distributed by Simone Bégouën. After reading it, Jeanne Mortier was so thrilled and moved that she wanted to meet its author. She decided to attend a public lecture on recent paleontological excavations in Burma, given by Teilhard at the Museum of Natural History in January 1939. Afterwards she offered her assistance to Teilhard. Their close collaboration really took off after the end of World War II, in 1946, when Teilhard had returned from China and lived in Paris. She then also organized small meetings on Teilhard's thought.[11] After he had made her the literary executrix for all his writings in 1951, she subsequently became the decisive figure in organizing the publication of Teilhard's collected works after his death. An immense gratitude is owed to her, since without her initiative and hard work, his writings might never have seen publication.

In March 1940, Max Bégouën wrote from Paris that they had produced 10,000 copies of Teilhard's essay "Sauvons l'Humanité"(1936)[12] after it had been published in abridged form in the review *Études*. A Russian translation and an English one are also mentioned.[13] If only we knew who were the recipients of all these copies, and what influence this essay may have exercised on its readers during the early years of the Second World War.

When writing this essay in 1936, Teilhard was deeply concerned with what was happening to the human race at a time of severe crisis. In his view humanity "has just entered into what is probably the most extensive period of transformation it has known since its birth" (SC, 128). The essay almost reads like a manifesto about the human future. It has a powerful threefold structure: What to believe? What to see? What to do? It encourages humanity's "spiritual concentration when confronted with the cosmic immensities disclosed to it by science, and with the collective power revealed to it by social organisation," not to create "a heartless, faceless, super-society" (SC, 148), but "to help, with all our strength, the birth of the new world that is trying to emerge" (SC, 142) from among a converging humanity.

The friendship between Teilhard and Max and Simone Bégouën was a deeply personal and lifelong one, lasting from 1915 until Teilhard's death in 1955. On departing from Marseilles in August 1937, Teilhard wrote to Max and Simone, "I could no longer work without you."[14] Learning almost twenty years later in Africa, where Max lived and worked then, about Teilhard's death, Max wrote a moving letter expressing everything he owed to Teilhard's influence and friendship. Teilhard was, and remained, "the guide" who gave him the "revelation of Life" and "the consciousness of being alive."[15]

This correspondence is unusual in that it explains through one personal example how some of Teilhard's new ideas about the transformation of the world, and the progress of life toward the future, were put into practice in a difficult political and economic environment. It shows how Max fought against the old ideas of French colonialism by organizing a new, cooperatively run rose plantation and small distillation plant for the French perfume industry in Morocco and French Guinea in West Africa. He received strong moral support from Teilhard's letters when battling with the French colonial administration who considered his ideas about indigenous cooperation as utopian. Here Teilhard's love for the whole of humankind and for the advancement of the species come out in full. His formative, practical influence on Max and his friends, as on many others, deserves a separate study which I cannot undertake here.

In 1949 Teilhard described his life in Paris as living from day to day, awaiting further decisions by his religious superiors about his future. He missed having a full-time appointment, but was nonetheless busy developing the "virus" of his thought in order to make it "more contagious" and enable it to be "filtering through."[16] This is a subtle but very suitable image for the way Teilhard's ideas began to circulate during his lifetime. They continued to do so after his death, and to some extent they are still penetrating contemporary culture in a similar manner. If we think about it, a virus is a small infectious agent, too small to be seen directly with a light microscope, able to replicate itself inside the living cells of all types of organism. Viruses are found in almost every ecosystem on Earth and are said to be the most abundant type of biological entity. The fact that they are poisonous perhaps makes this image less attractive; maybe Teilhard was above all taken with the ubiquity and invisible manner in which viruses powerfully and effectively multiply and spread themselves around, enacting major transformations wherever they get embedded. He wanted his thought to work in a similar manner and be equally effective in transforming the world.

The same virus metaphor is found in his retreat notes from the previous year, 1948, written in abbreviated form. He writes there: "The preoccupation of this year: to 'activate' the 'virus' K X . . . " (Cosmos Christ); "the objective: *to incorporate* Cosmogenesis into Christ." The editor of the *Notes de Retraites*, Gérard-Henry Baudry, points out that elsewhere Teilhard speaks of this as the process of "christification" and draws the reader's attention to Teilhard's last essay, "The Christic."[17]

The ideas that Teilhard expressed in his letters to the Bégouëns represent an early example of connecting the conscious self-reflection of human beings to the whole planet Earth and to the immensity of the universe. Already in 1926, he wrote from China that it was becoming more and more necessary to know Earth like we know our own body, and that the human mass, dispersed around the globe, represents a certain definite quantum of spiritual energy whose global maturation is necessary for the completion of each person on Earth.[18] He speaks of the "physical reality" of thought, and of his absolute belief in the forward march of thought ("or of Spirit, if you like").[19]

This forward movement is directly connected with the emergence and shaping of the future. Writing from Burma in January 1938, he expressed his growing desire to occupy himself more and more with the future.[20] He admits that "the future with all its personal, collective, political, and religious uncertainties appears to me like God's Sacrament par excellence, like the Divine being born."[21] When he comments in 1930 on Max's business ventures in Morocco, Teilhard speaks of a world on the way to unification, where the spiritual success of the universe is linked to all the zones of this universe, and especially to "the release of all possible energies of this universe." This relates to the complex, dynamic realm of interdependent human connections that bring into being "more freedom to act, to think, and to love."[22] It also relates to the theme of human energy, so extensively reflected upon in his 1937 essay "Human Energy."[23] And it is ultimately summed up in this simple statement: "Basically, nothing counts but the progress we can make, in isolation or together, in the vision and possession of all things."[24]

Writing soon again, Teilhard admits to Max in February 1938 that he is ready to fight for the ideas expressed in his essay "Human Energy." He discusses there the significance, organization, and maintenance of human energy, but also the transformative powers of love, "a higher form of human energy" (HE, 145). Teilhard says that what he has written there represents "the thought of today's true Christians." He considers it as sadly comical "to see clerics, devoted to the love of God" refuse to recognize these pages which, according to his knowledge, "represent the first attempt to assign a place to divine love in the structure of the modern world."[25]

Much later, in April 1951, Teilhard writes from Paris that he is more and more "preoccupied by questions of Human Energetics (questions about the 'taste' for Life, or even about the 'amorisation' of the World and of Evolution)." He mentions the possibility that, in association with Julian Huxley, a "Research Center for Human Energetics" might be developed in America."[26] Here he uses the French expression "goût de la Vie," whereas on other occasions he simply writes "goût de vivre"; yet both expressions seem to carry a similar meaning. In 1950 he devoted a whole essay to this topic, translated into English as "Zest for Living" (AE, 229–43). On other occasions, when discussing the importance of this drive for human life and evolution, the English equivalent is usually given as "zest for life," and I will retain this in my discussion here. Most important to note, however, is the association between the zest for life, the place of human energy in the unfolding of life, and the available energy resources for feeding the zest for life, and for activating human energies at the individual, social, and species level.

## What Is the Zest for Life?

The French word "goût" can be understood as a taste, a liking, a sense of enjoyment, as the appreciation of something—whether food, music, or nature, to mention some examples. This taste is connected with outer and inner senses, with a feeling, a predilection, a preference that motivates our actions. The English word "zest" refers to something similar, although it has also a wider semantic field. Teilhard uses the word "goût"—in the sense of "taste" or "zest"—throughout his writings.

According to *The New Oxford Dictionary of English,* the true origin of "zest" seems to be unknown. The word is said to come from the late fifteenth-century French word "zeste," meaning orange or lemon peel, both of which share a strong taste and are used for flavoring dishes when cooking. The contemporary meaning of zest is given as "great enthusiasm and energy," and also as "quality of excitement and piquancy."[27] Other meanings associated with zest might be eagerness, keenness, and also drive. All these words express a certain dynamic energy and movement, an aliveness that spurs us on, nourishes and sustains human attitudes, inspiring further action, growth, and development, or it is simply understood as an alignment with the flow of life. The zest for life is a drive that keeps us alive, engaged, committed to be involved with what is going on around us. It relates to an awakening to the fullness of life with all its joys and pains, its growth, diminishments, and sufferings.

With the immense knowledge humankind possesses at present, and the myriad problems the global human community faces today, we have to ask what it means to be truly human, to be fully alive in the twenty-first century. Experiencing the fullness of life is sometimes described as a "sense of plenitude,"[28] a sense of being fully awake and aware, of savoring, enjoying, and appreciating a rich spectrum of life's experiences within oneself, in others, and in one's environment. Children, with their exuberance, enthusiasm, curiosity, and playfulness, seem to have this sense almost more so than many disenchanted and overworked adults. Yet it is most important to nourish the zest of life throughout all stages of human development.

Growing into the fullness of life must be understood in the largest possible context today, that of evolutionary becoming. This now requires a strong ecological awareness, and a new ecological Earth-consciousness and responsibility. The sense of a fullness of life is related to a primal trust in life, a zest for life, an openness to the future, and a search for the necessary energy resources to feed this zest.

Another idea associated with the zest of life is the idea of flourishing, especially the flourishing of people and planet—of the whole human species on planet Earth. The original associations of the word flourishing can be traced back to flowers, gardens, and growth, so that we have here a very ecological concept that can be related to the whole web of life. Flourishing means to thrive and prosper. It refers to a dynamic drive rooted in a continuing source of energy which nurtures people's attitudes, motivation, and action. This very positive concept of flourishing is immensely attractive as it implies that we can go from strength to strength, even when the going may get difficult at times.

In order for people to flourish as persons and as communities, good relations with others have to be nurtured, the right external conditions must pertain. People cannot flourish in times of war, strife, and dissent. Humans cannot live a healthy, satisfactory life if they do not eat the right food, breathe clean air, drink clean water, and have the right education. So much poverty and starvation around the world is linked to the absence of these basic human necessities, so directly dependent on our most immediate environment. Human flourishing is not possible without other forms of flourishing, especially environmental and biological, but it also extends to economic, political, social, and spiritual flourishing.

Life in the widest sense is what humans experience and live for. But what is a truly *human* life? All life needs tending, nurturing, caring for, and human life especially requires physical, mental, moral, and spiritual care for body, mind, spirit, and soul. That means human life needs spirituality like the body needs breath and blood to flourish.

It has been said that Western society has now taken such an affirmative "turn to life," from honoring different ways of living to affirming one's individual lifestyle, that life itself has assumed the religious meaning formerly assigned to God. Thus we are observing the cult of a "new religion of life," much critiqued and strongly resisted by conservative and hierarchical religious institutions. Yet such a polarization between God and life is as artificial and unhelpful as other dichotomies, like the mutually exclusive contrast that is sometimes claimed to exist between religion and spirituality, for example. In theistic understanding, God is always a God of life, a living God who bestows life and sustains it, cares for the whole of life—the life of the earth, the life of nature, and all human life, past, present, and future. Christians affirm this belief every time they recite the Nicene Creed which states: "I believe in the Holy Spirit, . . . the giver of life."

Even in our times, so full of uncertainty and change, human beings still come into the world with a fundamental, underlying trust in life. It is an innate trust which in German is spoken of as *Ur-Vertrauen*—an elemental, primary, foundational trust that underlies all life and growth, a basic fundamental faith in the goodness of life, and in the world as our home. It is important to build on this primary trust, expand and consolidate it rather than become disenchanted and destroy it. "Trust life," Teilhard used to say; "life is never mistaken." This primary trust, this sense of being carried, affirmed, and supported, is so different from the *Ur-Angst* or existential anxiety that modern philosophers speak about. From a religious point of view, this trust is linked to a deep belief in being held and enfolded by something greater, of being cared for and protected by God's presence and loving care.

How can we ensure that this primary trust in life with which we are born is not diminished and lost, that it is encouraged to grow and build up into a courageous, active zest for life? We cannot advance the world and life's flourishing without such zest. But how can this be done? And where do we find the necessary resources for the development of the zest for life in the personal lives of people, and in the global community today?

The zest for life—the will to live and love life to the full, and contribute to its growth—is an indispensable requisite for the continuity of life, especially in the form of a higher, more conscious and spiritual life. It also shows itself in the development of a more integrated, stronger global human community that will give priority to promoting more equality, justice, and peace, as well as a planetary ethic. Enemy number one is indifference and boredom, the loss of a taste for life, the absence of inner resources, and the danger of dropping out of all commitments by not taking responsibility for one's own life and that of others. In Teilhard's view, we cannot advance the world and the flourishing of life on the planet without a zest for life. He described it as "nothing less than the *energy of universal evolution*" (AE, 231), but, at the human level, the feeding and development of this energy "is to some degree *our responsibility*" (AE, 232).

This theme preoccupied Teilhard until the day of his death. Toward the end of his last essay, the profoundly personal and mystical text "The Christic," completed in March 1955, one month before the end of his life, he speaks of "the primordial sources of the *Energy of Evolution*" which modern science has discovered, but also of the need for humanity "to find a way to increase the *Drive of Evolution*": "If humanity is to use its new access of physical power with balanced control, it cannot do without a rebound of intensity in its zest to act, in its zest to seek, in its zest to create" (HE, 96–97).[29] In this essay, as in so many previous ones, Teilhard emphasized once again that one of the key questions which humanity "in process of planetary arrangement"—or what we now call "globalization"—faces, is "a problem of spiritual *activation*" (HM, 96). This can be understood as feeding our drive to be fully alive and moving ahead, by enlarging our zest for life, by drawing on all available energy resources that we need for living, resources that are material and spiritual at the same time. It means to advance, support, and strengthen the zest for life in the whole of humanity and among all its members.

Addressing a wider audience in his essays, Teilhard often writes about the zest for life in general, open-ended terms, but in his own religious life and spiritual practice this zest for life is firmly grounded in his ardent faith in a personal God, and especially in the universal, the emergent Christ who provides the ultimate foundation that undergirds all life, all love and zest for life, all energies, and all processes of becoming. In his early *Retreat Notes* of 1919 Teilhard speaks of "le goût de Dieu"[30] the zest (or perhaps "desire"?) for God, the "zest" for being ("le goût de l'Être"), equated with "= the Absolute, = God, = Christ."[31] Twenty years later he refers to his *vision* of the "Super-Christ," the "Universal Christ" (the word "devotion" would be "much too sentimental and too weak," he adds). He continues: "Clearly, my only reason (zest ['goût'], passion) for living *now* is concentrated, 'materialised', around the discovery (and therefore, around the manifestation, propagation) of *the Universal Christ*." Teilhard is much attracted to the expression "To be in communion with becoming" ("Communier [fidélité, foi] au Devenir"). This becoming converges on "Christ-Omega." Another note adds, "The zest is assured through communion with Fire."[32] These remarkable expressions invite a larger theological elucidation of the zest for life and its spiritual activation. They also relate to Teilhard's highly original, and deeply mystical, Christology, a perspective I cannot pursue here. Several authors have explored the relationship between Christ and evolution,[33] but I shall now return to the question of how to feed the zest for life in the human community today.

## Feeding the Zest for Life: A New Imperative

Our new knowledge of evolutionary becoming and all that this implies—the immensities of space-time, the unimaginable complexities of living forms, including the history of the human species—provides a transformative, even revolutionary perspective on the understanding of human needs and potential, and what it means to have access to the fullness of life.

An evolutionary way of thinking teaches a new, dynamic way of looking at the world and ourselves, where the future is still open and we do not know where we are going. We are at a decisive junction in the history of the human species, at the crossing of a new threshold where matter and spirit, body and soul are being realigned and reconnected. Humans have always been called to attend to the "taste" for life, to nurture its zest, but the need to develop it to a much higher potency is now an evolutionary and spiritual imperative linked to the development of a new stage of consciousness. The Canadian ecofeminist theologian Heather Eaton speaks of the "revolution of evolution," that is to say, that when we take evolution seriously, this radically changes the reference point for all our thinking:

> We humans are not the central reference point—even for our own self-understanding. Awareness of Earth processes allows us to see our radical dependency on other organisms for basic survival, in addition to our kinship with, rather than difference from, other animals. Evolution bends the mind, expands the horizon, and reverses the reference points. Earth is not our context, it is our source.

She suggests that "we ground religious awareness first in the earth processes, second within the processes of human symbolic consciousness and only third within specific religious traditions."[34]

It is clear that the requirements for feeding the zest for life have become much more complex and specific. The activation of this energetic drive forward has become a much greater, more difficult, and more urgent, task since Teilhard first described this zest as "the ultimate mainspring of evolution" (AE, 232). He could hardly have imagined the complex diversity and diffusion of human groups and cultures we have come to know, nor the complexities of technological development and communication that have revolutionized the web of human connections around the entire globe—nor perhaps the intensity of hatred and violence, military aggression, financial greed and exploitation that tear apart the fabric of civil society and the possibilities of human fulfillment. I think if Teilhard were alive today, he would feel immensely challenged by the great perils and promises the human species faces at this decisive stage in its own evolution. Together with others, he would no doubt rise to this challenge by working out in much more detail what our responsibilities and opportunities for creative, innovative responses might be at the present time.

Our taste for life has a complex texture created by many different strands. It evolves through the influence of families, friends, communities, and culture. Education has an enormously important influence in shaping it, but so do our natural and cultural environments, the sciences, the arts, sports, and countless other factors. It was Teilhard's particular passion to draw special attention to the spiritual energy resources that we need to draw upon in order to feed the zest for life. Nowhere is this more strongly expressed than in his essay "The Zest for Living" (1950), which contains his most detailed treatment of the zest for life. It is worth noting that this essay represents the last of six contributions[35] written especially for the Paris group *"L'Union des Croyants,"* founded in 1947 as a French branch of the World Congress of Faiths,[36] the pioneering interfaith group set up by Sir Francis Younghusband in 1936 in London, and still in existence today. Teilhard was very sympathetic to, and supportive of, this group among whom he had several friends. This essay was primarily written as a talk addressed to members of this movement, people who had a religious orientation rather than being scientists or members of the general public.

It is not my intention to analyze this essay here, although I want to make several comments. Teilhard opens with the following definition:

> By "zest for living" or "zest for life," I mean . . . that spiritual disposition, at once intellectual and affective, in virtue of which life, the world, and action seem to us, on the whole, luminous–interesting— appetizing. (AE, 231)

This zest is characterized as "dynamic, constructive, and adventurous." At first sight, it might seem to affect only individual well-being, while it is, in fact, no less than an energy running through the whole evolutionary process. We can compare it to an immense wave that humans must take up and further develop. The most delicate part of this vital development "is *entrusted* to the expert knowledge and skill of *religions*" (AE, 232). At the same time Teilhard is fully aware of the need for a "profound refashioning and a dynamic sorting-out . . . in the field of 'creeds' and 'beliefs' " (AE, 239) of the earth's new religious needs, and of a general convergence of religions that we can observe today. He perceived important energy resources, an evolutionary stimulus, within the different currents of faith active on earth, and in the great mystical traditions, with their practice of contemplation and prayer. Thus the zest for life is presented as "the central and favored ligament . . . within . . . a supremely organic universe, a supremely intimate bond between mysticism, research, and biology" (AE, 242). The essay ends on this, but carries an additional note about *"neo-zest made explicit: Love* (higher form of zest!!)"

(AE, 243). At the end of his life, he said that to feed the zest for life ultimately means to energize to the full "both the powers of growth and life and the powers of diminishment and death" (HM, 99) at the heart of the dynamic process of becoming in which all humans are immersed. The important task of feeding the zest for life is a new imperative. It cannot be met without drawing on spiritual energy resources inside and outside ourselves, and this will require an immense effort.

The active awakening of the spiritual potential of human beings into a spiritually active approach to life is still very underdeveloped in contemporary society. We need to give far more attention to the education of the human spirit, and feed the zest for life in people by developing their spiritual literacy and awareness. Nurturing the human spiritual potential means the development of a spiritual awareness or consciousness, understood as a different, deeper way of "seeing," to which Teilhard de Chardin gave such emphatic witness. It is an all-embracing vision, a commitment to a depth dimension of human life, traditionally understood as a transcendent dimension. It enables human beings to see their experience in a larger context, having a greater vision by relating more widely, and responding more effectively, by taking "response-ability" toward themselves and others, the environment, nature, the earth, the human community, and Ultimate Reality, however named, often called the Spirit or, in theistic traditions, God.[37]

Nowhere does Teilhard speak more often about zest (goût) for action, evolution, super-living, and ultra-evolution of the human species than in the essays written during the last fifteen years of his life, collected in the volume *Activation of Energy*. His sense of urgency comes vividly across in the pages of this book where he reflects on the "main lines of a *spiritual energetics*" (AE, 295; my emphasis) that need to be developed to deal with the impetus of evolution, with its drive toward a further development of the human species. This energetics is understood as "the study of the conditions under which the human zest for auto-evolution and ultra-evolution" (AE, 295) can form a compact group to meet the requirements of "a world in a reflective state of self-transformation" (AE, 296). He explains in a note that this might also be called "psychodynamics," a term coined in analogy to "thermodynamics" (AE, 296), and of special interest to psychologists. Humanity is at the crossroads; it cannot be considered simply as a state that has been reached but must be approached "*as a work that has to be done.*" In his view, the future of humankind depends far more on "*a certain passion for hard work than on a certain wealth of material resources*" (AE, 333).[38] Reflecting on the convergence of humanity, and the role of energy in this process, Teilhard wrote in 1952 that it would be no exaggeration to say that the mankind of tomorrow, though standing on mountains of iron, of coal, of uranium, of wheat, would do no more than "tick over," if, by some mischance, there should be a weakening of its *zest* not simply for subsisting and surviving but for *super-living*.[39] (AE, 333)

The taste and zest for life, for all life, human and nonhuman, is essential for the future of people and the planet. Just as we are concerned to preserve the biodiversity of life-forms, so too we need to take conscious account of, and responsibility for, maintaining what might be called the rich "noospheric" diversity of religious and spiritual ideas, since they provide us with irreplaceable energy resources for feeding the zest for life.

## Conclusion

The zest for life is one of Teilhard's great ideas. It can help to transform the life of individuals by inspiring them to work for a better life for others, and contribute to the transformation of the life of humanity. The zest for life held an important place in Teilhard's own life, as can be seen from the advice given in letters to his friends, and from numerous passages in his essays. This zest can be encouraged and taught, and thus become a powerful incentive and practical help for living. This is especially important for young people who will create the future. To take stock and make use of the material and spiritual energy resources available on Earth is a gigantic task which human beings have to consciously strive to take on. Most important, the resources for building up and strengthening the global human community will include the powerful energies of love, and those of a new mysticism of action—topics that invite further reflections which cannot be pursued here.

Teilhard's thought represents a synthesis of the modern scientific worldview with deep religious and mystical insights. According to John Grim and Mary Evelyn Tucker, this mysticism is activated "in scientific investigation and social commitment to research as well as in comprehensive compassion for all life." Teilhard recognized

that the evolutionary perspective requires a shift in thinking and in moral commitment. . . . A primary question for Teilhard was how to valorize human action and inspire the zest for life amidst inevitable human suffering and the travail of natural disasters, as set within a picture of evolutionary space and time indifferent to life.[40]

With regard to the understanding of evolution, new perspectives are appearing today. Some scientists have begun to question the rather narrow materialistic interpretation of evolutionary processes by searching for "laws of self-organization and complexity"[41] in the development of life. A real paradigm shift is occurring in the move from a primary emphasis on physico-chemical perspectives to those of the complexity of biological systems and organisms which may result as much from self-organization and far-from-equilibrium dynamics as from Darwinian natural selection. The eminent theoretical biologist Stuart Kauffman argues that there are no "entailing laws" in evolution, since we live in a universe of radical emergence where we will not know or cannot ever know for certain where evolution will take us. He judges this situation as leading to a new worldview which he describes as "the re-enchantment of humanity." According to him, we live in a world of enablement, creativity, and often unprestatable opportunities that we partially create and co-create, with and without intent, but whose results we cannot know ahead, since the future becoming of life cannot be predicted. We need to develop new cultural forms and live "the well discovered life" that will serve our deeper humanity.[42] Teilhard's thought about the zest for life can certainly provide a powerful impetus for living such a life, and for working toward higher forms of life in the human community. It can also help to inspire educational and social programs that will put these ideas into practice.

May we hope that educators, planners, social thinkers, and activists, as well as political, scientific, and spiritual leaders, will take on Teilhard's suggestion to feed and increase the zest for life in the world, so as to advance the further evolution of the human species. A more thoroughly pursued and applied zest for life has the potential to generate much social, cultural, and spiritual change in the global community. It is encouraging to know that new emergence thinking among contemporary scientists, and discussions about the relationship between science and spirit,[43] are presently fuelling a renewed interest in the intellectual-spiritual synthesis and innovative theories of Teilhard de Chardin, a much misunderstood but powerful twentieth-century thinker of great originality who still has much to say to the present generation.

## Points to Ponder

+ Already in 1926, Teilhard wrote from China that it was becoming more and more necessary to know Earth like we know our own body, and that the human mass, dispersed around the globe, represents a certain definite quantum of spiritual energy whose global maturation is necessary for the completion of each person on Earth.

+ Teilhard speaks of the "physical reality" of thought, and of his absolute belief in the forward march of thought ("or of Spirit, if you like"). This forward movement is directly connected with the emergence and shaping of the future.

◆ "The future with all its personal, collective, political, and religious uncertainties appears to me like God's Sacrament par excellence, like the Divine being born."

◆ "Basically, nothing counts but the progress we can make, in isolation or together, in the vision and possession of all things."

◆ The zest for life is a drive that keeps us alive, engaged, committed to be involved with what is going on around us. It relates to an awakening to the fullness of life with all its joys and pains, its growth, diminishments, and sufferings.

◆ Human beings still come into the world with a fundamental, underlying trust in life . . . an elemental, primary, foundational trust that underlies all life and growth, a basic fundamental faith in the goodness of life, and in the world as our home.

◆ The zest for life shows itself in the development of a more integrated, stronger global human community that will give priority to promoting more equality, justice, and peace, as well as a planetary ethic. Enemy number one is indifference and boredom, the loss of a taste for life, the absence of inner resources, and the danger of dropping out of all commitments by not taking responsibility for one's own life and that of others.

◆ Humanity is at the crossroads; it cannot be considered simply as a state that has been reached but must be approached *"as a work that has to be done."* In his view, the future of humankind depends far more on *"a certain passion for hard work than on a certain wealth of material resources."*

## Questions for Discussion

1. What is the contribution of Teilhard's "zest for life" to Christian life? Contemporary culture?

2. What are the connections Teilhard makes between evolution, consciousness, and the rise of spiritual energy?

3. How can we understand Teilhard's "communion with becoming" in terms of the church's sacramental life, especially the Eucharist?

4. Is the zest for life a spiritual attitude or virtue, or is it intrinsic to the nature of the evolving cosmos itself?

# Notes

1. For example there is no entry for the term "zest for life" in Siôn Cowell, *The Teilhard Lexicon* (Brighton, OR: Sussex Academic, 2001). I have published an earlier essay on this theme in Thierry Meynard, S.J., ed., *Teilhard and the Future of Humanity* (New York: Fordham University Press, 2006), 3–19: "Feeding the Zest for Life: Spiritual Energy Resources for the Future of Humanity." The same volume also contains an essay by Mary Evelyn Tucker, "Zest for Life: Teilhard's Cosmological Vision," pp. 43–55, but the zest for life is only fleetingly referred to.

2. Paulo Freire, *Pedagogy of the Oppressed* (Harmondsworth, UK: Penguin, 1996).

3. Pierre Teilhard de Chardin, *Le rayonnement d'une amitié: Correspondance avec la famille Bégouën (1922–1955)*, ed. Michel Hermans and Pierre Sauvage with the collaboration of Marie Bayon de la Tour (Brusseles: Lessius, 2011).This correspondence contains ninety-six letters from Teilhard and ten letters from the Begouën family. References to this correspondence are noted as BegCor.

4. See BegCor, 15–16. In 1922, Henri de Bégouën was given the chair of prehistory at Toulouse University.

5. The development of twelve major works by Teilhard, written between 1933 and 1950 and reflected in this correspondence, is discussed by J.-P. Dumoulin's essay "Réflexions sur l'importance et l'originalité de cette correspondence," BegCor, 229–46.

6. See the collection of essays grouped together in Pierre Teilhard de Chardin, *Writings in Time of War*. Original French edition 1965.

7. See introduction to BegCor, 5; also 63.

8. See Patrice Boudignon, *Pierre Teilhard de Chardin. Sa vie, son oeuvre, sa réflexion* (Paris: Cerf, 2008), 161; the whole section 160–65 bears on the discussion of this method of diffusion of Teilhard's works, on which very little detailed information exists.

9. For example, on March 18, 1936, Teilhard writes from Beijing that Lucile has finished the translation of "How I Believe"; they will print some three hundred copies in a private edition on Chinese art paper. BegCor, 90.

10. BegCor, 179.

11. BegCor, 184. See also Boudignon, *Pierre Teilhard de Chardin*, 280–81. For a fuller account see P. Teilhard de Chardin, *Lettres à Jeanne Mortier* (Paris: Seuil, 1984), especially the Introduction *"Paroles d'un Témoin"* where she writes about her reaction to the reading of *The Divine Milieu:* "La lecture de ce livre éblouissant me fut un choc spirituel. Il me sortit du tunnel où m'avait enfoncée, après dix ans d'études thomistes, la certitude que la philosophie et la théologie médiévales, faute d'*aggiornamento* scientifique, parlaient une langue qui n'avait plus cours en notre temps. Elles tenaient l'Église amarrée au passé, alors que l'humanité, tirée par la science, voguait vers l'avenir à vitesse accélérée." *Lettres à Jeanne Mortier*, 9. Here is my translation of this passage: "Reading this brilliant book gave me a spiritual shock. It got me out of the tunnel I had been driven into after ten years of Thomistic studies that gave me the certainty that medieval philosophy and theology spoke a language that had little to do with our time, due to the absence of a scientific *aggiornamento*. They kept the Church moored in the past whereas humanity, drawn to science, was sailing with increasing speed toward the future."

12. Translated by the rather unsatisfactory title "The Salvation of Mankind. Thoughts on the Present Crisis," in SC, 128–50.

13. BegCor, 163.

14. BegCor, 113.

15. BegCor, 218. For the whole text of this extraordinary letter describing a deep friendship and inner transformation see BegCor, 218–22.

16. BegCor, 194 (my translation paraphrases the text).

17. P. Teilhard de Chardin, *Notes de retraites 1919–1954* (Paris: Seuil, 2003), 296 and note 11; hereafter abbreviated as NRet.

18. See BegCor, 25.

19. BegCor, 41.

20. BegCor, 126.

21. BegCor, 73.

22. BegCor, 52.

23. This essay is found in a book of the same title. See HE, 113–62.

24. BegCor, 36.

25. BegCor, 130.

26. See BegCor, 199–200.

27. Judith Pearsall, ed., *The New Oxford Dictionary of English* (Oxford: Clarendon, 1998), 2148.

28. Teilhard de Chardin uses this expression in his essay "The Heart of Matter" included in a book of the same title. For Teilhard the sense of plenitude is related to a particular, personal synthesis, but the expression can also be used in a more general sense.

29. My translation of "dans son goût d'agir, dans son goût de chercher, dans son goût de créer." The English translation simply reads "in its eagerness to act, to seek, to create." Taken from the essay "The Christic." See HM 80–102.

30. NRet, 61.

31. NRet, 58.

32. All quotations are found in NRet, 121 & 122.

33. See, for example, Ilia Delio, OSF, *The Emergent Christ: Exploring the Meaning of Catholic in an Evolutionary Universe* (Maryknoll, NY: Orbis Books, 2011) and *Christ in Evolution* (Maryknoll, NY: Orbis Books, 2008). A different approach is pursued by Celia Deane-Drummond, *Christ and Evolution: Wonder and Wisdom* (London: SCM Press and Minneapolis: Fortress Press, 2009).

34. Heather Eaton, "An Ecological Imaginary: Evolution and Religion in an Ecological Era," in Sigurd Bergman and Heather Eaton, eds., *Ecological Awareness. Exploring Religion, Ethics and Aesthetics,* Studies in Religion and the Environment, vol. 3 (Berlin: LIT, 2011), 12, 16.

35. Only four exist in print in Teilhard's collected works; two are short, unpublished papers. They are briefly discussed in Ursula King, *Teilhard de Chardin and Eastern Religions: Spirituality and Mysticism in an Evolutionary World* (New York: Paulist Press, 2011), 94–98. A more detailed analysis is provided in Ursula King, *The Spirit of One Earth: Reflections on Teilhard de Chardin and Global Spirituality* (New York: Paragon, 1989); see chapter 8, "Teilhard's Association with the World Congress of Faiths, 1947–1950."

36. Teilhard provided the inaugural address; see "Faith in Man" in P. Teilhard de Chardin, *The Future of Man* (London: Collins, 1965), 185–92.

37. These themes are discussed in more detail in Ursula King, *The Search for Spirituality: Our Global Quest for a Spiritual Life* (New York: BlueBridge, 2008).

38. This formulation may remind readers of Thomas Berry's approach presented in his influential book, *The Great Work: Our Way into the Future* (New York: Bell Tower, 1999).

39. The French text reads *"le goût,* non pas seulement de subsister et de survivre, mais *de super-vivre."*

40. John Grim and Mary Evelyn Tucker, "An Overview of Teilhard's Commitment to 'Seeing' as Expressed in His Phenomenology, Metaphysics, and Mysticism," in C. Deane-Drummond, ed., *Pierre Teilhard de Chardin on People and Planet* (London: Equinox, 2006), 55–73; see 67, 71 for the quotations.

41. This is the subtitle of Stuart Kauffman's book *At Home in the Universe: The Search for Laws of Self-Organization and Complexity* (Oxford: Oxford University Press, 1995). See also his book *Reinventing the Sacred: A New View of Science, Reason, and Religion* (New York: Basic, 2010).

42. Quoted from Stuart Kauffman, "The Reenchantment of Humanity: The Implications of 'No Entailing Laws,'" unpublished paper and notes from a lecture given at a conference on "Spirituality, Emergent Creativity, and Reconciliation," St Paul's University, Ottawa, May 23–26, 2012.

43. Just one example out of several is provided by Dave Pruett, *Reason and Wonder: A Copernican Revolution in Science and Spirit* (Santa Barbara: Praeger, 2012). See especially Part IV, "The Third 'Copernican' Revolution: Psychology/Spirituality," where three chapters deal with Teilhard de Chardin.

*Chapter 12*

# TEILHARD DE CHARDIN
*The Empirical Mystic*

## John C. Haughey, SJ

Although our project takes off from and goes beyond where Teilhard de Chardin went, I am curious about his prayer life because that seems to be the source of his creativity. Yes, his prayer was unique—whose isn't? But what if his was also a model and imitable way to approach and be approached by the Mystery? Many theologians and philosophers and scientists and "keepers of the keys" have been exasperated by Teilhard's writings since they expected something other than what is closer to nature poetry than to geology as such, or to religious naturalism than to theology, or to animism than to paleontology, etc. The same puzzlement faces someone like me who, while reading him, wonders what his praying was like. I have concluded that "empirical mystic" captures his spiritual uniqueness. Aside from this way of understanding him, I think his prayer has widespread relevance because many praying believers seem to be becoming like him. They are spending much time wondering, as am I, as more and more scientific findings fall into our laps. And many nonbelievers might be able to see themselves as already praying without even knowing that they are if they saw the connection between his wondering and theirs.

Prayer in the future will have to be more au courant with where our scientific knowledge of this world and the universe is going. For example, even a smattering of quantum thought or a whiff about the expansion of the cosmos—each is increasingly astonishing, so the place and role of the human species in the world needs continual updating. Science is becoming more and more successful at mapping out the beginnings and the boundaries of physicality. So locating ourselves somewhere on these maps is an increasing challenge. Teilhard de Chardin met and models this challenge. Faith needs reason and reason faith. Faith needs to believe that knowing gets us somewhere, and faith even further, and that reason flourishes where believing propels it. The hunt for data, especially scientific data, is a quest driven by faith in both the natural and the supernatural senses of that term. Faith and meaning and reasoning all accompany each other. Leave out one and the other two suffer.

Prayer is—among other things— an activity that is meaning seeking and meaning finding. We cannot live long without the meaning of what we're learning or seeking to learn. Most of the faith stories that our age embraces were born in the first axial age which was, of course, cosmologically innocent. We should not be. Teilhard connected the dots between faith and cosmological knowledge. The more the natural sciences drill down into the empirical, the thinner meaning gets. The value of the drilling can be wondered about eventually, unless there is the promise of meaning beyond the tip of the drill. Teilhard did his drilling within the divine milieu, and the more data he uncovered, the more energy he found for deeper drilling. This paper is not an exercise in apologetics nor will it be an exhortation to believe in God. Rather, given the magnitude and empirical complexity heretofore unimaginable of the empirical data of science, we need evidence that meaning can be probed all the way down (or is it up?) into infinity.

The empirical gets exhausting. It gets us to the next level of the proximate. But the proximate is always whole-deficient. Now that we know about the billion neurons in an adult brain and the trillion interconnections between them, how to explain mind and the achievements of intelligibility through intelligence lo these many years? Beyond the proximacy there is ultimacy, and prayer has been one way to access the realm of the not-yet-intelligible. It has been one of the ways of making wholes out of the separated parts. Science gets to parts; prayer seeks to get to wholes. If we approach Teilhard's thought as his prayer written down, we will understand him better than if we want to make him a theologian or a philosopher or a preacher or a scientist.

The first half of this article will unpack five of the unique ways Teilhard de Chardin went about wondering. His way of wondering was prayer, it seems. The things he went about wondering about were: (1) Matter; (2) Ahead/Above; (3) Eucharist; (4) Dark Adoration; (5) Le Tout. The second half of this article will enlarge on what he saw and see it as the Spirit at work in him. The matter/spirit nexus would not have been made by him except "in the Holy Spirit."

## Matter

The main matter of Teilhard's prayer was matter. His probing of physical reality seems to have been much more central to his prayer than the usual forms prayer takes in the church. He succinctly states the effect this manner of praying had for him: "by laying hold of earth I help myself to cling closely to you, Lord" (HU, 115). So thinking about his praying in the traditional terms of meditation or contemplation or resting in the Lord as these experiences have been described or prescribed in the past can miss something distinctive about him and his prayer. He believed that in the future prayer would no longer be a matter of the individual and heaven but of humanity and Earth.

*The Human Phenomenon* was one of Teilhard's first major publications. In it he explains how he sees two different kinds of energy in every instance of matter. One is, as it were, "inside," the other "outside." The inside had "spirit" which has it move in the direction of the *ahead*. He called this radial energy; it is moving toward complexity and eventually to consciousness. The second kind of matter has a tangential energy; the second law of thermodynamics would describe it as entropic. It is going downhill, being emptied out, dying, ephemeral; it is losing its grip. He does not always stay with radial and tangential as descriptors of energy; sometimes he distinguishes the difference as between psychic and physical energy (AM, 265).

For Teilhard, matter is complementary to spirit on Earth. For him, without matter there is no spirit and vice versa and, of course, without matter there would have been no prayer. It seems like this high regard for matter was going on in him from the beginning of his life when he found "so many different thoughts coming out of the same piece of bread," that is, the Eucharist. He has a whole hymn of praise to matter! Some of its lines: "Blessed be you, mighty matter, irresistible march of evolution, reality ever new-born; you who by constantly shattering our mental categories, force us to go ever further and further in our pursuit of the truth." Even more surprising: "Blessed be you, universal matter, immeasurable time, boundless ether, triple abyss of stars and atoms and generations: you who by overflowing and dissolving our narrow standards or measurements reveal to us the dimensions of God" (HU, 68–69). Matter, flesh, earth in general, nature and creation in all its variety goes in the direction of self-maintenance and self-sufficiency. So God makes stuff that makes itself, that organizes itself. But all of it also goes in the direction of self-emptying, entropy, death. And finally there is a confluence of spirit and matter. The endpoint of this matter-spirit interaction will be an eventual transfiguration of all that God has created when God will be "all in all."

## Ahead/Above

A spatial image that is particularly clarifying about his prayer is the connection between what he calls the Ahead and the Above. The dialectic between the Ahead and the Above is kept in play, he would say, by synthesis. With the Ahead and the Above consciously operating in tandem there can be union but still a union has to leave the differences different, and at the same time gathered and vectored toward Omega Oneness. Human consciousness for Teilhard is equipped to contribute to Omega, and the more the pursuit of the Ahead consciously seeks the Above, the more likely the contribution. It would be too simple to reduce the Above in Teilhard's thought to God. It is too simple because he realized the Ahead is already pregnant with the Above. Human consciousness naturally puts these together in innumerable ways. Doing so, he felt, is the right use and purpose of radial energy. Humans thereby can bring matter beyond where it can go on its own.

For Teilhard, the Above is already operating in the drive to the Ahead. Several factors in his background would have influenced this metaphor which was so central to his thought. One of these was the Thomist tradition, which would have taught him that the process of human intellection is a participation in the Divine Intellect. Another factor was his Jesuit training. Ignatius of Loyola encouraged "finding God in all things." Doing so would make it easier to believe that the co-laboring Spirit was operating in his subjectivity. A third factor was science, which helped him to experience God not as an object to be found apart from or beyond other objects but, as his more mature spirituality would articulate it, God everywhere. Reality is a Divine Milieu. He commented that "the great event of my life" was the moment when the rocks and his faith came together. "In an explosion of dazzling flashes," he said, he "felt caught between the two."[1]

## Eucharist

Teilhard's kind of praying began in his early experience with rocks and iron speaking to him but also with some bread saying to him that it is more than bread. In consuming the blessed bread, he began to envision and savor the future that God intends for all matter. So, while his preferred manner of praying was by probing matter and letting it have its say, understanding his prayer also needs to be seen in light of how he experienced Eucharist. His first writings about it put together a matter-energy-Eucharist troika. This was during the horrors of World War I in 1916. He was able to look up from the geysers of blood and torn guts all around him and do more than recoil, though recoil he did. He was able to have a sense of a converging whole. So where others saw only dismembered bodies, his communion with God which he had experienced from his youth, through the blessed bread and wine in particular, made him a unique kind of panentheist, a eucharistic kind, if you will.

Another dramatic articulation of his material way of seeing Eucharist was his "The Mass on the World" which he wrote in 1923 in the Ordos Desert in China, though the experience of the trenches had triggered it. Teilhard prayed there that Spirit/Fire will "breathe a soul into the newly formed, fragile film of matter with which the world is to be freshly clothed."[2] With this event he conveys how he connects the transubstantiation of the species of bread and wine with the transfiguration of all the world. Instead of bread and wine, he offered all the labor being done across the world that day with the sufferings that accompany them.

For him Eucharist functioned not only personally but cosmically, as he wrote: "The organic form of the universe divinized is Christ Jesus. Through the magnetism of his love and the effective power of his Eucharist, he gradually gathers into himself all the unitive energy scattered through the creation" (HU, 119). Notice again how the poetic imagination of Teilhard is not encased in yesterday's expression; radial energy becomes unitive energy.

The eucharistic bread was a primary source of this radial/unitive energy. As material, it is confected by human hands; as energy, it produces actions, like the actions of faith, hope, love, and worship. More abstractly, there was "God's creative action bringing to birth" what Teilhard described as "the upper pole of human co-reflexion" (AM, 270–71). This is where one of his inimitable terms, the "noosphere," comes into his rhetoric. The noosphere is the increment to "being" that consciousness produces. His Eucharist and prayer and zeal and research were all of a piece for him. One enlightened the other. In many texts this is evident. For example, from his *Hymn of the Universe* one gets increasingly insightful connections:

> By assisting in the spread of science and freedom I can increase the divine atmosphere, in itself as well as for me, that atmosphere in which it is always my one desire to be immersed. . . . May the kingdom of matter, then, under our scrutinies and our manipulations, surrender to us the secrets of its texture, its movement, its history. . . .

> May the universe offer to our gaz-e the symbols and the forms of all harmony and all beauty. (HU, 115–16)

The integration continues further on in the book: "For the sake of the world I would be more widely human in my sympathies and more nobly terrestrial in my ambitions than any of the world's servants. On the one hand I want to plunge into the midst of created things and, mingling with them, seize hold upon and disengage from them all that they contain of life eternal, down to the very last fragment, so that nothing may be lost" (HU, 128–29).

He has been famous for creating new terms. So if radial energy can become unitive energy, what does its destiny and, therefore, ours, look like? He sees all of reality heading toward what he called "Point Omega"; a teleology is "indispensable to the functioning of evolution." He analyzed the properties of this Omega finality as threefold. First, it has to be "objective." By this he means not only that it is an "ideal extension or projection of our concepts and desires" but that it "corresponds to a biological bringing together of our personalities." Second, "it preserves everything . . . that is most essential and incommunicable in each reflective element of the universe." And third, "it preserves everything *forever*," thereby rescuing "evolved humanity once and for all" from anything that would have it disappear into nonbeing (AM, 271).

His expectation was that at some point "humanity, in order to attain further co-reflexion and union, will be led progressively to distinguish an 'amorizing' kernel of the *transcendent* in the centre of an Omega at first regarded as simply *immanent*" (AM, 273). Hence a third inimitable term, "amorizing"; it conveys his description for the foundational love that undergirds all forms of evolution.

Teilhard did not explicitly think about ecology, but could have with his materialized sense of Eucharist. The erstwhile description of there being a transubstantiation of the species of bread and wine though the liturgical action of the community for him was connected with not only the work of human beings in the world but with the activities of all of nature. He doesn't say as much, but all of nature is a concelebrant in the liturgical actions of the celebrating community. Nature, therefore, needs to be reverenced in its own way and for itself just as the blessed bread and wine are. The divine has located itself in a material milieu. The material aspect of the sacrament might become even more evident if we adverted to its indebtedness to soil and grain and wheat and vines and grapes and the labors of bread- and wine-makers which eucharistic practice depends on. It requires the body of earth and the bodies of those who labor on it and the bodily presence of the congregation to have the bread and the wine become the new body representing the new creation.

What could also be added profitably to his eucharistic vision is an awareness of the dying that the wheat and grapes have gone through before one receives the blessed bread and wine: from the vine to the grape to the bunch to the wine to the blood . . . and we're not even counting their prehistory all the way back to the stars. There has been and still is a paschal mystery throughout both the prehistory and history of each of these ingredients before they and, in turn their recipients, are transformed into *kairos* time. So the dying and the rising do not end with the grapes becoming wine or the wheat becoming bread. Each is transformed to be consumed. So are those who consume them. No action is more paradoxical and para-doxological than that of receiving the bread and wine, of consuming and being consumed by it. The self-emptying God brings one into the paschal mystery through the Eucharist.

Teilhard's idea was that what the world in all its materiality needs, and what each human being in the world also needs, is to "consent to the communion that will enable it to find what it has come to seek" (HU, 115). It seems to me that all his writings can be read as a life-long disquisition on the *where* of God. As he puts it: "I must *search* and I must *find. What is at stake, Lord, is the element wherein you will to dwell here on earth; what is at stake is your existence amongst us*" (HU, 116). For him the Eucharist was the most tangible "element" of this presence and of its existence among us.

## Dark Adoration

One of the more intriguing comments Teilhard makes in relation to prayer is this observation: "There is much less difference than people think between research and adoration" (SC, 214–20). This comment is pregnant with meaning, both the meaning of our lives and of his life as a search to find God in all things. He spent long hours, days, months, years as a paleontologist at the grungy work of digging up bones and debris and pondering their silent message about us. Early on it was iron, then rocks, and eventually the bones—all had something to disclose, he believed, and he spent his whole lifetime deciphering what that was.

Teilhard called the lead-up to adoration "dark adoration," because it is still in the tunnel of inquiry. The objects being examined had not yet come into the light of day of insight and faith. When they did, they ceased to be dark and could formally become adoration . . . but not for long, since he was soon back to seeking more information and moving from acquiring it to adoration. Curiosity was his middle name. Information was endlessly and increasingly sought in a singularly passionate way by him. For him, as for most of us, the inquiry is in function of coming to insight and verification or judgment or conclusion, and to "is so" or "is not so." And all of this entailed, as I would put it, a kneeling down to acknowledge the co-laboring Spirit who accompanies consciousness. Gathering information did not become all-absorbing or virtually idolatrous as it can become if it shuts out other good ends, like family, coworkers, colleagues, love, mission, or one's own spirituality. His passion for knowledge did not swamp other goods, nor did it become disproportionately valued. Information was a relative good and it was kept relative by the Above Absolute.

His adoration wasn't always formal; to an outside observer of his behavior it would have looked more like wonder than praying. His continual pursuit of and the attainment of data was undertaken by him within a "divine milieu." It produced an ever-increasing enlargement of his consciousness that alternated between searching and finding, rummaging and marveling, hoping and being awed. One might go so far as to see him as a participant in God's enjoyment of each aspect of creation—often through some unearthed artifact.

Teilhard's way of giving glory to God was primarily by his thinking and choosing. It was these acts that made him and can make the rest of us reflect the One in whose image and likeness we have been made. And we can give greater glory to God by a consciousness that does the knowing and or choosing alive to its connection to God. So, if you will, it is ad *majorem* Dei Gloriam if one is aware of the divine milieu within which one is operating, whereas it is *ad minorem Dei gloriam* if one falls short of that awareness. We can also let ourselves experience God's enjoyment of what is, without a further formally religious act.

The Teilhardian suggestion is that we try to view matter in a new way by seeing its inner finality. Often enough he went from being immersed in the here and now to taking his work to a new level, and seeing it "like a Host ready to be charged with the divine influence, that is, with a real presence of the Incarnate Word" (DM, 98–99). One of his recommendations was that the eucharistic Host should not be perceived as merely a localized, external, temporary element "in an exile from which we are almost permanently obliged to live . . . (but to see that) the Host of bread is continually encircled more closely by another, infinitely larger Host, which is nothing less than the universe itself. . . . The world is the final and the real Host into which Christ gradually descends until his time is fulfilled. . . . 'Hoc est enim corpus meum.' Nothing is at work in creation except in order to assist, from near at hand or from afar, in the consecration of the universe" (SC, 64–66).

As we become more and more intrigued by the findings of science, more specifically, by the scale of data from macrocosmology and the infinitesimal findings being uncovered by microbiology, it seems like the liturgical community's offering of Jesus to the Father through the Spirit must begin to include in its scope this kind of information in some way. If we believe that Christ is in the process of "handing all things over to the Father," it seems that our liturgical actions should be commensurately knowledgeable about the varieties and complexities of what these are. Teilhard spent much of his life seeing wholes operating in the universe, e.g., cosmogenesis, anthropogenesis, etc., out of what would otherwise remain only piecemeal data. He did this by seeing that one is able "to lose oneself in the unfathomable, to plunge into the inexhaustible, to find peace in the incorruptible, to be absorbed in the definite immensity, to offer oneself to the fire . . . and to give one's deepest self to that whose depth has no end" (SC, 102). This is mysticism at its most attractive heights.

Not surprisingly Teilhard was sure that "an ultimate explanation of Cosmogenesis" could be found in what he called a "revealed Christogenesis" (SC, 189). He was sure that science needed something more than science to give it meaning, just as liturgical prayer also needed something more. His candidate for this was an awareness that "when all is said and done, it may well be, perhaps, faith in Christ that tomorrow will preserve in us the zest for evolution" (SC, 191).

## Le Tout

The act of naming an experience is making a whole. Whole making is what God equipped humans for, each in his or her own way. To fall short of whole seeking and whole making is to fall short of what is special about being human. An act of praying can make whole what otherwise falls short in our perception of it.

> The Absolute towards which we are ascending can wear only the face of the whole. . . . It is not I that have laboriously discovered the whole; it is the whole that has presented itself to me. . . . It is the attraction of the whole that has set everything in motion in me, has animated me and given organic form to everything. . . . It is because I feel the whole and love it passionately that I believe in the primacy of being and—that I cannot admit that life meets a final check—and that I cannot look for a lesser reward than this whole itself. (SC, 43–44)

Teilhard was never dislodged from believing that "the goal before Creation and attained by Creation is in the first place the whole. . . . If the world is to be thinkable, it must be centered . . . by the Divinity himself who has introduced us 'in et cum Mundo' into the triune heart of his immanence" (SC, 56). His focus and concern was with "the stuff of the universe," more specifically with "elementary matter, total matter, the evolution of matter" and the "psychic" dimension in all matter: in brief, God and matter. His faith and spirituality had him immerse himself in matter and energy. His probing of the nature of matter is key to understanding him and his "spiritual life."

I believe that Teilhard's discomfort with the church's liturgical prayer and teachings about prayer were that these were construed too supernaturally and not immanently enough. He took the incarnation into greater depths than his teachers had, and saw that God had subordinated the Godself to matter/spirit, as it were, or emptied itself into nature so that God and nature could be in communion for all eternity. And the response of adoration by humans is still the best evidence God has to see that "the plot is working" and that the offer has been accepted and that the deal has been clinched and that "God" hasn't been kidding "himself" all this time.

The church has spent a lot of its history trying to figure out the *who* of God as well as who is to be saved. I again have understood Teilhard to be inquiring into the *where* and how of God in the here and now, even in most unexpected things like the rocks (or in situations like being told he couldn't publish anything in philosophy or theology). I think he would feel his whole life was successful if it resulted in the church's understanding creation and incarnation in a much more wholistic way. I believe he imagined God lamenting: "Look! I'm here and I have committed myself to you here and now where you are and to all that is part of my ongoing creation." God commits Godself not only to creation but to its developing itself here and now. It takes an enlargement of consciousness to think this way about God. Wouldn't it be wonderful if from such an enlargement a commensurate degree of prayer was done?

Teilhard focused on nature as the where of God. This is not a denial of God's transcendence but it is taking God as seriously as God has taken nature—by creation and incarnation, both continuing to this day. Furthermore, the self-emptying God "obeys" the laws of nature. The kenotic character of each of the divine Persons is how there is a communion between them. Nature will be brought into this communion the same way Jesus was brought into flesh and his flesh was raised into indestructability.

One can't speak about Teilhard's prayer without noticing the impact of the Ignatian Spiritual Exercises on his life. Before entering the Jesuit order he was passionate about the hidden depths of matter, and the Exercises would have confirmed him in that passion. For example, Ignatius of Loyola recommends in the last meditation of the Spiritual Exercises that the retreatant ask the grace for what he calls an intimate knowledge of God, more specifically to see "how God works and labors in all creatures upon the face of the earth."[3] If anyone has received an answer to that grace full bore, it has been Teilhard. Teilhard went from bones to cosmogenesis, one could say, by practicing the "composition of place" as a way to do contemplation or meditation. Ignatius's recommendation for prayer is to take a scriptural scene or a text that would gather the mind around something imaginable so that the one praying wouldn't wander all over the place. In Teilhard's case he was usually focused on some empirical object, finding it or analyzing it and weighing its meaning in light of his wholistic categories. The discipline that it took for him to stay attentive to the particular can be overlooked because the vista that he ends up articulating in his work was so grand and imaginative.

## The Other Half of His Prayer

Though a visionary who saw profoundly into matter and the future, Teilhard was also a product of his time, and of the French Catholicism of his culture, and of the doctrinal development of the Catholic church in his time. The poverty of its doctrine was in the theology of the Spirit. So, unsurprisingly this was also the poverty in the body of his works. His corpus is developed Christologically and underdeveloped Spirit-ly. It is insufficiently Trinitarian. His Christology is so robust, the Spirit seems like an add-on. One of the reasons for this is his penchant for the genetic, for that which was just aborning—so there is anthropogenesis, cosmogenesis, noogenesis, orthogenesis, and Christogenesis. Helpful and true as all these are, the *not yet* can leave out the other half of the story which is the *already*, the *is*. The Spirit is a present presence, an architectonic presence here and now. Yes, the Spirit yesterday, today, and the same forever, if you will! The Cosmic Christ, maybe, but not without the Cosmic Spirit as the divine Presence in creation ever since there was a creation. The Spirit has been "the Lord and giver of life" all along. Yes, the personal characteristics of the Spirit were named for the first time by Jesus and most clearly manifest in the person of Jesus, but the Spirit was present in the universe from time immemorial.

Jesus promised that the Spirit would teach all truth, but it was the Spirit that taught Jesus all that he taught his listeners. Would there have been a Jesus if he had not been conceived by the Holy Spirit? Yes, Jesus is the way, the truth, and the life, but that is an abridgement that needs to be fleshed out. He was led by the Spirit into the way and he perfectly embodied the truths he was taught by the Spirit and is the source of life along with the Spirit. Christians believe in one Lord who is Father, Son, and Spirit. Our belief is in a Triune divinity!

The virtual absence of pneumatology in Teilhard's writings is paradoxical since, in some way, his whole corpus can be read as pneumatological. His work bears eloquent witness to the Spirit at work in him—one could say, even overtime. His "divine milieu" is full of rich imagery, but the absence of formal allusions to the Holy Spirit, in part, bears witness to the underdevelopment of pneumatology in the church of his time.

To show this Teilhardian pneumatology I will concentrate on just two essays done by him in 1936 and 1937 (both printed in HE), since they encapsulate for me three things I want to underscore in this chapter. One is that his work is a gold mine that hasn't been mined. Two, that one will not discover it unless one digs below the inductive method that obscures it; and three, that the evolutionary élan of all his writings makes it too easy to overplay the future and underplay the present.

The first of these essays was his "Sketch of a Personalistic Universe" done in Peking in 1936 and unpublished at the time, of course. In this essay he is certain that "the natural center of things" is the human personality—not as it is but as it will be if it loses itself "consciously in universal being." It must do so not by "standing on the shore and proving to ourselves that the ocean cannot carry us." No, "let us venture on its waters" (HE, 89). He believes that the mystery of the incarnation could, if appropriated, deliver this kind of cosmic consciousness which could and must develop, but that it has been too limited by "symbols of a juridical nature." This seems to be an allusion to the church's hegemony over these symbols and the need for its teachers and the faithful to enter into this cosmic consciousness.

The essay is full of brilliant but very sweeping assertions like this: "All that exists is matter becoming spirit. There is neither spirit nor matter in the world; the stuff of the universe is spirit-matter. No other substance but this could produce the human molecule" (HE, 57–58). Elsewhere he writes: "The physical structure of the universe is love"; it is "the fundamental power with which our life is woven"; this love "reveals itself to consciousness in three successive stages: in woman (for man); in society; in the All—by the sense of sex, of humanity and of the cosmos" (HE, 72). My sense is that none of this holds together if the personhood of the Spirit does not undergird his "personalistic universe," though no such ascription is made by him.

The second essay, "The Phenomenon of Spirituality," done a year later and also not published then, is even more tantalizing. He sees a "new physical science and a new philosophy" emerging and converging in "the stuff of the universe" (HE, 94). He sees this convergent/emergent spirit as the "thinking fringe" of the planet. This "phenomenon of spirit" (HE, 95), which he also calls "the phenomenon of spirituality," has a breadth that is as wide as the universe but also "a depth in the past" (HE, 96). Hence, "it is rooted over its whole surface in the abyss of past centuries. Spirituality is not a recent accident" (HE, 96). To add to this potpourri he notes that "from a purely scientific and empirical standpoint, the true name for 'spirit' is 'spiritualization'" (HE, 96). No less sweeping is this: "the phenomenon of spirit reveals a gradual and systematic passage from the unconscious to the conscious, and from the conscious to the self-conscious. It is a cosmic change of state" (HE, 96–97). Is the Spirit the source of this phenomenon? He finds three properties in this "phenomenon." First, it is irresistible: no power can prevent it. "If the world is really bound as a whole for consciousness, nothing could possibly oppose the growth of spirit" (HE, 98). Second, it is irreversible. Its goal is "the infinite ahead that it must succeed in propagating itself interminably" (HE, 98–99). It is boundless, unstoppable, and "for the progress of the spirit, the universe is completely *free ahead*" (HE, 99). It is "totalizing" (HE, 99); I'm not sure what that means.

Even more expansively, he sees three spheres of consciousness at work in the universe. The first is matter, which we wrongly regard as "inanimate, and this is the source of all our difficulties in understanding it" (HE, 101). But it is really "a state of consciousness so extended and fragmented that its elements are only visible to us in their statistical properties" (HE, 102). The second is plants and animals, where both individuality and consciousness appear. In the third sphere, with "man," the universe "becomes conscious of itself, *personalized*" (HE, 102). With man, the world is being transformed into spirit and into a "super-consciousness" (HE, 103). But paradoxically, personalized consciousness "has to become less conscious of itself" (HE, 103). "To complete ourselves, we must pass into a greater than ourselves. Survival and also 'super-life' await us in the direction of a growing consciousness and love of the universal" (HE, 105).

He then develops the morality needed for this vision of "spirituality." He states: "It is imperative that the goal shall shine with enough light to be desired and held in view. . . . The God we are seeking must satisfy two conditions if He is to be capable of sustaining and directing the phenomenon of spirit" (HE, 109). The first of these is that "He shall combine in his singularity the evolutionary extension of all the fibers of the world in movement" (HE, 109). The second is that the cosmic synthesis that God effects "shall act in the course of this synthesis as a first nucleus of independent consciousness; (this is) a supremely personal God from whom we are the more distinguishable the more we lose ourselves in Him" (HE, 109). This is a formula for grasping the contradictory conditions for "the cosmic genesis of the spirit," namely, being able to combine "a universal God to be realized by effort, and yet a personal God to be submitted to in love" (HE, 109).

Here Teilhard has "situated the stuff of the universe in consciousness" (HE, 110) because "only our hypothesis of a cosmos in spiritual transformation" can make sense of "two opposed elements (spirit and matter) in a series of linked combinations covering the expanse between thought and consciousness" (HE, 110). He writes: "The definitive discovery of the phenomenon of spirit is bound up with the analysis (which science will one day finally undertake) of the 'mystical phenomenon,' that is of the love of God" (HE, 112).

All of this seems like a very inductive way of seeing the Spirit without bringing the person of the Spirit into the process of the emergence/convergence which he has laid out here. Why did he not do this? He had a sense that "the time has passed in which God could simply impose Himself upon us from without, as master and owner of the estate. Henceforth the world will only kneel before the organic center of its evolution" (HE, 110). But the Spirit I understand does not impose itself from without. It accompanies all that is made from within what is made, as all the particular things in the universe go about their seeming self-organization.

One very revealing self-disclosure about how he sees himself vis-à-vis pneumatology is this: "Let others, fulfilling a function more august than mine, proclaim Your splendors as pure Spirit; as for me, dominated as I am by a vocation which springs from the inmost fibers of my being, I have no desire, I have no ability to proclaim anything except the innumerable prolongations of Your incarnate Being in the world of matter; I can preach only the mystery of your flesh, You the Soul shining forth through all that surrounds us" (HU, 36–37). This comment seems to me to be very revealing both about his blind spot about pneumatology as well as his contribution to it. Why would the pneumatology of others be "more august" than his "innumerable prolongations"? And isn't he loading up the person of Jesus with far too much to handle if the Spirit isn't the other half of the necessary agency? This overload is easy to document. Two of his statements will suffice to convey this position: "To Christify matter sums up the whole venture of my innermost being" (HM,

47). If that doesn't convey it, this should: "It is a matter, not of superimposing Christ on the world, but of pan-Christizing the universe."[4] These moves seem to me to leave the unique human personhood of Jesus behind, or in midair. His feet come back down into his humanity by bringing the role of the Spirit into the picture.

So I end this chapter both delighted with the importance Teilhard assigned to matter, while at the same time less satisfied with the ways he connected spirit/matter with Spirit. It might be unfair to blame Teilhard for not having developed a pneumatology, since that doctrine has been and still is largely underdeveloped by theologians and the church. Nonetheless, his seeing spirit and matter in the conflated way he did begs for a more developed pneumatology than we find in his work. To take the long view, one might go back to the first four centuries after the resurrection and Pentecost, which were full of passionate discourse (to say the least) about the Trinity. The followers of Christ were trying to sort out who God was, given the claims about Jesus in the communities that believed in him. But the Spirit was why they could believe in him, and the Spirit was prompting and inspiring the whole process. The Spirit was why Jewish monotheism developed into a Trinitarian monotheism. It was not a journey taken on a smooth road. It had to be walked through, eked out even, over treacherous terrain that went every which way before the meanderings were made straight. It doesn't do justice to our forebears or to the beautiful mystery of the Trinity to leave it theologically underdeveloped. In practice this lack of development produces a Christological unitarianism.

The beauty of the Divine Mystery has become too coagulated by the conceptual clarities that have developed around Christology. These always need to be aerated by the wind-like freedom of the Spirit and to be completed by pneumatology. Just as "no one can say 'Jesus is Lord' except by the Holy Spirit" (1 Cor 12:3), no one could have seen the matter/spirit nexus as deeply as Teilhard did unless accompanied in his inquiry by that same Spirit.

## Points to Ponder

◆ A teleology is "indispensable to the functioning of evolution."

◆ What the world in all its materiality needs, and what each human being in the world also needs, is to "consent to the communion that will enable it to find what it has come to seek."

◆ Teilhard's way of giving glory to God was primarily by his thinking and choosing. It was these acts that made him and can make the rest of us reflect the One in whose image and likeness we have been made.

- ◆ Reflect on Teilhard's words: "to lose oneself in the unfathomable, to plunge into the inexhaustible, to find peace in the incorruptible, to be absorbed in the definite immensity, to offer oneself to the fire . . . and to give one's deepest self to that whose depth has no end."

- ◆ To fall short of whole seeking and whole making is to fall short of what is special about being human.

- ◆ God commits the Godself not only to creation but to its development here and now.

- ◆ For Teilhard, Eucharist functioned not only personally but cosmically, as he wrote: "The organic form of the universe divinized is Christ Jesus. Through the magnetism of his love and the effective power of his Eucharist, he gradually gathers into himself all the unitive energy scattered through the creation."

- ◆ The divine has located itself in a material milieu.

## Questions for Discussion

1. How do you understand the relationship between Jesus Christ and the Spirit?

2. Does Teilhard's cosmic Christology introduce a new understanding of matter and spirit on the natural level that might change the way we understand the divine Persons?

3. Where is the first person of the Trinity in Teilhard's theology of evolution? Does his "pan-Christic" universe weaken the Trinity or is he advocating a new relationship of the Trinity with creation in light of evolution?

## Notes

1. Thomas M. King, *Teilhard's Mass: Approaches to "The Mass on the World"* (New York: Paulist, 2005), 128–29.

2. Celia Dean-Drummond, ed., *Pierre Teilhard de Chardin on People and Planet* (London: Equinox, 2006), 114.

3. Ignatius, *The Spiritual Exercises of St. Ignatius*, trans. Louis Puhl (Chicago: Loyola University Press, 1951), 236.

4. Quoted by David H. Lane, *The Phenomenon of Teilhard: Prophet for a New Age* (Macon, GA: Mercer University, 1996), 78.

*Part Four*

# A NEW VISION
# OF SCIENCE

We might say that at this moment, as in
the time of Galileo, what we most urgently
need in order to appreciate the convergence of the universe is much less new
facts . . . than a new way of looking at the
facts and accepting them. A new way
of seeing, combined with a new way of
action—that is what we need.

—TEILHARD DE CHARDIN
*Activation of Energy*

# Chapter 13

# TEILHARD DE CHARDIN

## *New Tools for an Evolutive Theory of the Biosphere*

### Ludovico Galleni

Teilhard de Chardin published more than forty-five hundred pages of scientific writings, most of them during his years in China and mainly published in Chinese scientific journals. This material was recovered by Nicole and Karl Schmitz-Moorman and is now available to researchers (OS). Within these papers I have searched for the presence of a theory of evolution which could be confronted with the revision of Darwinism called the modern synthesis,[1] using the epistemological theory described by Imre Lakatos. His scientific research program allows for reciprocal interactions between science and theology. I have sought a similar line of research in Teilhard's technical papers on paleontology and geology, with the intention of discovering his program of research with regard to the theory of evolution and to highlight the quality of his investigations.

The main contribution of Lakatos to contemporary epistemology was to find an alternative both to Popper's trivial falsificationism and to Kuhn's theory of scientific revolutions.[2] According to Lakatos, a scientific research program (SRP) cannot be falsified by a single experiment because it has a complex structure. Contrary to Kuhn, there is no necessity of a scientific revolutionary change: theories can be confronted, discussed, and integrated but they can coexist as happens for theories related to the complex events of biological evolution.[3] In a SRP there is a central core ("hard core" in Lakatos's terminology) describing the aspects of the theory which cannot be eliminated because their failure would represent the end of the theory. The central core is not only based on experiments and observations but also on metaphysical considerations, here intended with the literal meaning of *meta ta physika*.[4] For instance, Galileo clearly stated that God wrote the book of nature in the language of mathematics, and this is the metaphysical aspect of the central core of Galileo's method. This metaphysical statement allowed Galileo to describe many aspects of nature using mathematical laws. Looking back to the twentieth-century discussion about chance and necessity, the

221

conclusions of Jacques Monod are not determined (as he maintained) by the correct use of scientific objectivity, but on the contrary, by the metaphysical core of its atheistic existentialism. In this case, as in many other examples, the metaphysical part is implicit and must be brought to light. The epigraph of *Chance and Necessity*, from *Le mythe de Sisyphe* of Albert Camus—"One must imagine Sisyphus happy"—is a clear indication of Monod's philosophical position. [5]

In our opinion, Teilhard's method is as scientific as that of Galileo or Monod, but it is more explicit and evident than theirs. What is the SRP in Teilhard's hypothesis on evolution? First of all it is possible to summarize the hard core in a few words: evolution is *moving toward* complexity and consciousness. This is the main law of Teilhard's SRP; it is the very basis of its hard core, and it is a true Galilean law because it is grounded in observations and it is subject to experimental confirmation. The theological and philosophical aspects of Teilhard's SRP are easily explained: the philosophical idea of moving toward is related to the Lamarckian suggestion that evolution is moving toward progress and complexity: a scientific counterpart of the general *moving toward* progress of the illuminist philosophy.[6] From a theological point of view, the history of salvation is a history of moving toward redemption; in the final analysis this means the salvation of every individual in the heavens thanks to Christ's sacrifice.

In the traditional biblical vision of nature and humankind there is a gap between the general laws of the universe and the human perspective of salvation. Actually, from the moment of creation until the appearance of humankind there was a perfect and static universe; only after humanity's Fall can history be characterized as moving toward redemption. Evolution, on the contrary, solves the gap because we have a general moving of matter and life toward an increase of order and complexity and then a moving toward alliance and salvation thanks to the presence of the freely thinking and freely acting creature. The moving toward is the unifying concept and it is the metaphysical part of the hard core of Teilhard's SRP.

The experimental section of Teilhard's central core is defined by the general law of complexity and consciousness, intended as a general movement toward complexity and consciousness that is to be investigated scientifically. The aim of this paper is to show that the experimental part of the central core of Teilhard's SRP is well inside the Galilean methods. The law is described thanks to a first group of observations and paleontological findings, then it is defined as a general law, using mathematical methods (the natural curve of complexities, presented in Teilhard's *Man's Place in Nature*) and then it is confirmed by further findings. The use of Lakatos's epistemological theory of scientific research programs illustrates the reciprocal interactions between science and theology in Teilhard's papers.[7] Teilhard's SRP was described in our previous papers and now we will report its results in order to present Teilhard's contributions to the theories of evolution, mainly the concept of the biosphere considered as a whole evolving system.

## Heuristic Perspectives

In Teilhard's SRP the moving toward is the unifying concept, and its experimental perspectives are defined by the general law of complexity and consciousness, intended as a general movement of matter toward complexity and of life toward complexity and consciousness. This law is investigated with scientific methodologies.[8] The scientific research program consists of a central core and a protective belt indicating the novelties proposed by the program and its suggestions for the researcher: the heuristic content of the program. We described three different heuristic perspectives.

*The First Heuristic Perspective of the Protective Belt:*
*Parallelisms versus Convergence*

Teilhard's first experience as a professional paleontologist is related to the work of his doctoral thesis in the laboratory directed by Marcellin Boule in Paris. Boule was one of the most influential paleontologists and paleoanthropologists in continental Europe and gave his pupil a good background in quaternary vertebrate paleontology. Teilhard described the mammals of the deposits of Quercy and other French deposits in his doctoral thesis. In these deposits Teilhard described bones from the genus *Plesiadapis* (OS I, 273–77) and from two genera reported to the Tarsidae family: *Pseudoloris* and *Tarsius* (OS I, 223–45). They both are primates, but *Plesiadapis* represents their first morphological adaptation, the so-called sciuroid stage. Their general morphology is clearly similar to those of the squirrel; *Tarsius*, on the contrary, is clearly the phyletic line arriving at monkeys.

Teilhard knew very clearly the distinction between convergence and parallelisms, a distinction with which every good paleontologist is familiar: *Plesiadapis* was a convergence with the squirrel morphology. On the contrary *Tarsius* developed a line of evolution parallel to those of the other primates. Teilhard described this example of parallelism: the evolution toward a more wide brain, presented in the line of Tarsidae, was independently presented in the line of the other monkeys and in the line bringing to humankind's progenitors (OS I, 215–16).

The distinction between convergence and parallelisms is capital. Convergence means the similarity in morphological structures obtained for adaptation to the same habitat. In this case both the oldest primates and the squirrel were morphologically similar; they were adapted to arboreal life. Convergence, on the other hand, does not imply any connection with the general mechanism of moving toward. On the contrary, parallelisms are related to the fact that different phyletic branches originate from the same roots and evolve in a parallel way; that is to say, the same characteristics evolve independently because of their inner structure. In the case of Tarsidae, the evolution moved toward forms with larger brains and was parallel to the other primate's branches. Also these branches, as a matter of fact, moved toward an increase of the brain.

Very early during his scientific career Teilhard showed that he had clearly in mind the differences between parallelisms and convergence. For this reason his choice of following the researches on parallelisms represented the acquisition of an experimental tool.

From the very beginnings of evolutionary theories, parallelisms were one of the main topics of discussion. The discussion concerned the explanatory adequacy of natural selection; parallelisms were considered to be a proof of the action of mechanisms different from natural selection.

According to both Darwin and Wallace, there is a continuing origin of biological variability, and the environment acts on these variations, choosing individuals with more adaptive characteristics. Natural selection works first of all through a wide search of possibilities and then through the choice of the environment. This is the conceptual basis of Darwinian chance: the source of variability is completely independent from the choosing agents. Darwin described it with the "architect's metaphor" and it is graphically reported in the only diagram of *The Origin of Species*.[9] Evolution is described as diverging segments originating from a point. Each segment represents graphically the search for variability, but only one among the segments goes on, and it is subjected to another spot of search for variability, descent with modifications, and continuing diversifications of the phyletic branches.

Parallelisms suggest the existence of different mechanisms other than natural selection. The topic was proposed by an English zoologist working with Thomas Huxley and a collaborator of Darwin, St. George Jackson Mivart.[10] In 1871 he published a book, again on the origin of species where evolution was considered an accepted fact, but many events described in evolution appeared difficult to interpret in terms of natural selection. It is a fascinating book because most of the difficulties of natural selection described and discussed in the last one hundred and fifty years are already presented there, for instance, the origin of complex structures, the saltationist theory, the long stasis and rapid changes, and there is also a long discussion on parallelisms. Parallelisms mean that when a morphological level is reached, then the following steps are at least in part determined, and if an original group is divided into branches, these branches are compelled to evolve similar morphological features.

Mivart reported many examples of parallelisms. The first regarded the parallel evolution of marsupials and placental mammals. Mivart's interpretation asked for more deterministic mechanisms than those based on natural selection and suggested the possibilities of making prevision regarding future discoveries. When a phyletic branch was well known and described in its characteristics, then it was possible to make a prevision about the forms presented in the parallel branches. At the end of the nineteenth century an Italian botanist, Pier Andrea Saccardo, published a paper describing the fungi which would be discovered in the future thanks to the use of the parallelism concept.[11]

At the beginning of the 1920s a Russian botanist and geneticist, N. I. Vavilov, developed (complementary to Teilhard) a proposal for parallelisms. His idea was more related to those of Mivart and Saccardo, and to a more deterministic model of evolution. His ambition was to become the Mendeleyev of evolutionary biology. Mendeleyev, thanks to the deterministic rules of chemistry, was able to describe the characteristics of the elements of a line, knowing the characteristics of the upper line.[12] This was also the hope of Vavilov: the knowledge of the characteristics of the species of a genus allowed the description of the morphology of the species of the parallel genus.[13]

Teilhard, in his first papers on parallelism, used this concept in a different way. His interest is mainly in the description of events compatible with the hypothesis of evolution as a moving toward, more specifically, as a moving toward complexity and consciousness. He looked for the description of events rather than searched for mechanisms, because parallelism was the experimental proof of the moving toward. We have just reported that his first example is the moving toward cerebralization of Tarsidea, a moving toward which took place side by side with that of the other phyletic branches of the primates.

## The Second Heuristic Perspective: Biology as the Science of Complexity and the Emergence of Qualities during Evolution

Teilhard's research program is based on the techniques of a paleontologist working at a larger-scale level from those of the authors of the modern synthesis mainly based on the population level. The larger scale was used in order to bring out the presence of parallelisms. The necessity of a more general approach in science is reported, first of all, in the letters exchanged with the French geologist Jean Boussac during WWI where the necessity of a global approach to geology was discussed.[14] The exchange was abruptly interrupted by the death of Boussac, but Teilhard started to think about the possibilities of a different approach in paleontology.[15] Curiously, in these letters, the geologist (Boussac) suggests that the priest (Teilhard de Chardin) read the mystic Angela da Foligno in order to investigate the totality concept better and to transfer it to science. The relationships between a metaphysical part (Angela da Foligno, the mystic vision) and an experimental part (the global approach to geology) could be related to working on the general suggestions useful to reconstruct Teilhard's scientific research program.

After the war Teilhard started his Chinese period because of the collaboration between the Huango-Paio Museum in Tien Tsin and its director and founder, the Jesuit Émile Licent, and the Paris Institute of Paleontology directed by M. Boule.[16] In China Teilhard was a participant in many expeditions organized by Père Licent, and in the desert of the Ordos he had the mystical experience of totality. It is interesting that when he was in Tien Tsin he wrote about the necessity of a global approach to biology, considered as the science of the infinitely complex and about the necessity of a different scale of investigation in order to describe different mechanisms in evolution. The hope expressed by Teilhard was that geology and paleontology passed quickly from the analysis of this or that layer or of this or that fossil to a more general and global technique of investigation.

The next passage was the proposal of the science of geobiology intended at first as the science of continental evolution. The geobiological method stated that, following the evolution of a peculiar animal group on a large geographical (continental) and temporal (millions of years) scale, it was possible to describe mechanisms and events which were not acting at a lesser scale. After a few years, Teilhard started to work with the geological survey of China in Peking and on the so-called Peking Man. One of his tasks was the relative dating of its bones. He looked carefully at the strata where the human remains had been dug up, and at similar strata such as the so-called reddish clays, and there he found the best example of parallelism: that of the mole rats of the Chinese Pleistocene. This is the proof that Teilhard used a true scientific research program based on the Galilean method. First of all we meet the observations on *Tarsidea* and a research program based on the general idea of evolution as a moving toward; then we find the definition of a general law: the complexity-consciousness law proved by the findings of parallelisms; finally we arrive at the confirmation of the law through the definition of the continental approach and then the finding and description of parallelisms in mole rats.[17] Teilhard described the example of mole rats as a group orthogenesis and provided a good deal of evidence from these findings. In Teilhard's words:

> From this point of view, taken as a whole, they become just as useful and illuminating in the line of "Group-differentiation" and "Group-

orthogenesis" as for instance the *Drosophila* fly does in the line of Heredity.

Regarded at first as an odd and aberrant type of Asiatic Rodents, the Siphneidae turn out to be a choice object for research, and perhaps the starting point for new methods of analysis, in the field of General Science. (OS VIII, 3727)

We have discussed many times the meaning of the term "orthogenesis" in Teilhard's scientific papers: the original meaning of the term was that of directionality of evolution. However, to avoid any tautological risks based on a directionality described a posteriori, it was intended by Teilhard to be taken as a parallel evolution. The moving toward of orthogenesis was proved by the evidence that many different evolutive branches just separated from a common step, reaching the same morphological stages independently.[18] In the description of mole-rat evolution Teilhard found this:

The original peduncle of the *Siphneidae* soon divided into three branches that followed independent evolutionary lines. In all three there independently appeared similar traits: an increase in size, inception of continuous growth of molars and a fusion of the cervical vertebrae.[19]

His conclusions were that changes appeared independently in just separated phyletic branches and that these examples provided examples of directionality in evolution. To these examples he applied the term orthogenesis, intended to describe such things as the appearance of similar tracts in branches just separated, and this definition was free from any teleological or unscientific meaning.[20] G. G. Simpson questioned strongly the idea of orthogenesis, stating that orthogenesis was without a scientific meaning in a historical science, like paleontology. When different fossil forms of different periods are discovered, then clearly there is a line linking them, and then there is always the possibility of describing directionality. Teilhard was able to avoid this criticism by giving to the term orthogenesis the meaning of parallel evolution. The mole rats, for example, demonstrate that the use of the continental scale suggests the existence of new elements in evolution. Of course, Teilhard proposed many more examples of parallelisms, such as the emergence of hypsodonty many times in rodents and the parallel evolution of teeth in *Machairodus*, an example from *felidae* evolution (OS IX, 4097–135).[21] When parallelisms are found, it is possible to speak of orthogenesis.

We are now ready to introduce the third heuristic point of Teilhard's research program: the theory of the biosphere. At the very beginning of this investigation, Teilhard describes the distinction between aggregation and organization. The interactions between objects happen in two different ways.

First of all is aggregation, as, for instance, in the origin of stars or of a crystal, where interstellar dusts (stars) or molecules (crystals) combine to make larger objects. They present internal regular structure and the possibility of increasing in dimension only from outside and without a precise boundary. Moreover, they enlarge but they remain ontologically themselves.

Organization is completely different. Apparently the processes are the same, because they are interactions among objects of the same hierarchical level, but in organization there is the origin of an object ontologically different. The interactions among molecules give rise to objects with different characteristics, based on new and unpredictable relationships among the parts. These new objects have well defined boundaries, and the relations among the parts develop a precise *telos*: that of the survival of the object and of the peculiar categories of objects: i.e., the survival of the single and the reproduction. The possibilities of an increase in dimension are not related to the apposition from the outside of new quantities of the same components such as one finds in the case of crystals. On the contrary, from the outside there is a selective passage of molecules through the boundary and then the material is incorporated inside the objects. As a matter of fact, they become components of the object and they acquire its *telos*.

The great novelty in evolution is the emergence of complex objects or new systems, according to Von Bertallanfy's definition. These new objects cannot increase in dimension by appositions of new elements but only by interacting and giving rise to new ontological objects: from the protobionts to the primitive cells, from the primitive cells to prokaryotic cells, from prokaryotic cells to eukaryotic cells, to pluricellular organisms, to species, ecosystems, and so on. There is an emergence of new ontological entities and qualities which makes the difference between aggregation and organization and the origin of complex objects. However, working on evolution, there is also the necessity to find the final object to be investigated using the techniques of complexity. Teilhard proposed a way to measure complexity in order to find the proof of the moving toward, but also to look for an asymptotic value where the curve of complexity is moving. The value corresponds to the biosphere: this is the final complex object to be investigated in order to find the general laws of evolution, those laws which characterize the rising of complex objects thanks to organization all over the universe. Life is not any more an epiphenomenon but the essence of the phenomenon: it is the result of the general laws of evolution as described in Teilhard's program.

## The Third Heuristic Perspective: A General Theory of the Biosphere

The theory of the biosphere is the next passage after the idea of continental evolution and is a tool to give an empirical definition to the idea of complexity.

The biosphere is the final complex object in order to describe the general laws of evolution. As a system, the biosphere is made up of parts and relations among the parts, and it is delimited by boundaries, actually not so sharply defined as those of a cell or of an organism, but still present and active. See, for instance, the greenhouse effect of the upper atmospheric layers. Geobiology is, in Teilhard's scientific program, the general science of the evolution of the biosphere, and continental evolution is only a tool to study the evolving biosphere at a lesser scale but without distortions.

Geobiological research was carried out at the Institute of Geobiology in Peking, and the results of the geobiological methods were published in many papers and then in the journal founded by Teilhard and Pierre Leroy, *Geobiologia*. In his first papers, Teilhard gives attention to continental evolution:

> The Institute of Geobiology, established in Peking in 1940, continues the work of the Haungho–Peiho Museum, founded by Emile Licent in Tientsin in 1914. Its purpose is to study the interdependent Evolution of Land and Life on the Asiatic Continent considered as a semi-independent nucleus of the Earth Crust. Therefore in its publications the Institute specializes in those geological and biological facts that have continental significance. (OS VIII, 3638)

He also wrote:

> Due to the particular composition of the material in hand, this Memoir is not so much a description of disconnected new fossil forms, but rather, in outline, the "continental history" of three Asiatic Rodents families, namely: the Castoridae, the Rhizomidae, and, most interesting of all, the Siphneidae. (OS VIII, 3639)

After a few years, in 1943, in the foreword of the first issue of *Geobiologia*, the journal dedicated to publishing papers in geobiology, there is a clear passage toward the biosphere with respect to continental evolution:

> The world of life, taken as a whole, forms a single system bound to the surface of the earth, a system whose elements, in whatever order of association they may be considered, are not simply thrown together and moulded upon one another like the grains of sand, but are organically interdependent like the stream-lines of a hydrodynamic system, or like molecules caught in capillary surfaces. (OS IX, 3757)

These sentences must be emphasized because we have now the global approach and the system concept related to the biosphere.

Teilhard stated that geobiology is the science reuniting all the other sciences of evolution such as paleontology, ecology, and biogeography. Because of its method there is a more general and planetary method of investigation:

1. The study, first of all, of the organic links of every description which are recognizable between living beings considered *in their totality as a single closed system*; and,

2. Secondly, the study of the physical chemical links by which the birth and development of this living envelop are bound up with the history of the planet. (OS IX, 3758)

Defined as the "science of the biosphere," it is a development of the previous definition of geobiology. The science of continental evolution is now extended to the whole biosphere considered as a system, because it is closed (see again the presence of a boundary: the upper active layers of the atmosphere) and is characterized by the interactions among parts in order to maintain stability.[22] This is a very innovative approach to evolution!

## Teilhard's Scientific Legacy: The Latin School of Evolution

Teilhard was not an isolated researcher in the Chinese subcontinent with few friends in the small Institute of Geobiology, but the founder of a true paleontology school. By the end of World War II, Teilhard was back in France where the Jesuit theological school of Lyon-Fourvière was active. It was one of the places where the new theology, at the very basis of the Second Vatican Council, was elaborated. Here he joined in discussions with theologians Henri de Lubac, Jean Danielou, and others. He was also present in the scientific discussion starting from the meeting held in Paris in paleontology and evolution organized by Jean Piveteau (OS X, 4276–80). In Italy he went to see the place where the fossil man of *Saccopastore* had been excavated, and he discussed many aspects of the mechanisms of evolution with the Italian human paleontologist Alberto Carlo Blanc, focusing mainly on Blanc's cosmolisis theory.

Blanc published the Italian translation of some of Teilhard's papers, and in his foreword presented Teilhard's works.[23] First of all he underlined the importance of the presence of so many Catholic scientists having a clear vision of evolution, such as distinguished paleontologists and paleoanthropologists such as Teilhard, l'Abbè Breuil, H. Obermaier, and J. Bouyssonie. Then he confronted his own and Teilhard's hypothesis of evolution. The cosmolisis theory of Blanc was a transposition in a general theory of evolution of the main results of Vavilov's researches on the origin of cultivated plants. The original population was characterized by a high level of genetic variability, and then human cultivations diversified and canalized this variability thanks to the use of artificial selection. Blanc extended the model to a general process of natural canalization, resulting in different specialized branches originating from a high-variability group. In a more general vision the canalization was due to the action of natural selection acting on a high variability population.

Teilhard was less interested in population genetics. There was not an idea of a high polymorphic basal population, but on the contrary of a common morphological ground. From this common starting point the different branches evolved developing separately similar characters. The basal high genetic diversity was not a key point in Teilhard's vision of moving toward and parallelisms, as it was for Vavilov and Blanc. Teilhard presented his researches in the 1947 meeting on paleontology and evolution in Paris. That was the occasion for a discussion among paleontologists both of the Anglo American school—mainly those inside the modern synthesis, first of all G. G. Simpson—and of the Latin school, first of all Piveteau and Teilhard.

We want to remember again the discussion between Teilhard and Simpson about parallel evolution.[24] For Simpson, parallel evolution is only one of the many lateral events of evolution, and its mechanism is clearly based on natural selection. It is a peculiar case of orthoselection. On the contrary, Teilhard, as in the discussion with Blanc, was not interested in mechanisms but in the description of parallelisms. These parallelisms were not—and this is actually the main difference from Simpson—a lateral event but the main event in evolution. Can so wide and general a mechanism be explained only by the local action of natural selection? It is the same question of Mivart who proposed that the parallelisms were one of the difficulties of natural selection.

In 1955 a new meeting was held in Paris, but Teilhard was not able to come from New York where he had been sent in exile by the Roman Catholic authorities in order to remove him from the activities of the French "*nouvelle théologie.*" He had serious health problems and died in New York a few days after the meeting. In any event, his paper was read at the meeting and later published (HM, 268–74). It highlighted the importance of orthogenesis intended as parallel evolution and the necessity of looking for genetic mechanisms, mainly based on the idea of some kind of gene additive, perhaps a first hint toward gene amplification.[25]

In the 1950s a group of Latin paleontologists started to meet regularly in Sabadell, near Barcelona, discussing evolution and its mechanisms. Among them were the Catalan M. Crusafont-Pairó, the Italian P. Leonardi, and the Frenchman J. Piveteau. The Latin school finds its very beginning there. In Sabadell the discussions were mainly related to the possibilities of relationships between the moving toward and the equilibriums of ecosystems. The general maintenance of equilibriums in ecosystems and of the biosphere was discussed as possible motors of evolution. Ramon Margalef, one of the most worldwide-known ecologists, wrote that his idea of the ecological theory of the biosphere started from his participation at the Sabadell meeting and from the discussion regarding Teilhard's theory.[26]

During the discussion Teilhard was referred to as "*querido amico y excellente maestro*" (beloved friend and excellent mentor), and his ideas were discussed and developed.[27] Crusafont-Pairó proposed that the *moving toward* was not only a *moving toward* complexity and cerebralization, but also a *moving toward* freedom: the capacity of choice with respect to the environment increases with the increase of cerebral attitude. From a more technical point of view, Crusafont, together with another Catalan paleontologist, J. Truyols-Santonja, published a paper on directionality of evolution discussing a synthesis between Teilhard's ideas of parallelisms and those of Vavilov and Blanc.[28] The observations were mainly related to the evolution of carnivores based on the specialization of teeth. From a basal group with large diversity, the *Cynodictidae*, described in Teilhard's paper on the carnivorous of Quercy deposits, the evolution toward the hypocarnivores (*Ursidae* for instance) and the hyper carnivores (*Felidae*) was described measuring the teeth, and there was clearly an evolution toward the specialization on both sides. What is relevant, and this is the novelty of the paper, is that the average measured on the basal group remained quite constant in time. In the opinion of Crusafont and Truyols this was an example of stability in evolution: they recovered Vavilov and Blanc's statement that the evolution was mainly a mechanism of specialization from a basal group with high diversity, but there were constraints showed by the average stability. Their conclusion was that the forms of the different biocenosis were distributed around a mean similar to that of the basal group.[29]

The paper was published in *Evolution*, the journal edited by G. G. Simpson. The methods, that is, the careful measurements of teeth and the mean calculated at various stages of carnivorous evolution, were considered a sufficient proof of the skillfulness of the authors and of the quality of the paper. Discussion of the paper is a proof of its cultural impact. Simpson was impressed by the accuracy of the method, the measurements in dental parameters, but he strongly refuses the paper as proof of directionality and orthogenesis.[30] On the contrary, according to Crusafont and Truyols, the stability of the average is an experimental proof that evolution is not a casual dispersion from a basal step, but a moving toward, in this case toward the mean stability due to the maintenance of the equilibriums of the ecosystems.

In the open discussions during the Sabadell meeting, a word often used was "harmony." Many aspects of evolution were explained referring to the harmony of nature. The term harmony was a colloquial term often substituted for the scientific terms of equilibrium and stability. We infer that these words refer to the system theory developed partially by Teilhard and in all its richness by Von Bertallanfy. Stability of the biological system was one of the motors of evolution. Regarding the Latin countries, in Italy Vito Volterra proposed the equations describing prey/predator balances and equilibrium conditions, and Umberto D'Ancona a mathematical modeling of ecosystems. Finally, one of the participants at the Sabadell meeting, the Italian geologist and paleontologist Piero Leonardi, recovered the ecological modeling of Volterra and D'Ancona, proposing the existence of a general symbiotic relationship regarding the whole biosphere.[31]

In these last years Teilhard's synthesis received its final perspective. Studying the biosphere as a whole evolving object, there is the emergence of the moving toward complexity related to the maintenance of the biosphere equilibrium. Using the Lovelock concept of stability and feedback, the stability of the biosphere is maintained thanks to the continual evolving of living beings.[32] Again, the idea of a global vision in evolution, in this case the maintenance of the equilibrium of ecosystems and of the biosphere, was used to explain a peculiarity in evolution related to the concept of moving toward.

## Recent Confirmations of Teilhard's Research Program

We have just discussed the perspective of Teilhard's SRP and its development. Here we give a short summary about the more general perspective related to the moving toward concept. Stability of the biosphere was revised from Lovelock in a perspective related to the concept of the system of Von Bertallanfy and to its application on biology and sociology made by C. H. Waddington. The concept of biosphere stability goes back to the very beginning of the Latin school thanks to the Italian geologist Antonio Stoppani. In his geological theories in the second half of the nineteenth century, he investigated life at a planetary level and its interactions with physical and chemical parameters, showing the stability of the main parameters of the biosphere which allow the survival of life on Earth.[33] From this point of view, we suggest a new and decisive heuristic perspective in the Teilhard research program. Could the maintenance of biosphere equilibriums be the true motor of evolution and of the moving toward complexity and consciousness? In the light of continuously changing parameters, the increase in diversity and in complexity is the suitable tool for stability maintenance. Moreover, mathematical models of biosphere evolution gave new suggestions. The presence of catastrophic events such as mass extinctions is fundamental because they create new ecological niches and give the opportunity for new adaptive radiations. These events are related to the mechanism of biosphere evolution itself and are not correlated to external accidental events.[34]

These models are clearly in contrast with S. J. Gould's hazardous mechanisms of external impacts. The search for the general laws in biosphere evolution, clearly related to Teilhard's research program, gives us some information regarding the presence of less casual models than those proposed.[35] Also, some of the present-day novelties in evolution could be related to Teilhard.[36] First of all, the links between the evo-devo theory and paleontology are of interest. Metamery is determined in very different animal groups by the same genes which are present at the very beginning of animal evolution or at least when head/tail directionality is developed. From this moment it is easy to reach the metameric organization, and it emerges two or three times in animal evolution. The origin of metamery is the best example of the importance of parallelisms. These topics were recently developed, again in the perspective of parallelisms, by Simon Conway Morris in his discussion about the Burgess Shale fossil deposits.[37] A second confirmation is related to the new revision of placental mammals' evolution. In this case the new phyletic tree based on the results of molecular and chromosome investigations clearly showed that placental mammals could be divided in four taxonomic entities based on the four continental regions recently separated. The continental approach gives us new information about animal evolution.

The final confirmation, however, of the moving toward cerebralization and of the complexity consciousness law is the discovery of the bacterial nanobrain. In this case we have a group of molecules adjacent to the part of the bacterial membrane opposite to the flagellum and in the direction of the movement. These molecules are able to discriminate the presence of an attractive or repellent substance, to calculate its gradient, and then to send a message to the flagellum in order to maintain or to change the direction of movement. The nanobrain is able to receive information from the extern, to elaborate the information and then to send a message to the locomotors organelles. This is exactly the function of the brain in the primitive Metazoan. It is the confirmation of the heuristic values of the moving toward complexity and consciousness as a general Galilean law. The bacteria are no longer the example of limited evolutionary possibilities, but on the contrary the example that evolution is everywhere exploring the possibility of moving toward cerebralization, and the moving toward as a general empirical law finds one of its best confirmations here.[38]

A complete theory of the biosphere as a complex evolving object has yet to be developed.

Lovelock's ideas of the presence of stability based on feedback still must be firmly demonstrated, but the biosphere modeling is, in any event, a confirmation of Teilhard's hypothesis on the importance of studying the biosphere in order to understand evolutionary mechanisms. Mass extinctions are not related to external fortuitous impacts, but are a consequence of the general laws of the biosphere. The next step could be to develop a biosphere modeling with the hope of demonstrating that the moving toward complexity is related to the maintenance of biosphere stability. As a matter of fact, we would be in the presence of a top-down mechanism. The necessity of maintaining the stability of the whole is influencing the evolution of the parts, and this evolution is actually the evolution of living—and the result is the moving toward complexity and consciousness.[39]

## Points to Ponder

♦ Evolution is moving toward complexity and consciousness.

♦ The "moving toward" is the unifying concept and it is the metaphysical part of the hard core of Teilhard's scientific research programs.

♦ Teilhard looked for the description of events rather than searched for mechanisms.

♦ Teilhard wrote about the necessity of a global approach to biology, considered as the science of the infinitely complex.

♦ Teilhard's concept of moving toward is not only moving toward complexity and cerebralization but also a moving toward freedom: the capacity of choice with respect to the environment increases with the increase of cerebral attitude.

♦ The increase in diversity and in complexity may be the suitable tool for stability maintenance.

## Questions for Discussion

1. What have you learned about Teilhard as a scientist? Does his theology resonate with his approach to science?

2. What new aspects of evolution are discussed here? Do they help you understand the science of evolution more clearly?

3. Does Teilhard's scientific research program allow a bridge to be formed between science and religion in an original way?

## Notes

*Acknowledgments*: Thanks are due to Dr. Donald Viney and to Ilia Delio, OSF, for their suggestions and criticisms and to Jonathan Key for his revision of the English manuscript.

1. Ernst Mayr and William B. Provine, eds., *The Evolutionary Synthesis: Perspectives on the Unification of Biology* (Cambridge, MA: Harvard University Press, 1998).

2. Imre Lakatos, *The Methodology of Scientific Research Programmes,* in *Philosophical Papers,* vol. 1, ed. J. Worrall and G. Curries (Cambridge: Cambridge University Press, 1978).

3. Ludovico Galleni, *Darwin, Teilhard de Chardin e gli altri . . . le tre teorie dell'evoluzione* (Pisa: Felici, 2012).

4. Ludovico Galleni, "Teilhard de Chardin's Multicentric Model in Science and Theology: A Proposal for the Third Millennium," in *The Legacy of Pierre Teilhard de Chardin,* ed. J. Salmon, SJ, and J. Farina (New York: Paulist, 2011), 59–78.

5. Jacques Monod, *Le hazard et la nécessité* (Paris: Seuil, 1970).

6. Michael Ruse, *From Monad to Man: The Concept of Progress in Evolutionary Biology* (Cambridge, MA: Harvard University Press, 1996), 42–83.

7. Ludovico Galleni and Marie-Claire Groessens-Van Dyck, "A Model of Interaction between Science and Theology Based on the Scientific Papers of Pierre Teilhard de Chardin," in *Religion and the Challenges of Science,* ed. W. Sweet and R. Feist (Burlington, VT: Ashgate, 2007), 55–71.

8. Ludovico Galleni, "Teilhard de Chardin: *Moving Towards* Humankind?" in *Biological Evolution: Facts and Theories,* ed. G. Auletta, M. Leclerc, and R. A. Martinez (Rome: Gregorian Biblical Press, 2011), 493–516.

9. Charles Darwin, *The Origin of Species by Means of Natural Selection* (London: John Murray, 1859).

10. St. George J. Mivart, *On the Genesis of Species* (London: MacMillan, 1871).

11. Pier Andrea Saccardo, *I prevedibili funghi futuri secondo la legge d'analogia* (Padua: Ferrari, 1896).

12. The reference to Mendeleyev is a clear demonstration that the search for parallelisms has nothing to do with the theory of intelligent design or a similar nonscientific hypothesis. It is only the proof that some scientists, and Teilhard among them, looked for different mechanisms other than that of natural selection.

13. Reprinted in Nicolai I. Vavilov, *Origin and Geography of Cultivated Plants* (Cambridge: Cambridge University Press, 1992).

14. Galleni, "Teilhard de Chardin's Multicentric Model," 63.

15. Pierre Teilhard de Chardin and J. Boussac, *Lettres de guerre inédites* (Paris: ŒIL, 1986).

16. Ludovico Galleni and Marie-Claire Groessens-Van Dyck, "Lettres d'un paléontologue—Neuf lettres inédites de Pierre Teilhard de Chardin à Marcellin Boule," *Revue des Questions Scientifiques* 172 (2001): 5–104.

17. Galleni and Van Dyck, "A Model of Interaction."

18. Ludovico Galleni, "Relationships between Scientific Analysis and the World View of Pierre Teilhard de Chardin," *Zygon* 27 (1992): 153–66.

19. See Galleni, "Relationships between Scientific Analysis and the World View of Pierre Teilhard de Chardin," 160.

20. Galleni, "Relationships between Scientific Analysis and the World View of Pierre Teilhard de Chardin," 160–62.

21. Ludovico Galleni, "How Does the Teilhardian Vision of Evolution Compare with Contemporary Theories?" *Zygon* 30 (1995): 43.

22. Unhappily, too often Teilhard is forgotten by the scientific community. Recently a new journal, whose title is *Geobiology,* was published, but among the forerunners Teilhard is not mentioned. ("Geobiology" is the English translation of "Geobiologia.") See Galleni, "Teilhard de Chardin: *Moving Towards* Humankind?" 507.

23. See Pierre Teilhard de Chardin, *L' avvenire dell'Uomo* (Rome: Partenia, 1947).

24. Galleni, "Relationships between Scientific Analysis and the World View of Pierre Teilhard de Chardin," 153–66.

25. Galleni, "How Does the Teilhardian Vision of Evolution Compare," 25–45.

26. Ramon Margalef, "Miquel Crusafont, a la recerca del temps passat," *Paleontologia i evolució* 26–27 (1993): 7–8.

27. Ludovico Galleni, "Teilhard de Chardin and the Latin School of Evolution: Complexity, Moving Towards and the Equilibriums of Nature," *Pensamiento* 67 (2012): 689–708.

28. Miguel Crusafont-Pairó and Jaime Truyols-Santonja, "A Biometric Study of the Evolution of Fissiped Carnivores," *Evolution* 10 (1965): 314–32.

29. Crusafont-Pairó and Truyols-Santonja, "A Biometric Study."

30. George G. Simpson, "A Review of Masterometry," *Evolution* 19 (1965): 249–55.

31. Piero Leonardi, *L' evoluzione dei viventi* (Brescia: Morcelliana, 1950).

32. See Ludovico Galleni, "Levels of Organization and Evolution, from Teilhard de Chardin to Lovelock," *Studies in Science and Theology* 4 (1996): 109–15, and Francesco Santini and Ludovico Galleni, "Stability and Instability in Ecological Systems: Gaia Theory and Evolutionary Biology," in *Scientists Debate Gaia,* ed. S. H. Schneider, J. R. Miller, E. Crist, and P. J. Boston (Cambridge, MA: MIT Press, 2004), 353–62.

33. Ludovico Galleni, "Teilhard's Science of the Biosphere," in *Rediscovering Teilhard's Fire,* ed. K. Duffy, S.S.J. (Philadelphia: Saint Joseph's University Press, 2010), 197–206.

34. Vieri Benci and Ludovico Galleni, "Stability and Instability in Evolution," *Journal of Theoretical Biology* 194 (1998): 541–49.

35. See Stephen J. Gould, *Wonderful Life: The Burgess Shale and the Nature of History* (New York: W.W. Norton, 1989).

36. See Galleni, "Teilhard de Chardin: *Moving Towards* Humankind," 493–516, and Galleni, "Teilhard de Chardin and the Latin School of Evolution," 689–708.

37. Conway Morris, *The Crucible of Creation* (Oxford: Oxford University Press, 1998).

38. Galleni, "Teilhard de Chardin and the Latin School of Evolution," 704–5.

39. Galleni, "Teilhard de Chardin: *Moving Towards* Humankind," 512–13.

# CONCLUSION

Teilhard de Chardin had a vision for a new world rising up from the old one. He saw far into the future with such depth and clarity that others mistook him to be eccentric or delusional. He was largely ignored by his fellow Jesuits and suppressed by the church, but like the prophets of old, he could not be silenced and courageously wrote down what he saw. He trusted his insights sufficiently to leave his writings to his closest confidantes, who believed in Teilhard's prophetic gifts.

We are the heirs of a brilliant mind who may well be the primary architect of a new church in an emerging world. Through the eyes of Teilhard we see that the old wineskins of Christianity can no longer hold the new wine of our time. The construction of Christian doctrine, including our understanding of God, creation, salvation, and redemption, was done in ages past, based on a cosmology that is no longer true. This does not mean that our doctrine is irrelevant; the core principles are still held to be revelatory of divine mystery. Our understanding of these core principles, however, principles of a living God, evokes new insights and dimensions consonant with our place in this expanding universe.

The world that belongs to God, and to which God continues to commit Godself, continues to change, and we can only deepen our understanding of this God-world relationship by exploring the complexities of change. Theology is not a series of abstract concepts conjured up by human speculation; it is personal reflection on the living God who shares divine life with us. When theology is divorced from cosmology we wind up with an empty concept of God. Without worldly engagement we are left with a *Deus otiosus,* an idle God of dead philosophers. An organic theology in tune with the living world brings us more deeply into the mystery of a living God.

Teilhard was keenly aware that our metaphysics, the underlying principles of reality, are out of touch with the world as modern science now describes it. Theology has not kept abreast of modern physics, and we continue to talk about God as if we still live in a stable, fixed cosmos. We do not lived in the ancient Ptolemaic cosmos, however, nor can we go back to that cosmos. Evolution is a forward-moving process; there is no turning back. God is up ahead, the future into which we are moving.

The essays in this volume have all addressed—in one way or another—the process of moving forward. John Haught has described a metaphysics of the future as our sole support, while Kathy Duffy has illuminated the beauty of wisdom at work in the cosmos. Ilia Delio has shown that God and secularity are intertwined in the incarnation, rendering nothing on Earth profane.

239

Denis Edwards has highlighed Teilhard's influence on Karl Rahner and hence on the modern church, while François Euvé has pointed to humanity as part of the unfolding web of life. Don Viney and David Grumett have brought to light the importance of Teilhard's new metaphysical view of reality, and Ed Vacek has reconceived moral decision making in an evolutionary universe. Bill Dinges and Ilia Delio have shown that Christianity is thoroughly secular and thus consonant with the new spirituality. Ursula King continues to awaken us to Teilhard's zest for life, the energy and passion we need to evolve this earth into a greater unity, and John Haughey has grappled with the Holy Spirit in Teilhard's evolutionary Christology. Finally, Ludovico Galleni has illuminated Teilhard's scientific research program as an original approach to the task of science itself.

These areas of theology, metaphysics, philosophy, spirituality, ethics, and science are Teilhard's windows to a new reality, a new vision of God and cosmos which continues to deepen, as long as we remain open to the freedom of love. It is a thoroughly incarnational vision that recognizes a novel breakthrough in the person of Jesus, which continues in and through us. Teilhard's evolutionary vision is a breathtaking one that will need to be continuously distilled in generations to come. By alerting us to the insights of modern science and a world of change, he awakens us to a new age: law-filled faith must now yield to the spirit-filled adventure of evolution. Humankind is the growing tip of this evolutionary trend. We must attune ourselves to the birthing of Christ and trust in the power of love to lead us onward to a new reality.

# TIMELINE OF TEILHARD'S LIFE*

**1881:** Birth on May 1 at Sarcenat on May 1 in France, near Orcine and Cler-mont-Ferrand. Fourth of eleven children—eight of his brothers and sisters would precede him in death. Sarcenat is in the Massif Central amidst extinct volcanos, the tallest of which is Puy-de-Dôme (4800 ft).

**1902:** Graduates Licence ès Lettres. He had passed baccalauréat exams in philosophy (1897) and in mathematics (1898) and entered the Jesuit novitiate in 1897.

**1905–1908:** Three years teaching in Jesuit college in Cairo, Egypt, with three geological field trips. Teilhard learned in 1907 that because of his finds of shark teeth in Fayoum, a new species of shark was named for him, Teilhardia.

**1910–1912:** Study of theology at Hastings, England. Ordained a priest in 1911. During this period he read Henri Bergson's *Creative Evolution* (1911) and was greatly influenced by it. Bergson's book would later appear on the church's Index of Forbidden Works. In 1912, Teilhard participated in the digs at Piltdown with Charles Dawson. "Piltdown man" revealed as a hoax in 1953.

**1915–1918:** Stretcher bearer during the Great War. Two of Teilhard's brothers killed in action. Teilhard was awarded the Croix de Guerre and the Médaille Militaire and was eventually (1921) made a Chevalier de la Légion d'Honneur for his bravery in battle. During the war Teilhard wrote letters to his cousin Marguerite Teillard-Chambon and sent her many of his essays; these essays caught the notice of his Jesuit superiors because of their unorth-odox theology (e.g., no Adam and Eve, no original sin, no creation *ex nihilo*), but he was still allowed to take his final vows as a Jesuit.

**1919–1922:** Takes final vows as a Jesuit and completes formal education (certificates in geology, botany, zoology, and a doctorate in geology). In 1922 Teilhard wrote "Note on Some Possible Historical Representations of Original Sin" as a private reflection, not meant for publication, but for the consider-ation of theologians. This document somehow made its way to Rome and was a contributing factor in Teilhard's being "exiled" to China in 1926.

**1923:** April 1923 to September 1924, in China, writes "La Messe sur le Monde" ("The Mass on the World").

---

*A special thank you to Professor Donald Viney for providing the materials on Teilhard's life and original works and letters.

**1924–1925:**  Teaches at the Institut Catholique in Paris. Extreme popularity with students that alarms his superiors because of his unorthodox views on evolution and original sin. During July 1925 (week of the Scopes Trial in America), the crisis of obedience: Teilhard obliged to sign a statement of repudiation of his ideas on original sin. Some of his friends advised Teilhard to leave the Jesuits—Abbé Breuil said, "Vous êtes mal marié. Divorcez-la!" However, Auguste Valensin advised Teilhard to sign the confession, not as a statement of the condition of his soul—which, Valensin argued, God alone could judge—but in order to signal his obedience to the Jesuits. Teilhard signed the statement. It was during this period that Teilhard introduced the word "noosphere" (*nous* = mind), the layer of reflective life embracing the biosphere, though still dependent on it.

**1926–1939:**  In these years Teilhard makes six more trips to China, spending much of his time there. He writes his spiritual masterpiece, *Le Milieu Divin* (*The Divine Milieu*), trying in vain to revise it so as to please the church censors. In 1929, he begins a life-long friendship with Lucille Swan (1890–1965), often discussing his work with her. He plays a major role in the expedition that discovered *Sinanthropus* (so-called Peking Man) in 1929–30 and, in 1931–32, participates in the Croisière Jaune (the Yellow Expedition) in China. His trips to and from China allow him opportunities for geological and paleontological study in Ethiopia, Manchuria, France, the United States, England, Java, and India. He is awarded the Gregor Mendel Medal in Philadelphia in 1937. In 1938 Teilhard begins writing his magnum opus, *Le Phénomène Humain* (The Human Phenomenon), finished 1940. For Teilhard, disbelief in evolution is unthinkable; it is a light illuminating all facts, but especially "the human phenomenon." The God *En Haut* (Above) is identified with the aim, *En Avant* (Ahead), of the evolutionary process, which Teilhard calls "Omega Point."

**1939–1946:**  Teilhard is stranded in China as he waits out World War II. During these years he and his close friend and fellow Jesuit, Pierre Leroy, set up the Institute of Geobiology. He also lectures at the French embassy on "The Future of Man" and he founds the journal *Geobiologia*.

**1946–1951:**  These eventful years are spent mostly in and around Paris. In 1946 he does some lecturing, but in 1947 he suffers a heart attack. October 1948 finds Teilhard in Rome seeking ecclesiastical approval for the publication of *Le Phénomène Humain* and for permission to accept an invitation to a Chair at the Collège de France—Teilhard prepared himself "to stroke the tiger's whiskers." Both requests are denied. In early 1949 Teilhard gave one of a series of six planned lectures at the Sorbonne, but an attack of pleurisy cut short the lectures. Teilhard wrote the lectures into a book, *Le Groupe Zoologique Humain* (translated as *Man's Place in Nature*); again, however, Rome refuses permission to publish.

**1950:**   Despite the fact that the church denied Teilhard permission to publish his religious-philosophical works, many of these works were widely known in Catholic circles because Teilhard authorized multiple copies to be made and distributed—these were referred to as Teilhard's "*clandestins*." Two books were published prior to Teilhard's death which used these *clandestins* to launch criticisms of Teilhard's ideas. *L'Evolution Redemptrice du P. Teilhard de Chardin* (Les Editions du Cèdre, 1950) was the first, published anonymously, although the author was probably Abbé Luc Lefèvre. However, the more important event of 1950 was the release in August of Pope Pius XII's encyclical *Humani Generis*. Some people believed that the encyclical was directed at Teilhard. If Teilhard believed this, he never let on. Be that as it may, the encyclical affirmed the historical truth of the first eleven chapters of Genesis, expressed skepticism about the truth of evolution, and denied altogether the evolution of the soul (as opposed to the body). Teilhard wrote a partial response to the encyclical and sent it to Rome. [See the note at the end of this Timeline.] Despite this, Teilhard wrote a letter to his Jesuit superior assuring him of his complete fidelity. In 1950 Teilhard also completed his autobiographical essay, "Le Cœur de la Matière" ("The Heart of Matter").

**1951–1955:**   Teilhard felt the pressure to leave France and was allowed to accept a research position with the Wenner-Gren Foundation in New York City. In 1952, the second of two books critical of his ideas appeared, Abbé Louis Cognet's *Le Père Teilhard de Chardin et la Pensée Contemporaire*. Teilhard wrote to Père Leroy, "It's a shame I can neither explain nor answer him." In 1952 a conference on evolution was held at Laval University in Quebec to which the great evolutionists of the day were invited, with the exception of Teilhard. Teilhard referred to these as "Catholic games." In these final years Teilhard remained active, traveling across the United States as well as overseas to South Africa and South America. He made his final trip to France in the summer of 1954 where he visited the Lascaux caves with Père Leroy. In early 1955 Teilhard declined an invitation to speak at a symposium at the Sorbonne. A little later in the year, Rome took the precaution of denying him permission to attend the symposium. At the same time, he heard that Rome had denied permission to publish a German translation of some of his published scientific articles.

**1955:**   April 10. Teilhard dies of a heart attack in New York City on Easter Sunday in the afternoon.

**1955–1976:** By the end of 1955, Éditions de Seuil had published the first of thirteen volumes of Teilhard's work, beginning with *Le Phénomène Humain* (1955) and ending with *Le Cœur de la Matière* (1976). After consulting a Jesuit canon lawyer to insure that he would remain faithful to the church to the end, Teilhard bequeathed his literary remains to his secretary, Mademoiselle Jeanne Mortier. It was Mlle. Mortier who ensured that the Roman censors would not have the last word.

*Note:* "Monogenism and Monophyletism: An Essential Distinction." Teilhard argues that science debates the question of monophyletism versus polyphyletism (i.e., single vs. multiple evolutionary branches giving rise to humans). Science cannot *directly* address the hypothesis of monogenism (i.e., human origins from an individual Adam). However, *indirectly*, the scientist can say that all we believe we know about biology renders an individual Adam untenable—e.g., Adam would be *born adult*.

# Originals and English Editions of Teilhard's Works and Letters

*T1 – T13 refer to volume numbers (tomes) in the French editions.*

| | | |
|---|---|---|
| 1955 | T1 *Le phénomène humain* | |
| 1956 | T2 *L'apparition de l'homme* | |
| | T8 *Le groupe zoologique humain* | |
| | *Lettres de voyage, 1923–1939* | |
| 1957 | T3 *La vision du passé* | |
| | T4 *Le milieu divin: essai de vie intérieure* | |
| 1958 | *Construire la terre* (multi-lingual edition) | *Building the Earth* [also published 1965] |
| 1959 | T5 *L'avenir de l'homme* | T1 *The Phenomenon of Man* [revised 1965] |
| 1960 | | T4 *The Divine Milieu: An Essay on the Interior Life* |
| 1961 | *L'Hymne de l'univers* | |
| | *Genèse d'une pensée: lettres 1914–1919* | |
| | *Lettres de voyage, 1923–1955* | |
| 1962 | T6 *L'énergie humain* | *Letters from a Traveler* [Lettres de voyage (1961)] |
| 1963 | T7 *L'activation de l'énergie* | |
| | *Lettres d'Égypte (1905–1908)* | |
| 1964 | | T5 *The Future of Man* |
| 1965 | T9 *Science et Christ* | T2 *The Appearance of Man* |
| | T12 *Écrits du temps de la guerre* | *Hymn of the Universe* |
| | *Lettres d'Hastings et de Paris, 1908-1914* | *Letters from Egypt, 1905–1908* |
| | | *The Making of a Mind: Letters from a Soldier-Priest, 1914–1919* |
| | *Lettres à Léontine Zanta* | |
| 1966 | *Je m'explique* (ed. Jean-Pierre Demoulin) | T3 *The Vision of the Past* |
| | | T8 *Man's Place in Nature* |
| 1967 | | *Letters from Paris, 1912–1914* |

| 1968 | Accomplier l'homme. Lettres inédites (1926–1952) [letters to Ida Treat and Rhoda de Terra] | T9 Science and Christ<br><br>T12 Writings in Time of War*<br><br>Letters from Hastings, 1908–1912<br><br>Letters to Léontine Zanta<br><br>Letters to Two Friends, 1926–1952 [Treat / de Terra] |
|---|---|---|
| 1969 | T10 Comment je crois | T6 Human Energy |
| 1970 | | T7 Activation of Energy<br><br>Let Me Explain (ed. Jean-Pierre Demoulin) |
| 1971 | Œuvres scientifiques (11 volumes)<br><br>Journal 1915–1919, Tome 1 (Cahiers 1–5) | T10 Christianity and Evolution |
| 1973 | T11 Les directions de l'avenir | Prayer of the Universe [excerpts from T12] |
| 1974 | Lettres intimes à Auguste Valensin, Bruno de Solages, Henri de Lubac, André Ravier | |
| 1975 | | T11 Toward the Future |
| 1976 | T13 Le cœur de la matière<br><br>Lettres familières de Pierre Teilhard de Chardin mon ami. Les dernières années, 1948–1955 (ed. Pierre Leroy) | |
| 1978 | | T13 The Heart of Matter |
| 1980 | | Letters from My Friend Teilhard de Chardin, 1948–1955 (ed. Pierre Leroy) |
| 1984 | Lettres à Jeanne Mortier | |
| 1988 | Lettres inédites à l'Abbé Gauderfroy et à l'Abbé Breuil | |
| 1989 | Pèlerin de l'avenir: Le Père Teilhard de Chardin à travers sa correspondence (1905-1955) | |
| 1994 | Letters of Teilhard de Chardin and Lucile Swan [originals mostly in English] | |
| 1999 | | T1 The Human Phenomenon |
| 2011 | La rayonnement d'une amitié: Correspondance avec la famille Bégouën (1922–1955) | |

* Writings in Time of War omits seven essays from French original that are found in two other works: "Christ in the World of Matter" and "The Spiritual Power of Matter" (in Hymn of the Universe [1965]); "Nostalgia for the Front," "The Great Monad," "My Universe," "Note on the Presentation of the Gospel in a New Age," and "The Names of Matter" (in The Heart of Matter [1978]).

# CONTRIBUTORS

**Patrick H. Byrne** is currently Professor at Boston College. His teaching and research and publication interests include philosophy of service learning and social justice; the relationships between science, evolution, and religion; and the thought of Bernard Lonergan, Albert Einstein, and Aristotle. His recent publications include "Wholeness through Science, Justice and Love," in *In Search of the Whole: Twelve Essays on Faith and Academic Life,* ed. John C. Haughey, SJ (2011); "Is the Universe on Our Side? Scientific Understanding and Religious Faith," *The Lonergan Review* 3 (2011); "Bernard Lonergan's Transformation of the Darwinian Worldview" (with Frank Budenholzer), in *Darwinism and Catholicism* (2009); *The Dialogue Between Science and Religion: What We Have Learned from One Another?* (2005); "Evolution, Randomness and Divine Purpose: A Reply to Cardinal Schörnborn," (2006); "The Good under Construction and the Research Vocation of a Catholic University" (2013); and *Analysis and Science in Aristotle* (1997). He is currently working on a book on the ethics of Bernard Lonergan.

**Ilia Delio,** OSF, is Director of Catholic Studies and Visiting Professor at Georgetown University. Prior to joining Georgetown she was Professor and Chair of Spirituality Studies at Washington Theological Union and taught in the areas of spirituality, Franciscan theology, and science and religion. She holds a doctorate in pharmacology from New Jersey Medical School–Graduate School of Biomedical Sciences, and a doctorate in historical theology from Fordham University. She is the author of thirteen books and numerous articles. Her most recent book, *The Unbearable Wholeness of Being: God, Evolution and the Power of Love,* was recently published by Orbis Books (2013).

**William D. Dinges** is Ordinary Professor of Religious Studies in the School of Theology and Religious Studies, Director of Religion and Culture Area, and a fellow of the Institute for Policy Research and Catholic Studies at the Catholic University of America. He is co-author with Dean Hoge, Mary Johnson, SND de N, and Juan Gonzales Jr., of *Young Adult Catholics: Religion in the Culture of Choice* (University of Notre Dame Press, 2001). His research interests include religious movements, religion and globalization, fundamentalism, religion in America (Catholicism in particular), spiritual questing, and religion and ecology. Dr. Dinges has a long-standing interest in Catholic traditionalism and was a contributor on the topic to the American Academy of Arts and Sciences Fundamentalist Project. He is currently completing a book on the cultural construction of the phenomenology of the sacred in the Latin Tridentine liturgy.

**Kathleen Duffy**, SSJ, is Professor of Physics, Director of the Interdisciplinary Honors Program, and Director of the Institute for Religion and Science at Chestnut Hill College, editor of *Teilhard Studies*, and serves on the advisory boards of the American Teilhard Association and Cosmos and Creation. She has published several book chapters and articles on Teilhard, has edited a volume of essays about his life and work, *Rediscovering Teilhard's Fire* (2010), and is presently writing a book about Teilhard's mysticism.

**Denis Edwards** is Associate Professor in the Department of Theology of Flinders University in South Australia. He teaches for Catholic Theological College and is a priest in residence in Tranmere parish. Recent books include *Breath of Life: A Theology of the Creator Spirit* (2004), *Ecology at the Heart of Faith* (2006), and *How God Acts: Creation, Redemption and Special Divine Action* (2010). In 2012 he received the Medal of the Order of Australia (OAM) for service to the Catholic Archdiocese of Adelaide and to theological education.

**François Euvé**, SJ, is Professor of Systematic Theology at the Jesuit Faculties in Paris, where he holds the Chair Teilhard de Chardin. He is also editor in chief of *Études*. His publications include *Penser la création comme jeu* ( 2000), *Darwin et le christianisme* (2009), and *Les jésuites et les sciences* (2013).

**Ludovico Galleni** is Professor of General Zoology, University of Pisa, and Professor of Science and Theology, Istituto Superiore di Scienze religiose di Pisa. Presently his research interests are related to the relationships between biological evolution and Christian theology, and also the scientific papers of Pierre Teilhard de Chardin.

**David Grumett** is Chancellor's Fellow in Christian Ethics and Practical Theology in the School of Divinity, University of Edinburgh. He has published many books, chapters, and articles on modern French Catholic theology, including *Teilhard de Chardin: Theology, Humanity and Cosmos* (2005).

**John C. Haughey**, SJ, is a researcher and writer at Colombiere Jesuit Center. Research Fellow at Georgetown University Law Center. He is a former professor of religious ethics at Loyola University Chicago, was appointed by Vatican's Council on Christian Unity to serve as member of its international dialogues with Pentecostalism and World Evangelical Alliance. His scholarship has been in the area of university education with an emphasis on the meaning of what constitutes the Catholic intellectual tradition. In addition, he has been drawing on contemporary theology to develop a better understanding of the relationship between a theology of Spirit and recent scientific findings, and has examined business in light of spirituality. He has authored or edited a number of books, including *Where is Knowing Going?* (2009), which won first place by the Catholic Press Association. His most recent manuscript, in collaboration with eight other authors, is on transhumanism, on what theology has to say to technology and the sciences.

**John F. Haught** is Distinguished Research Professor of Theology, Georgetown University. He was formerly Professor in the Department of Theology at Georgetown University (1970–2005) and Chair (1990–95). His area of specialization is systematic theology, with a particular interest in issues pertaining to science, cosmology, evolution, ecology, and religion. He has written nineteen books and has authored numerous articles and reviews. He lectures internationally on many issues related to science and religion. In 2002 he was the winner of the Owen Garrigan Award in Science and Religion, in 2004 the Sophia Award for Theological Excellence, and in 2008 a Friend of Darwin Award from the National Center for Science Education. He testified for the plaintiffs in the Harrisburg, Pennsylvania "intelligent design trial" (Kitzmiller et al. v. Dover Area School District). In fall 2008 he held the D'Angelo Chair in the Humanities at St. John's University in New York City. In April 2009 he received an honorary doctorate from Louvain University in Belgium. He and his wife, Evelyn, have two sons and live in Falls Church, Virginia.

**Ursula King** is Professor Emerita of Theology and Religious Studies and Senior Research Fellow at the Institute for Advanced Studies, University of Bristol. She is also Professorial Research Associate, Department of the Study of Religions, School of Oriental and African Studies, and Fellow of Heythrop College, both at the University of London. She has held several visiting chairs in the United States and Norway, and been awarded honorary doctorates by the universities of Edinburgh, Oslo, and Dayton, Ohio. She gave the 1996 Bampton Lectures at the University of Oxford, published as *Christ in All Things: Exploring Spirituality with Teilhard de Chardin* (1997), and wrote the biography *Spirit of Fire: The Life and Vision of Teilhard de Chardin* (1996). Her most recent books are *Teilhard de Chardin and Eastern Religions: Spirituality and Mysticism in an Evolutionary World* (2011) and *The Search for Spirituality: Our Global Quest for a Spiritual Life* (2008).

**Edward Vacek**, SJ, currently holds the Stephen Duffy Chair in Systematic Theology in the Department of Religious Studies at Loyola University New Orleans. Previously he taught for thirty years at the Weston Jesuit School of Theology and at Boston College. He is the author of *Love, Human and Divine* (1994) and has published over sixty articles in professional and popular journals.

**Donald Wayne Viney** holds the rank of University Professor of Philosophy at Pittsburg State University (Kansas), where he has taught since 1984. He publishes primarily on philosophy of religion with a focus on process-relational philosophy and theology.

# INDEX

251